Acquiring English Sentence Stress
Pitch and Musical Sensitivity

—Saeko Sasaki—

The Eighth Installment of the
EPSJ English Phonetics Series

MARUZEN PLANET

The EPSJ English Phonetics Series

Published by Maruzen Planet Co., Ltd, Tokyo

Copyright © 2016 by Saeko Sasaki

All rights reserved. No part of this publication may be reproduced or transmitted in any form or by any means, electronic or mechanical, including photocopying, recording or any information storage or retrieval system, without permission in writing from the author.

Saeko Sasaki
E-mail: saeko1234@aol.com

First published 2016

ISBN 978-4-86345-310-4 C3382

Printed in Japan

Contents

Preface vii
Message (Dr. John C.L. Ingram) ix
Acknowledgements xi
List of figures xiii
List of tables xxi
List of abbreviations xxv

Introduction 1

1 **Fundamental concepts** 5
  1.1 Characteristics of stress 5
    1.1.1 Word stress 5
    1.1.2 Sentence stress 6
      1.1.2.1 Stress shift 8
      1.1.2.2 Weak form 10
  1.2 Definitions of stress 11
  1.3 Previous research on English stress 18
  1.4 Comparison of English prosodic features and Japanese prosodic features 24
    1.4.1 Stress accent languages and pitch accent languages 24
    1.4.2 Intonation languages and word-pitch languages 25
    1.4.3 Stress-timed rhythm and mora-timed rhythm 26
  1.5 Relationship between music and language 27

2 **Pitch contour of sentence stress in American English** 29
  2.1 Purpose 29
  2.2 Method 29
    2.2.1 Informants 29
    2.2.2 Materials 29
    2.2.3 Recording method 30
  2.3 New F_0 contour 31

2.4	Discussion	39
2.5	Summary	40
2.6	Devised F_0 contours	41

3 Perception of sentence stress and pitch change by native speakers of American English   67

- 3.1 Introduction   67
- 3.2 Experiment   67
  - 3.2.1 Purpose   67
  - 3.2.2 Method   67
  - 3.2.3 Materials   67
  - 3.2.4 Method of synthesis   69
  - 3.2.5 Method of perception test   74
- 3.3 Stress perception by native speakers of American English (Group A)   78
  - 3.3.1 Background theory   78
  - 3.3.2 Test of incorrect answer rate   78
  - 3.3.3 Test of difference in incorrect answer rate between words   86
- 3.4 Details of answers   92
- 3.5 Test of difference in incorrect answer rate between Sentence 1 and Sentence 2   108
- 3.6 Total perception rate of Sentence 1 and Sentence 2   109
- 3.7 Summary   110

4. Perception of pitch change with a comparison of native speakers of American English and Japanese   111

- 4.1 Introduction   111
- 4.2 Experiment   112
  - 4.2.1 Purpose   112
  - 4.2.2 Method   112
- 4.3 Stress perception by Japanese learners of English (Group B)   112
  - 4.3.1 Background theory   112
  - 4.3.2 Test of incorrect answer rates   113
  - 4.3.3 Test of difference in incorrect answer rate between words   117
  - 4.3.4 Test of difference in incorrect answer rate between Sentence 1 and Sentence 2   125
  - 4.3.5 Total perception rate of Sentence 1 and Sentence 2   126
- 4.4 Comparison of incorrect answer rate between American subjects and Japanese subjects   127

	4.4.1	Test of difference in incorrect answer rates of words between American subjects and Japanese subjects	127
	4.4.2	Test of difference in incorrect answer rates of sentences between American subjects and Japanese subjects	139
4.5		Details of answers from American subjects and Japanese subjects	141
4.6		Test of difference in incorrect answer rate between American subjects and Japanese subjects (total of Sentence 1 and Sentence 2)	146
4.7		Summary	148

5. Perception of pitch change with a comparison of native speakers of American English, British English and Japanese — 149

5.1		Introduction	149
5.2		Experiment	149
	5.2.1	Purpose	149
	5.2.2	Method	149
5.3		Stress perception by native speakers of British English (Group C)	150
	5.3.1	Background theory	150
	5.3.2	Test of incorrect answer rates	151
	5.3.3	Test of difference in incorrect answer rates between words	154
5.4		Test of difference in incorrect answer rates of words between American subjects and British subjects	161
5.5		Comparison of pitch movements between American subjects and British subjects	172
5.6		Details of answers from American subjects, Japanese subjects and British subjects	175
5.7		Total perception rates of Sentence 1 and Sentence 2 by British subjects	179
5.8		Test of difference in incorrect answer rates of sentences between American subjects and British subjects	180
5.9		Test of difference in incorrect answer rates of words between British subjects and Japanese subjects	182
5.10		Test of difference in incorrect answer rates of sentences between British subjects and Japanese subjects	192
5.11		Test of difference in incorrect answer rates between American subjects, Japanese subjects and British subjects (total of Sentence 1 and Sentence 2)	195
5.12		Summary	197

6 Relationship between perception of pitch change in speech and ability to distinguish pitch levels in music — 199
- 6.1 Introduction — 199
- 6.2 Purpose — 200
- 6.3 Experiment 1 — 200
- 6.4 Experiment 2 — 201
- 6.5 Method — 208
- 6.6 Analysis — 210
  - 6.6.1 Correlation coefficient between the perception rates of piano tones and the perception rates of synthesized utterances — 210
  - 6.6.2 Regression line of the perception rates of piano tones and the perception rates of synthesized utterances — 214
  - 6.6.3 Test of correlation coefficient between the perception rates of piano tones and the perception rates of synthesized utterances — 215
- 6.7 Summary — 216

7 Relationship between perception of sentence stress and ability to distinguish pitch levels in music — 217
- 7.1 Introduction — 217
- 7.2 Purpose — 217
- 7.3 Method — 217
- 7.4 Analysis — 221
  - 7.4.1 Correlation coefficient between the perception rates of piano tones and the perception rates of sentence stress — 221
  - 7.4.2 Regression line of the perception rates of piano tones and the perception rates of sentence stress — 224
  - 7.4.3 Test of correlation coefficient between the perception pates of piano tones and the perception rates of sentence stress — 226
- 7.5 Summary — 226

Conclusion — 227

References — 231
Index — 237

Preface

This book examines whether pitch variations play an important role in both producing and perceiving sentence stress (nucleus, contrastive and emphatic stress) in English. Although word stress has been studied (D.B.Fry, 1955, 1958, 1965; Nakatani and Aston, 1978; Beckman, 1986), sentence stress has not been researched extensively. This book examines the effect of changes in pitch on the emphasized word in a sentence. This book also examines the relationship between the perception of the emphasized word in English and musical sensitivity.

The author devised a new pitch contour "F_0 contour S" (Sasaki, 2002 a). Using this pitch contour, pitch patterns of native speakers of English and native speakers of Japanese can be compared visually. From "F_0 contour S", we find that sentence stress is not produced by Japanese learners of English who do not speak English well. Students should be instructed in English pitch patterns visually in order to speak English naturally. It is effective for students to be instructed both aurally and visually about the difference of pitch patterns between native speakers of English and native speakers of Japanese using "F_0 contour S".

This book is based on my PhD dissertation presented to and approved by Kanto Gakuin University in 2004. The dissertation's title is "*Fundamental Frequency Pattern and Sentence Stress in English: From Acoustic Point of View.*" Chapter 6 of the dissertation, entitled 'Relationship between Perception of Fundamental Frequency Patterns and Music Ability', has not been included here because the subjects' music ability was based on a subjective self-evaluation. In follow-up studies, the relationship between the subjects' ability in music and the perception of pitch changes (Sasaki, 2008) and the relationship between the subjects' ability in music and the perception of sentence stress (Sasaki, 2009) were analyzed. These studies were used to write Chapters 6 and 7 of this book.

Message

Prosodic features play a critical role in first language acquisition and second language learning. This is now well established. Yet we are still a long way from a detailed understanding of how languages with rather different prosodic systems, such as those of Japanese and English, impact upon second language learners perception and production of prosodic contrasts in the second language. This monograph, which is an elaboration with further research of the author's 2004 PhD dissertation, makes a significant contribution to this growing field of study.

Prosody is often defined as the music of language, raising the inevitable question of how musical training affects learners' ability to perceive and produce prosodic contrasts in the second language.

Following quite a comprehensive review of classical phonetic studies of acoustic and articulatory correlates of English word stress, discussion turns to English stress at the sentence level (accent marking) and how it differs from and may relate to prosodic systems of accent marking, timing and information highlighting in Japanese.

The focus of experimental interest in the research reported here is the perception and production of contrastive and emphatic stress by Japanese learners of English. The author seeks to investigate Japanese learners of English sensitivity to pitch peaks (f0 perturbations) as cues to emphatic and contrastive stress in the speech of selected speakers of standard American and British English.

She develops a method of visually displaying this cue in isolation from others that may be present in the signal, presumably with the intention of using this feature for instructional feedback of learners, though this is not explicitly discussed in the text. She employs speech synthesis to systematically vary the placement and extent of f0 perturbation in order to assess learners' ability to identify the locus of contrastive stress in synthesized utterances modeled on American and British speakers. In the later chapters she develops an objective measure of musical pitch sensitivity and correlates this with the performance of language learners' ability to utilize pitch pattern as a cue to stress in resynthesized English speech. This monograph is very clearly written and explores questions that take us to the heart of issues that currently preoccupy phonetic research in second language learning.

March 28, 2016

Dr. John C.L. Ingram

Former Senior Lecturer
Phonetics & Phonology
The University of Queensland

Acknowledgements

I would like to thank all those who generously gave their time advising and assisting me during the preparation of this book.

I would especially like to thank Professor Kazuo Misono of the Graduate School of Humanities, Kanto Gakuin University, who provided valuable instruction and expert guidance as my supervisor. Professor Fumio Hirasaka, Professor Seigo Tanimoto, Professor William I Elliott and Professor David Minton of the same university also provided generous support and encouraged me when I was a graduate student.

Dr. John C.L. Ingram of Phonetics & Phonology, the University of Queensland, generously read the manuscript and offered valuable suggestions. Ms. Chitoshi Kurokawa who is a lecturer of Kokugakuin University, kindly assisted me with devising piano pitch tones for my research.

I would also like to thank Professor Masaki Tsuzuki of Aichi Gakuin University who is the president of the English Phonetic Society of Japan (EPSJ). This book is published as the eighth installment of the EPSJ English Phonetics series. I am truly grateful to all those who participated in the experiments and to the large number of people who helped me in so many ways to write this book.

Lastly, the writing of this book has been supported by the grant-in-aid of Seseragi Foundation.

Figures

2.1	F_0 contour and waveform of "Ignore the gloom and **DOOM**" by A1	31
2.2	F_0 contour and waveform of "Ignore the gloom and **DOOM**" by A2	31
2.3	F_0 contour and waveform of "Ignore the gloom and **DOOM**" by A3	31
2.4	F_0 contour and waveform of "Ignore the gloom and **DOOM**" by J1	31
2.5	F_0 contour and waveform of "Ignore the gloom and **DOOM**" by J2	31
2.6	F_0 contour and waveform of "Ignore the gloom and **DOOM**" by J3	31
2.7	F_0 contours of "Ignore the gloom and **DOOM**" by three American informants severally and averaged	35
2.8	F_0 contours of "Ignore the gloom and **DOOM**" by three Japanese informants severally and averaged	35
2.9	The average F_0 contours by American and Japanese informants uttering "Ignore the gloom and **DOOM**"	35
2.10	The changes in F_0 between the stressed syllable "**DOOM**" and the preceding syllable "and" by three American informants severally and averaged	37
2.11	The changes in F_0 between the stressed syllable "**DOOM**" and the preceding syllable "and" by three Japanese informants severally and averaged	37
2.12	Comparison of the changes in F_0 of the stressed syllable between American informants and Japanese informants	37
2.13	F_0 contours of "Ignore the gloom and doom" by three American informants severally and averaged	37
2.14	F_0 contours of "Ignore the **GLOOM** and doom" by three American informants severally and averaged	38
2.15	F_0 contours of "Ignore the **GLOOM** and doom" by three Japanese informants severally and averaged	38

2.16	The average F_0 contours of "IgNORE the gloom and doom" by American and Japanese informants	39
2.17	F_0 contours of "Avoid every kind of evil." by three American, three Japanese and averaged	42
2.18	F_0 contours of "AVOID every kind of evil." by three American, three Japanese and averaged	43
2.19	F_0 contours of "Avoid EVery kind of evil." by three American, three Japanese and averaged	44
2.20	F_0 contours of "Avoid every kind of Evil." by three American, three Japanese and averaged	45
2.21	F_0 contours of "Avoid every kind of evil?" by three American, three Japanese and averaged	46
2.22	F_0 contours of "AVOID every kind of evil?" by three American, three Japanese and averaged	47
2.23	F_0 contours of "Avoid EVery kind of evil?" by three American, three Japanese and averaged	48
2.24	F_0 contours of "Avoid every kind of Evil?" by three American, three Japanese and averaged	49
2.25	F_0 contours of "Ignore the gloom and doom." by three American, three Japanese and averaged	50
2.26	F_0 contours of "IgNORE the gloom and doom." by three American, three Japanese and averaged	51
2.27	F_0 contours of "Ignore the GLOOM and doom." by three American, three Japanese and averaged	52
2.28	F_0 contours of "Ignore the gloom and DOOM." by three American, three Japanese and averaged	53
2.29	F_0 contours of "Ignore the gloom and doom?" by three American, three Japanese and averaged	54
2.30	F_0 contours of "IgNORE the gloom and doom?" by three American, three Japanese and averaged	55
2.31	F_0 contours of "Ignore the GLOOM and doom?" by three American, three Japanese and averaged	56
2.32	F_0 contours of "Ignore the gloom and DOOM?" by three American, three Japanese and averaged	57
2.33	F_0 contours of "But you love me!" by three American, three Japanese and averaged	58
2.34	F_0 contours of "But YOU love me!" by three American, three Japanese and averaged	59
2.35	F_0 contours of "But you LOVE me!" by three American, three Japanese and averaged	60
2.36	F_0 contours of "But you love ME!" by three American, three Japanese and averaged	61

2.37	F₀ contours of "But you love me?" by three American, three Japanese and averaged	62
2.38	F₀ contours of "Do you love me?" by three American, three Japanese and averaged	63
2.39	F₀ contours of "Do **YOU** love me?" by three American, three Japanese and averaged	64
2.40	F₀ contours of "Do you **LOVE** me?" by three American, three Japanese and averaged	65
2.41	F₀ contours of "Do you love **ME**?" by three American, three Japanese and averaged	66
3.1	F₀ contour of "**AVOID** every kind of evil" by A1	68
3.2	F₀ contour of "Ig**NORE** the gloom and doom" by A1	68
3.3	Synthesized F₀ contour of "Avoid every kind of evil" ('steady')	70
3.4	Synthesized F₀ contour of "A*void* every kind of evil"	70
3.5	Synthesized F₀ contour of "Avoid *ev*ery kind of evil"	71
3.6	Synthesized F₀ contour of "Avoid every *kind* of evil"	71
3.7	Synthesized F₀ contour of "Avoid every kind of *e*vil"	71
3.8	Illustration of Figure 3.3, "Avoid every kind of evil" ('steady')	71
3.9	Illustration of Figure 3.4, "A*void* every kind of evil"	72
3.10	Illustration of Figure 3.5, "Avoid *ev*ery kind of evil"	72
3.11	Illustration of Figure 3.6, "Avoid every *kind* of evil"	72
3.12	Illustration of Figure 3.7, "Avoid every kind of *e*vil"	72
3.13	Synthesized F₀ contour of "Ignore the gloom and doom" ('steady')	73
3.14	Synthesized F₀ contour of "Ig*nore* the gloom and doom"	73
3.15	Synthesized F₀ contour of "Ignore the *gloom* and doom"	73
3.16	Synthesized F₀ contour of "Ignore the gloom and *doom*"	73
3.17	Illustration of Figure 3.13, "Ignore the gloom and doom" ('steady')	73
3.18	Illustration of s Figure 3.14, "Ig*nore* the gloom and doom"	74
3.19	Illustration of Figure 3.15, "Ignore the *gloom* and doom"	74
3.20	Illustration of Figure 3.16, "Ignore the gloom and *doom*"	74
3.21	The incorrect answer rate of each word by AEs (Group A) <Sentence 1>	79
3.22	The incorrect answer rate of each word by AEs (Group A) <Sentence 2>	80
3.23	Estimated value of the incorrect answer rate for each word by AEs (Group A) <Sentence 1>	85
3.24	Estimated value of the incorrect answer rate for each word by AEs (Group A) <Sentence 2>	86
3.25	Comparison of the incorrect answer rates <Sentence 1>	91
3.26	Comparison of the incorrect answer rates <Sentence 2>	91

3.27	F_0 contour of "Avoid every kind of **E**vil" by informant A1	92
3.28	The comparison of the utterance time between when A1 places stress on "A**VOID**" (the top bar) and when A1 places stress on "**E**vil" (the bottom bar)	93
3.29	Answers of Higher "*e*vil"	94
3.30	F_0 contour of Sentence 1 with no stressed words by informant A1	95
3.31	Answers of 'steady' <Sentence 1>	96
3.32	Answers of Higher "A*void*"	96
3.33	F_0 contour of "Avoid **EV**ery kind of evil" by informant A1	97
3.34	Answers of Higher "*ev*ery"	97
3.35	F_0 contour of "Avoid every **KIND** of evil" by informant A1	98
3.36	Answers of Higher "*kind*"	98
3.37	F_0 contour of Sentence 2 with the stress on "**DOOM**" by informant A1	99
3.38	The comparison of the utterance time between when A1 places stress on "Ig**NORE**" (the top bar) and when A1 places stress on "**DOOM**" (the bottom bar)	100
3.39	Answers of Higher "*doom*"	101
3.40	F_0 contour of Sentence 2 with no stressed words by informant A1	102
3.41	Answers of 'steady' <Sentence 2>	102
3.42	F_0 contour of Sentence 2 with the stress on "**GLOOM**" by informant A1	103
3.43	Answers of Higher "*gloom*"	104
3.44	Answers of Higher "Ig*nore*"	104
3.45	Comparison of the incorrect answer rates between Sentence 1 and Sentence 2	109
3.46	The perception rate of Sentence 1 and Sentence 2	109
4.1	The incorrect answer rate of each word by Js (Group B) <Sentence 1>	115
4.2	The incorrect answer rate of each word by Js (Group B) <Sentence 2>	115
4.3	Estimated value of the incorrect answer rate for each word by Js (Group B) <Sentence 1>	116
4.4	Estimated value of the incorrect answer rate for each word by Js (Group B) <Sentence 2>	117
4.5	Comparison of the incorrect answer rates of words in Sentence 1 by Js	123
4.6	Comparison of the incorrect answer rates of words in Sentence 1 by AEs	123

List of figures xvii

4.7	Comparison of the incorrect answer rates of words in Sentence 2 by Js	124
4.8	Comparison of the incorrect answer rates of words in Sentence 2 by AEs	124
4.9	The incorrect answer rates of Sentence 1 and Sentence 2 by Js	125
4.10	Total perception rate of Sentence 1 and Sentence 2 by Js	126
4.11	Results of testing to determine whether there are significant differences in the incorrect answer rates of words in Sentence 1 between AEs (A) and Js (B)	137
4.12	Results of testing to determine whether there are significant differences in the incorrect answer rates of words in Sentence 2 between AEs (A) and Js (B)	138
4.13	The incorrect answer rates of Sentence 1 by AEs and Js	140
4.14	The incorrect answer rates of Sentence 2 by AEs and Js	141
4.15	Answers by AEs (Left) and Js (Right) when "_e_vil" was set to higher in F_0	142
4.16	Answers by AEs (Left) and Js (Right) in the case of 'steady' in Sentence 1	142
4.17	Answers by AEs (Left) and Js (Right) when "A_void_" was set to higher in F_0	142
4.18	Answers by AEs (Left) and Js (Right) when "e_v_ery" was set to higher in F_0	143
4.19	Answers by AEs (Left) and Js (Right) when "_kind_" was set to higher in F_0	143
4.20	Answers by AEs (Left) and Js (Right) when "_doom_" was set to higher in F_0	144
4.21	Answers by AEs (Left) and Js (Right) in the case of 'steady' in Sentence 2	144
4.22	Answers by AEs (Left) and Js (Right) when "_gloom_" was set to higher in F_0	144
4.23	Answers by AEs (Left) and Js (Right) when "Ig_nore_" was set to higher in F_0	145
4.24	Comparison of the incorrect answer rates between AEs and Js (total of Sentence 1 and Sentence 2)	148
5.1	The incorrect answer rate of each word by BEs (Group C) <Sentence 1>	152
5.2	The incorrect answer rate of each word by BEs (Group C) <Sentence 2>	153
5.3	Estimated value of the incorrect answer rate for each word by BEs (Group C) <Sentence 1>	153
5.4	Estimated value of the incorrect answer rate for each word by BEs (Group C) <Sentence 2>	154

5.5	Comparison of the incorrect answer rates of words in Sentence 1 by BEs	161
5.6	Comparison of the incorrect answer rates of words in Sentence 2 by BEs	161
5.7	Results of testing to determine whether there are significant differences in the incorrect answer rates of words in Sentence 1 between AEs (A) and BEs (C)	170
5.8	Results of testing to determine whether there are significant difference in the incorrect answer rates of words in Sentence 2 between AEs (A) and BEs (C)	171
5.9	F_0 contour of "AVOID every kind of evil" by informant B1 (British informant)	172
5.10	F_0 contour of "AVOID every kind of evil" by informant A1 (American informant)	172
5.11	F_0 contour of "Avoid EVery kind of evil" by informant B1	173
5.12	F_0 contour of "Avoid EVery kind of evil" by informant A1	173
5.13	F_0 contour of "Avoid every KIND of evil" by informant B1	173
5.14	F_0 contour of "Avoid every KIND of evil" by informant A1	173
5.15	F_0 contour of "Avoid every kind of Evil" by informant B1	173
5.16	F_0 contour of "Avoid every kind of Evil" by informant A1	173
5.17	F_0 contour of "IgNORE the gloom and doom" by informant B1	174
5.18	F_0 contour of "IgNORE the gloom and doom" by informant A1	174
5.19	F_0 contour of "Ignore the GLOOM and doom" by informant B1	174
5.20	F_0 contour of "Ignore the GLOOM and doom" by informant A1	174
5.21	F_0 contour of "Ignore the gloom and DOOM" by informant B1	174
5.22	F_0 contour of "Ignore the gloom and DOOM" by informant A1	174
5.23	Answers by AEs (A), Js (B) and BEs (C) when "A_void_" was set to higher in F_0	177
5.24	Answers by AEs (A), Js (B) and BEs (C) when _ev_ery was set to higher in F_0	177
5.25	Answers by AEs (A), Js (B) and BEs (C) when "_kind_" was set to higher in F_0	177
5.26	Answers by AEs (A), Js (B) and BEs (C) when "_e_vil" was set to higher in F_0	178
5.27	Answers by AEs (A), Js (B) and BEs (C) in the case of 'steady' in Sentence 1	178
5.28	Answers by AEs (A), Js (B) and BEs (C) when "Ig_nore_" was set to higher in F_0	178
5.29	Answers by AEs (A), Js (B) and BEs (C) when "_gloom_" was set to higher in F_0	178
5.30	Answers by AEs (A), Js (B) and BEs (C) when "_doom_" was set to higher in F_0	179

5.31	Answers by AEs (A), Js (B) and BEs (C) in the case of 'steady' in Sentence 2	179
5.32	The perception rate of Sentence 1 and Sentence 2	180
5.33	Results of testing to determine whether there is a significant difference in the incorrect answer rates in Sentence 1 between AEs and BEs	181
5.34	Results of testing to determine whether there is a significant difference in the incorrect answer rates in Sentence 2 between AEs and BEs	182
5.35	Results of testing to determine whether there is a significant difference in the incorrect answer rates of words in Sentence 1 between Js (B) and BEs (C)	191
5.36	Results of testing to determine whether there is a significant difference in the incorrect answer rates of words in Sentence 2 between Js (B) and BEs (C)	192
5.37	Results of testing to determine whether there is a significant difference in the incorrect answer rates in Sentence 1 between Js and BEs	194
5.38	Results of testing to determine whether there is a significant difference in the incorrect answer rates in Sentence 2 between Js and BEs	194
5.39	The significant difference in perception rates between AEs, Js and BEs	196
6.1	Examples of piano tones	201
6.2	F_0 contour and waveform of A1 stressed on "**NOW**"	203
6.3	F_0 contour and waveform of B1 stressed on "**NOW**"	203
6.4	No prominent synthesized contour	203
6.5	Illustration of contour in Figure 6.4	203
6.6	"_You_" is set to 26.9 Hz higher	203
6.7	"_You_" is set to 55.5 Hz higher	203
6.8	"_may_" is set to 26.9 Hz higher than "you"	204
6.9	"_may_" is set to 55.5 Hz higher than "you"	204
6.10	"_go_" is set to 26.9 Hz higher than "may"	204
6.11	"_go_" is set to 55.5 Hz higher than "may"	204
6.12	"_in_" is set to 26.9 Hz higher than "go"	204
6.13	"_in_" is set to 55.5 Hz higher than "go"	204
6.14	"_now_" is set to 26.9 Hz higher than "in"	204
6.15	"_now_" is set to 55.5 Hz higher than "in"	204
6.16	Illustration of contour in Figure 6.6	207
6.17	Illustration of contour in Figure 6.7	207
6.18	Illustration of contour in Figure 6.8	207
6.19	Illustration of contour in Figure 6.9	207

6.20	Illustration of contour in Figure 6.10	207
6.21	Illustration of contour in Figure 6.11	207
6.22	Illustration of contour in Figure 6.12	207
6.23	Illustration of contour in Figure 6.13	207
6.24	Illustration of contour in Figure 6.14	207
6.25	Illustration of contour in Figure 6.15	207
6.26	Questionnaire	209
6.27	Regression line of x and y (Data from Table 6.6)	215
7.1	Questionnaire	220
7.2	Regression line of x and y (Data from Table 7.5)	225

Tables

2.1	Background of the six informants	30
2.2	Change of emphasis in test sentences	30
2.3	F_0 of "Ignore the gloom and **DOOM**" by three American informants and their average F_0	32
2.4	F_0 of "Ignore the gloom and **DOOM**" by three American informants where the beginning of each sentence was set at 100 Hz	33
2.5	F_0 of "Ignore the gloom and **DOOM**" by three Japanese informants and their average F_0	33
2.6	F_0 of "Ignore the gloom and **DOOM**" by three Japanese informants where the beginning of each sentence was set at 100 Hz	34
2.7	The changes in F_0 between the stressed syllable and the preceding syllable by three American informants	34
2.8	The changes in F_0 between the stressed syllable and the preceding syllable by three American informants where the beginning of each sentence was set at 100 Hz	34
2.9	The changes in F_0 between the stressed syllable and the preceding syllable by three Japanese informants	36
2.10	The changes in F_0 between the stressed syllable and the preceding syllable by three Japanese informants where the beginning of each sentence was set at 100 Hz	36
3.1	List of change in stress in synthesized utterances	75
3.2	Background of the forty subjects	76
3.3	Perception test sheet	77
3.4	The incorrect answer rate of each word by AEs (Group A) <Sentence 1>	79
3.5	The incorrect answer rate of each word by AEs (Group A) <Sentence 2>	79
3.6	Estimated value of the incorrect answer rate for each word by AEs (Group A) <Sentence 1>	85

3.7	Estimated value of the incorrect answer rate for each word by AEs (Group A) <Sentence 2>	85
3.8	Details of answers in Sentence 1	105
3.9	Details of answers in Sentence 1 (%)	105
3.10	Details of answers in Sentence 2	107
3.11	Details of answers in Sentence 2 (%)	107
3.12	Comparison of the incorrect answer rates between Sentence 1 and Sentence 2	108
3.13	The perception rate of Sentence 1 and Sentence 2	109
4.1	The incorrect answer rate of each word by Js (Group B) <Sentence 1>	113
4.2	The incorrect answer rate of each word by Js (Group B) <Sentence 2>	114
4.3	Estimated value of the incorrect answer rate for each word by Js (Group B) <Sentence 1>	116
4.4	Estimated value of the incorrect answer rate for each word by Js (Group B) <Sentence 2>	116
4.5	The incorrect answer rates of Sentence 1 and Sentence 2 by Js	125
4.6	Total perception rate of Sentence 1 and Sentence 2 by Js	126
4.7	The numbers of correct and incorrect answers by AEs (Group A) and Js (Group B) when "_e_vil" was set to higher in F_0	128
4.8	The numbers of correct and incorrect answers by AEs (Group A) and Js (Group B) when F_0 was decreased uniformly ('steady') in Sentence 1	129
4.9	The numbers of correct and incorrect answers by AEs (Group A) and Js (Group B) when "A_void_" was set to higher in F_0	130
4.10	The numbers of correct and incorrect answers by AEs (Group A) and Js (Group B) when "_e_very" was set to higher in F_0	131
4.11	The numbers of correct and incorrect answers by AEs (Group A) and Js (Group B) when "_kind_" was set to higher in F_0	132
4.12	The numbers of correct and incorrect answers by AEs (Group A) and Js (Group B) when "_doom_" was set to higher in F_0	133
4.13	The numbers of correct and incorrect answers by AEs (Group A) and Js (Group B) when F_0 was decreased uniformly ('steady') in Sentence 2	134
4.14	The numbers of correct and incorrect answers by AEs (Group A) and Js (Group B) when "_gloom_" was set to	

	higher in F_0	134
4.15	The numbers of correct and incorrect answers by AEs (Group A) and Js (Group B) when "Ig*nore*" was set to higher in F_0	135
4.16	Significant differences in the incorrect answer rates of words in Sentence 1 between AEs (A) and Js (B)	139
4.17	Significant differences in the incorrect answer rates of words in Sentence 2 between AEs (A) and Js (B)	139
4.18	The incorrect answer rates of Sentence 1 by AEs and Js	140
4.19	The incorrect answer rates of Sentence 2 by AEs and Js	141
4.20	Comparison of the incorrect answer rates between AEs and Js	147
5.1	The incorrect answer rate of each word by BEs (Group C) <Sentence 1>	151
5.2	The incorrect answer rate of each word by BEs (Group C) <Sentence 2>	151
5.3	Estimated value of the incorrect answer rate for each word by BEs (Group C) <Sentence 1>	153
5.4	Estimated value of the incorrect answer rate for each word by BEs (Group C) <Sentence 2>	153
5.5	Correct and incorrect answer rates by AEs (Group A) and BEs (Group C) when "*e*vil" was set to higher in F_0	162
5.6	Correct and incorrect answer rates by AEs (Group A) and BEs (Group C) when F_0 was decreased uniformly ('steady') in Sentence 1	163
5.7	Correct and incorrect answer rates by AEs (Group A) and BEs (Group C) when "A*void*" was set to higher in F_0	164
5.8	Correct and incorrect answer rates by AEs (Group A) and BEs (Group C) when "*ev*ery" was set to higher in F_0	165
5.9	Correct and incorrect answer rates by AEs (Group A) and BEs (Group C) when "*kind*" was set to higher in F_0	165
5.10	Correct and incorrect answer rates by AEs (Group A) and BEs (Group C) when "*doom*" was set to higher in F_0	166
5.11	Correct and incorrect answer rates by AEs (Group A) and BEs (Group C) when F_0 was decreased uniformly ('steady') in Sentence 2	167
5.12	Correct and incorrect answer rates by AEs (Group A) and BEs (Group C) when "*gloom*" was set to higher in F_0	168
5.13	Correct and incorrect answer rates by AEs (Group A) and BEs (Group C) when "Ig*nore*" was set to higher in F_0	169
5.14	The perception rate of Sentence 1 and Sentence 2	179
5.15	The incorrect answer rates of Sentence 1 by AEs and BEs	181
5.16	The incorrect answer rates of Sentence 2 by AEs and BEs	182

5.17	Correct and incorrect answer rates by Js (Group B) and BEs (Group C) when "_e_vil" was set to higher in F_0	183
5.18	Correct and incorrect answer rates by Js (Group B) and BEs (Group C) when F_0 was decreased uniformly ('steady') in Sentence 1	184
5.19	Correct and incorrect answer rates by Js (Group B) and BEs (Group C) when "A_void_" was set to higher in F_0	185
5.20	Correct and incorrect answer rates by Js (Group B) and BEs (Group C) when "_e_very" was set to higher in F_0	186
5.21	Correct and incorrect answer rates by Js (Group B) and BEs (Group C) when "_kind_" was set to higher in F_0	186
5.22	Correct and incorrect answer rates by Js (Group B) and BEs (Group C) when "_doom_" was set to higher in F_0	187
5.23	Correct and incorrect answer rates by Js (Group B) and BEs (Group C) when F_0 was decreased uniformly ('steady') in Sentence 2	188
5.24	Correct and incorrect answer rates by Js (Group B) and BEs (Group C) when "_gloom_" was set to higher in F_0	189
5.25	Correct and incorrect answer rates by Js (Group B) and BEs (Group C) when "Ig_nore_" was set to higher in F_0	189
5.26	The incorrect answer rates of Sentence 1 by Js and BEs	194
5.27	The incorrect answer rates of Sentence 2 by Js and BEs	194
5.28	Comparison of the incorrect answer rates between AEs, Js and BEs (Total of Sentence 1 and Sentence 2)	195
6.1	List of recorded synthesized utterances: Statement 1 and Statement 2	205
6.2	List of recorded synthesized utterances: Question 1 and Question 2	206
6.3	List of piano tones	206
6.4	List of synthesized F_0 variations in Hz	208
6.5	Perception rates of piano tones and of synthesized utterances	210
6.6	Distribution of perception rates of piano tones and of synthesized utterances	211
6.7	The analysis result of Table 6.6	212
7.1	Change of emphasis in test sentences	218
7.2	List of sentences by native speakers of English	219
7.3	Perception rates of sentence stress by 150 Japanese subjects	222
7.4	Perception rates of sentence stress and of piano tones	223
7.5	Distribution of perception rates of piano tones and of sentence stress	223
7.6	The analysis result of Table 7.5	224

List of Abbreviations

AE: one native speaker of American English
BE: one native speaker of British English
AEs: native speakers of American English
BEs: native speakers of British English
Js: Japanese learners of English

Group A: forty native speakers of American English
Group B: one hundred and sixteen Japanese learners of English
Group C: thirty-six native speakers of British English

F_0: Fundamental frequency
F_0 contour S: F_0 contour devised by the author

Sentence 1: "Avoid every kind of evil."
Sentence 2: "Ignore the gloom and doom."

Statement 1: "You may go in now."
Statement 2: "I always knew you were alive."
Question 1: "Are you all well?"
Question 2: "Now where are we going?"

Introduction

Although written language is not connected with 'prosodic features', every spoken language has 'prosodic features' peculiar to the language. 'Prosodic features' are also called 'suprasegmental phonemes', which are features that distinguish one language from another (Ohyama, Suzuki, *et al.*, 1989).

Intonation is one of the 'suprasegmental phonemes'. Intonation is physically defined as the pattern of pitch (fundamental frequency) variation and in a broad sense, as a total tone phenomenon exhibiting among others as stress, pitch, and pause. In Cruttenden (2001:301), Gimson states that "intonation makes a most important contribution to the accentual patterning of English (pitch variation serving to accent and hence make salient those information points to which the speaker wishes to draw attention)". English has an aspect of 'intonation language', and so intonation affects not only the impression of good natural English-speaking but also the meaning. Learners whose goal is to speak English fluently and whose goal is a level of 'minimal general intelligibility' should both learn English pitch variations (Imai, 1989; Cruttenden, 2001). Learners who want to speak English naturally need to control pitch variations of the whole utterance in English well (Fujisaki, Sugito, *et al.*, 1982).

It is important for instructors of English to teach certain basic features of English, such as 'rhythm', 'word stress', 'consonant cluster', 'linking', 'assimilation', 'elision', 'sentence stress', and 'pitch variation'. This book focuses on pitch variation on sentence stress among these features of English. Teachers should also teach the features of English that are not found in the learner's native language. Japanese prosodic features and English prosodic features are compared in section 1.4 in this book.

Since acoustic research on word stress was undertaken by the leading British experimental phonetician, D.B.Fry (1955), various studies on word stress have been conducted and have revealed that stressed syllables are marked not only by greater intensity, but also by a higher fundamental frequency (F_0), greater duration, or more clearly defined vowel qualities than unstressed syllables (Fry, 1955, 1958, 1965; Lieberman, 1960; Nakatani and Aston, 1978; Beckman, 1986). Among these factors, pitch (F_0) and duration are said to be especially powerful factors in the perception of word stress (Roach, 2000). On the other hand, sentence stress has not been researched extensively.

Music seems to enhance spatial-temporal reasoning abilities, such as mathematics and science (Rauscher, *et.al.*, 1997). Is there also a relationship between music and language? Only a few studies on the relationship between language and music (Patel, 2008; Pastuszek-Lipinska, 2007; Magne, *et al.*, 2006) have been conducted.

The first objective of this book is to show visually how pitch variation plays an important role in producing prominent stress in a sentence. The second objective is to show statistically how pitch variation plays an important role in perceiving the focused word in a sentence. The third objective of this book is to examine the relationship between the perception of music and the perception of English sentence stress (nucleus, nuclear stress, tonic syllable, tonic stress).

The term 'pitch' is sometimes used instead of 'fundamental frequency' in this book as well for the convenience of general readers. Strictly speaking, the term 'pitch' should be used to refer to a perceptual phenomenon and 'fundamental frequency' used to refer to a physical measure of the lowest periodic component of vocal fold vibration (Kent and Read, 1992:230,232). 'Fundamental frequency' is abbreviated as 'F_0'. I use the term 'sentence stress', but the term 'nucleus' or 'nuclear stress' also can be used because there is only one stressed syllable in each utterance used in this book.

The most important characteristic of this book is that the author succeeded in devising a new pitch contour in order to compare visually the pitch patterns on the stressed syllables of native speakers with those of non-native speakers. The difference of pitch patterns on the stressed syllables is not clearly comparable by the available speech processing software because the length and pitch of utterance naturally differs from person to person. Therefore, I made the length of utterance of each word the same by calculation without changing the shape of pitch patterns and made it possible to compare the pitch patterns of each word. Next, all utterances were set to start at the same pitch and the pitch patterns of plural subjects were displayed on a coordinate axis to show clearly how stressed syllables are higher in pitch than the preceding syllables. The whole pitch patterns are also easily compared between subjects. Furthermore, I drew the informants' average pitch contours by calculating digital data. The averaged pitch contours of native speakers of English group and the averaged pitch contours of Japanese learners of English group are drawn and compared visually on a coordinate axis (Chapter 2). This is based on research undertaken by Sasaki (2002a).

The aim of this book is threefold. Firstly, how pitch changes on the stressed syllables in a sentence produced by native speakers of English is examined from the production point of view (Chapter 2).

Secondly, the role of pitch variation in perceiving sentence stress (contrastive accent) in English is examined from the perception point of view. Pitch is controlled by the speech processing software to examine acoustically whether the large pitch changes are perceived as stressed syllables by 40 native speakers of American English (AEs), 36 native speakers of British English (BEs), and 116 Japanese learners of English (Js) (Chapters 3−5). This is based on research undertaken by Sasaki (2002b, 2003a, 2004c).

Thirdly, whether there is a relationship between musical sensitivity and ability to perceive pitch variation in English (Chapter 6) and a relationship between musical sensitivity and ability to perceive English sentence stress (contrastive accent) are examined (Chapter 7). These are based on research undertaken by Sasaki (2003b, 2004a, 2005, 2006, 2008, 2009).

This book is comprised of seven chapters. In Chapter 1, characteristics of stress (section 1.1), definitions of stress (section 1.2), previous research on English stress (section 1.3), comparisons of English prosodic features and Japanese prosodic features (section 1.4), and relationship between music and language (section 1.5) are discussed before stating the experimental results in Chapters 2−7. In Chapter 2, how pitch changes on the stressed syllable and whole pitch patterns in each sentence are visually shown.

In Chapter 3, the latest method of synthesizing speech was applied. The two imperative utterances by a native speaker of English were recorded and the fundamental frequency (F_0, pitch) was controlled in nine different ways in the higher F_0 syllable by speech processing software. Forty AEs listened to the nine stimulus types of synthesized utterances five times played at random in order to examine acoustically whether they perceive sentence stress on the higher syllable in F_0.

In Chapter 4, 116 Js listened to the same synthesized utterances and the result was compared with the result of AEs. In Chapter 5, 36 BEs listened to the same synthesized utterances and the result was compared with the results of AEs and Js.

In the experiment undertaken in Chapters 3−5, some listeners did not perceive stress on the higher syllable in F_0. I hypothesize that a listener who is unable to perceive pitch changes in synthesized utterances will also have a low ability to distinguish between high and low pitches in music.

The purpose of Chapter 6 is to examine the relationship between ability to perceive pitch changes in synthesized utterances (changes in F_0) and ability in music (ability to distinguish between pitch levels). The two declarative and the two interrogative utterances of a native speaker of English were synthesized using Praat. The F_0 parameter was changed so that one high-F_0 syllable was produced in each sentence. Forty-four stimulus types of synthesized utterances were recorded twice randomly and eighty-one Js listened to these synthesized utterances and thirty-six piano tones at controlled pitch levels twice at random.

Chapter 7 examines the relationship between ability to perceive sentence stress in English and ability to distinguish between pitch levels in music. Forty types of declarative and interrogative utterances with emphasis placed each time on a different word were uttered by two native speakers of English and recorded twice randomly. One hundred and fifty Js listened to the forty utterances and thirty-six piano tones twice at random.

This book emphasizes the importance for Japanese learners of English to be instructed in the pitch patterns of English, especially pitch patterns of the focused word in a sentence in order to speak English naturally.

1 Fundamental concepts

In Chapter 1, characteristics of stress (section 1.1), definitions of stress (section 1.2), previous research on English stress (section 1.3), comparison of English prosodic features and Japanese prosodic features (section 1.4) and the relationship between music and language (section 1.5) are discussed before stating the experimental results in Chapters 2−7.

1.1 Characteristics of stress

Suprasegmental phonemes, i.e. stress, pitch, length, tone, rhythm, and intonation function the same way as segmental phonemes, i.e. vowels and consonants. What this means is that a different stress in uttering a sentence can produce a different meaning in much the same way that different phonemes are interpreted as different words. For example, a **_HOT_ dog** means a hot frankfurter and a **_HOT DOG_** means a dog that is hot (stressed syllables are shown in capital and bold). The speech sounds [aɪbɛgjuə(r)pardn] can be understood as two different meanings depending on 'intonation'. If it is said with a rising intonation at the end of the utterance, it may be interpreted as "I beg your pardon?", meaning "Would you mind repeating that again, please?", while with a falling intonation "I beg your pardon." may mean "I'm sorry" (Misono, 1995:318). Tone of voice and context will determine what the intended meaning and effect will be.

1.1.1 Word stress

In Cruttenden (2001:300), Gimson states that "the correct accentual patterns associated with English words must be given an important and early place in any teaching programme. The correct accentual patterns of words should be learnt as they are first acquired."

Stress applied to a word is called 'word stress' and stress within a word group or sentence is called 'sentence stress'. The syllable or word that stands out from its neighbors is called 'prominent'.

Words in Japanese sometimes have no accent. However, in any English word with more than one syllable, one syllable is marked as having the main stress. The stress marked in a dictionary is called 'lexical stress'. In a polysyllabic word, the strength of a syllable differentiates it from other syllables. The number of degrees of stress differs between dictionaries and publications. When four degrees of stress are adopted, the kind of stress-mark is listed in order of strength as follows (Misono, 1995:277,278):

primary stress	[´] acute accent mark
secondary stress	[ˆ] circumflex accent mark
tertiary stress	[`] grave accent mark
weak stress	[˘] breve accent mark

In General American English, secondary stress is more often used than in British English (RP). For example (Misono, 1995:278),

	GA	RP
dictionary	[ˈdɪkʃənˌɛrɪ]	[ˈdɪkʃənərɪ]
preparatory	[prɪˈpærəˌtourɪ]	[prɪˈpærətərɪ]

In a noun phrase, prominent stress (nuclear stress) is assigned to the last stressed syllable. For example, 'black board' (=board which is black) normally has stress on the second element 'board'. The compound noun 'blackboard' (=board for writing on with chalk), on the other hand, takes primary stress on the first element 'black' (Fudge, 1984:134).

1.1.2 Sentence stress

Apart from 'word stress', stress on a word group or sentence is called 'sentence stress'. In an utterance in English, stressed words and unstressed words rhythmically occur at equal intervals (isochrony). This rhythm is called 'stress-timed rhythm'. Unstressed words are pronounced using a weak form or reduced form. 'Word stress ... differs from sentence-stress in that the stressed syllable of a word is not always given special prominence in pronunciation' (Fudge, 1984:1).

Laver (1994:514,515,517) explains the terms 'sentence stress', 'nuclear stress', 'emphatic stress' and 'nucleus' as follows:
"**Sentence stress** is simply another term for the placement of the nuclear intonational tone." "**Nuclear stress** is a term used by generative phonology (e.g. in Chomsky and Halle 1968) for the location of greatest syllabic prominence on phrases." "The function of **emphatic stress** is to call the listener's attention to a given syllable or word with greater insistence than is afforded merely by neutral patterns of intonation or lexical stress. In

the case where intonation and lexical stress are neutral, with a falling nuclear tone being placed on the lexically stressed syllable of the last content word in the utterance, as in the English utterance *The dog ate the biscuit*, emphatic stress can be used to give special emphasis to this syllable, as in *The dog ate the BIScuit*, with a wider pitch excursion, greater loudness and possibly a longer duration for the realization of the vowel." "Emphatic stress can also be used to highlight a syllable not normally receiving lexical stress ... in order to draw the listener's attention to a choice made by the speaker between potentially competing forms." "The nucleus is the perceptually most prominent part of the syllable."

Gillian Brown, *et al.* (1985:31) state that it is well known that in British studies what is called the 'tonic' or 'nuclear' tone is what in American work is called 'primary stress'.

It is generally accepted that 'lexical items' (content words) are more likely to receive stress than 'grammatical items' (function words). Nouns are more likely to receive stress than verbs and adverbs among the different classes of lexical items. 'Content words' and 'function words' are listed as follows:

- Content words: nouns, most verbs (excluding 'be' and 'have'), adjectives, most adverbs, demonstratives (this, that), interrogatives (who, when) and exclamations.
- Function words: articles, common conjunctions (and, if), prepositions, auxiliary verbs, modal verbs, personal pronouns (I, him), possessive adjectives (my, his), relative pronouns (who, which) and infinitive.

However, the following 'function words' usually receive stress. Demonstrative pronouns: this, that, these, those are usually stressed. For example: **THESE** are **Ex**cellent.

As demonstrative adjectives, the same words are less likely to be stressed. For example: Do you LIKE these FLOWERS?

When wh-words (who, which, what, whose, why, when, where, and how) are used as interrogatives, whether in direct or in indirect questions, they are usually stressed. However, they are not stressed when they are used as relatives. For example: This is the place where she lives.

Auxiliary and modal verbs are usually unstressed, but when they form negatives with n't, they are accentable, e.g. isn't.

A tone-group always has one prominent syllable which is called 'nucleus' or 'tonic'. If there is only one stressed syllable in a tone-group, then that syllable is the 'nucleus'. When there are several stressed words in a tone-group, 'nucleus' often falls on the last content word. Other stressed

8   Fundamental concepts

syllables in a tone-group may be less important and lose their pitch-prominence in order to keep the rhythmic beat.

The unstressed syllables at the beginning of tone-groups are called 'prehead'. The part of the stressed syllables between 'prehead' and 'nucleus' is called 'head'. The part of the syllables after 'nucleus' is called 'tail'.

In English, pitch is usually graduated on four levels (Misono, 1995:308). These are as follows:

/4/ extra high
/3/ high
/2/ mid
/1/ low.

The normal pitch which is used at the beginning of the utterance is /2/. /1/ is used at the end of the utterance in a falling tone. /3/ is used on the focused syllable or pitch peak in the utterance or used at the end of the utterance in a rising tone. /4/ is used when emphasis or surprise is added to /3/.

1.1.2.1 Stress shift

In the *Longman Pronunciation Dictionary* (2000), 'stress shift' is defined as follows:

> 1. Some words seem to change their stress pattern in connected speech. Although in isolation we say **fundamental** with the primary stress on [ment] and **Japanese** with the primary stress on [niˈz], in connected speech these words often have a different pattern. For example, there might be greater stress on [fʌnd] than on [ment], or greater stress on [dʒæp] than on [niˈz]. This phenomenon is known as **stress shift**. ([ ] is added by the author.)
> 2. A phrase usually receives late stress. The placing of primary stress on the last element of the phrase means that the basic stress of the first element is weakened: combining ˈweekly and ˈlessons gives the phrase ˌweekly ˈlessons. So you might expect that ˌfundaˈmental plus miˈstake would give fundaˌmental miˈstake, and that ˌJapaˈnese plus ˈlanguage would give Japaˌnese ˈlanguage.
> 3. But these stress patterns are unbalanced. To balance them, native speakers of English usually switch round the stress levels in the first element, and say ˌfundamental miˈstake, ˌJapanese ˈlanguage.
> 4. The same thing happens in a phrase such as ˌvery ˈlazy plus ˈpeople. Stress shift produces ˌvery lazy ˈpeople.
> 5. In principle, stress shift can apply to any word that has a secondary stress before its primary stress. In practice, though, it is most likely

to apply to those which are regularly followed in a phrase by a more strongly stressed word: most adjectives, but only certain nouns (Wells, 2000:742).

'Nucleus' often falls on the last lexical item of a tone-group. However, in the ordinary utterance, the location of 'nucleus' often shifts in a tone-group. Some of the reasons are listed as follows:

(1) Response
   A: "ˈWho ˈshot the ˈburglar?"
   B: "ˈMary shot the burglar." (Normal stress pattern: "ˈMary ˈshot the ˈburglar.") (Misono, 1995:296.)

(2) New information
   In general, new information receives the nucleus and information that has already been mentioned (old information) is pronounced with low pitch and weak stress. If the last content word contains old information, then the nucleus goes on the last content word that contains new information.

(3) Emphasis
   "Girls ˈand boys cried." means not only girls but also boys cried. A frequent function of "even" and "only" is to focus on what follows, with a nucleus often placed on the item which is brought into focus as follows:
   "ˈEven ˈshe can operate it".

(4) Contrast
   Function words can receive nucleus when contrastive. For example;
   "The cat is ˈunder the table, not ˈon the table." (Misono, 1995:297.)
   Old information can receive the nucleus if it is being contrasted with another item. Contrastiveness can override lexical stress. For example;
   "Did you say ˈsixteen or ˈseventeen?"   *"ˈSeventeen."*
   "We have tea, coffee and beer."   *"I'd prefer ˈbeer, please."*

(5) Structure, Rhythm
   In ordinary utterance in English, 'rhythmic stress' precedes 'lexical stress'. 'Lexical stress' shifts in the word in order to avoid a stress clash. For example;
   "I'll ˈtalk to you aˈbout it this afterˈnoon." (Maidment, 2002.)
   "I've inˈvited him to ˈafternoon ˈtea." (Maidment, 2002.)
   "I start this ˌafterˈnoon. I start by the ˈafterˌnoon ˈtrain." (Misono, 1995:298.)

10   Fundamental concepts

1.1.2.2 Weak form
Stressed syllables are usually uttered in 'strong form' or 'stressed form'. On the other hand, unstressed syllables are uttered in 'weak form', 'reduced form' or 'unstressed form'. There is a great difference in English between 'strong form' and 'weak form'. For example, the word "to" can be pronounced [tuː] (strong form) or [tə] (weak form). In the sentence, "Whom did you speak to?", "to" is pronounced [tuː] (strong form). In the sentence, "He went to the park", "to" is pronounced [tə] (weak form) (Misono, 1995:287-291).

Gimson states that the "rhythm of English (be it a single word or connected speech) with the related obscuration of weak syllables is a prime distinguishing feature of the language's pronunciation. In fact, in connected speech, unaccented syllables, a majority of which include reduced vowels, considerably outnumber those carrying primary or secondary accents" (Cruttenden, 2001:300). Gimson also states that it "is regarded as essential that the accentual characteristics of English (including rhythmic features and the associated obscuration of weak syllables) should be retained, as well as the ability to produce the common consonant clusters" (Cruttenden, 2001: 309).

Roach (2000) states as follows:

> It is possible to use only strong forms in speaking, and some foreigners do this. Usually they can still be understood by other speakers of English, so why is it important to learn how weak forms are used? There are two main reasons; first, most native speakers of English find an "all-strong-form" pronunciation unnatural and foreign-sounding, something that most learners would wish to avoid. Second, and more importantly, speakers who are not familiar with the use of weak forms are likely to have difficulty understanding speakers who do use weak forms; since practically all native speakers of British English use them, learners of the language need to learn about these weak forms to help them to understand what they hear (Roach, 2000:112).

In *The Pronunciation of American English*, Bronstein (1960) states as follows:

> A first-grade child may read the words of a sentence as though each word is of equal import, giving to each word equal stress. Such reading, sounding as if it were a series of items on a grocery list, does not convey the information expected from a normally spoken sentence. With the child's ability to read will come his use of the varied stress pat-

terns we associate with literate, intelligible reading and speaking (Bronstein, 1960:257).

1.2 Definitions of stress

There are two ways to approach the characteristics of stressed syllables. One is to consider what the speaker does to produce stressed syllables and the other is to consider what features of sounds make a syllable seem to a listener to be stressed. That is to say, stress can be studied either in terms of production or perception.

The terms 'stress', 'accent' and 'prominence' are ambiguous. Some publications do not distinguish 'stress' from 'accent' (Roach, 2000). Others distinguish 'stress' from 'accent' (Wells, 2000). Some definitions of stress are introduced as follows:

(1) *A Dictionary of Linguistics & Phonetics* (2003)
In *A Dictionary of Linguistics & Phonetics* (2003), 'stress' is defined thus:

> The usual distinction is between stressed and unstressed syllables, the former being more PROMINENT than the latter (and marked in TRANSCRIPTION with a raised vertical line, [']. The prominence is usually due to an increase in LOUDNESS of the stressed syllable, but increases in LENGTH and often PITCH may contribute to the overall impression of prominence. In popular usage, 'stress' is usually equated with an undifferentiated notion of 'emphasis' or 'strength' (Crystal, 2003:435).

(2) *Longman Pronunciation Dictionary* (2000)
In the *Longman Pronunciation Dictionary* (2000), 'stress' is defined thus:

> 1. A **stressed** syllable is one that carries a **rhythmic beat**. It is marked by greater loudness than unstressed syllables, and often by pitch-prominence, or greater duration, or more clearly defined vowel qualities.
> 2. An **accent** is the placement of intonational pitch-prominence (=higher or lower pitch than the surroundings) on a word. Speakers choose to accent certain words (or to de-accent others) because of the particular meaning they wish to convey in a particular situation. Accents can be located only on stressed syllables. Thus to accent the word **collapse** [kəˈlæps] the pitch- prominence goes on the syllable

[læps], but in **tumble** [ˈtʌmbə] on the syllable [tʌm]. ([ ] is added by the author.)
3. The stresses marked in LPD are **lexical** (=potential) stresses. Whether they are realized as accents depends on intonation.
4. LPD recognizes two levels of stress.
   primary stress (ˈ): When a word is said in isolation, this is where the nuclear tone (= sentence accent) goes. A word or phrase has only one primary stress.
   secondary stress (ˌ): In a word or phrase that potentially has more than one stress, this symbol marks the place of a stress other than the primary one. If this syllable is **before** the primary stress, it may also bear an accent. See STRESS SHIFT.
5. In the first edition of LPD, a distinction was made between secondary (ˌ) and tertiary (ˌ) stress. In this second edition the distinction has been abandoned (Wells, 2000:741).

In the *Longman Pronunciation Dictionary* (2000), 'Compounds and phrases' are defined thus:

1. A two-element **compound** is typically pronounced with **early** stress: that is to say, its first element has more stress than its second.
   ˈ**bedtime** [ˈbed taɪm] ....
   Although many compounds are written as single words, others are written as two words.
   ˈ**Christmas card** ... ˈ**music** ˌ**lessons** ....
2. On the other hand, a **phrase** is typically pronounced with **late** stress: that is to say, the second of two words has more stress than the first.
   ˌ**next** ˈ**time** ... ˌ**several** ˈ**books** ....
3. These stress patterns, and all others, can be changed if the speaker wants to emphasize a particular contrast (to focus on a particular element).
   I ˌdon't want ˌmusic ˈlessons – ˌJust some ˌtime to ˈpractice! ...
4. Some expressions, grammatically compounds, are nevertheless pronounced with late stress (= as if they were phrases)....
   ˌ**cheese** ˈ**sandwiches**
   a ˌ**pork** ˈ**pie** ....
   However, expressions involving **cake**, **juice** and **water** take early stress....
   ˈ**orange juice** ....
5. Names of roads and streets all take late stress except those involving **street** itself, which take early stress....
   ˌ**Oxford** ˈ**Square**, ˌ**King** ˈ**Avenue** .... (Wells, 2000:163).

1.2 Definitions of stress

(3) Roach (2000)

Roach (2000:93) states that "…. we can study stress from the point of view of production and of perception; the two are obviously closely related, but are not identical". From a speaker's point of view, Roach states as follows:

> The production of stress is generally believed to depend on the speaker using more muscular energy than is used for unstressed syllables. Measuring muscular effort is difficult, but it seems possible, according to experimental studies, that when we produce stressed syllables, the muscles that we use to expel air from the lungs are often more active, producing higher subglottal pressure. It seems probable that similar things happen with muscles in other parts of our speech apparatus (Roach, 2000:93-94).

From a listener's point of view, Roach states as follows:

> Many experiments have been carried out on the perception of stress, and it is clear that many different sound characteristics are important in making a syllable recognizably stressed. From the perceptual point of view, all stressed syllables have one characteristic in common, and that is prominence. Stressed syllables are recognized as stressed because they are more prominent than unstressed syllables. What makes a syllable prominent? At least four different factors are important.
> i) Most people seem to feel that stressed syllables are louder than unstressed; in other words, loudness is a component of prominence….
> ii) The length of syllables has an important part to play in prominence. If one of the syllables in our "nonsense word" ba:ba:ba:ba is made longer than others, there is quite a strong tendency for that syllable to be heard as stressed.
> iii) Every voiced syllable is said on some pitch; pitch in speech is closely related to the frequency of vibration of the vocal folds and to the musical notion of low- and high-pitched notes. It is essentially a perceptual characteristic of speech. If one syllable of our "nonsense word" is said with a pitch that is noticeably different from that of the others, this will have a strong tendency to produce the effect of prominence. For example, if all syllables are said with low pitch except for one said with high pitch, then the high-pitched syllable will be heard as stressed and the others as unstressed. To place some moment of pitch (e.g. rising or falling) on a syllable is even more effective.

iv) A syllable will tend to be prominent if it contains a vowel that is different in quality from neighbouring vowels. If we change one of the vowels in our "nonsense word" the "odd" syllable biː will tend to be heard as stressed. This effect is not very powerful nor [sic] very important, but there is one particular way in which it is relevant in English (Roach, 2000:94-95).

Prominence, then, is produced by four main factors: (i) loudness, (ii) length, (iii) pitch and (iv) quality. Generally these four factors work together in combination, although syllables may sometimes be made prominent by means of only one or two of them. Experimental work has shown that these factors are not equally important; the strongest effect is produced by pitch, and length is also a powerful factor. Loudness and quality have much less effect (Roach, 2000:95).

From the perceptual point of view, all stressed syllables have one characteristic in common, and that is prominence. Roach (2000:100) has "avoided using the term *accent*, which is found widely in the literature on stress." The main reasons are as follows:

i) It increases the complexity of the description without, in my view, contributing much to its value.
ii) Different writers do not agree with each other about the way the term should be used.
iii) The word 'accent' is used elsewhere to refer to different varieties of pronunciation (e.g. "a foreign accent"); it is confusing to use it for a quite different purpose – to a lesser extent we also have this problem with the word 'stress', which can be used to refer to psychological tension (Roach, 2000:100-101).

(4) Ladefoged (2001)
Ladefoged (2001) states as follows:

In nearly every language ...what we hear as stress is more a matter of increasing the pitch and length of the syllables concerned than of increasing their loudness. From the speaker's point of view it involves extra effort, an extra push of air out of the lungs, and increased tension of the vocal folds. What is most important to the listener is the increase in pitch that occurs, not the increase in loudness (Ladefoged, 2001:23).

The act of pushing more air out of the lungs ... makes the amplitude of the vibrations of the vocal folds larger and hence louder; it increases the pitch; and it usually makes the syllable longer. ...the vocal folds vibrate because the air from the lungs pushes them apart and then sucks them together again. A large push will result in their being pushed apart more rapidly; and a greater flow of air between them will cause them to be sucked together more rapidly. The result is that they will vibrate at a higher frequency, and the pitch will go up. The increase in pitch is the major cue to the position of the stressed syllable in an English word (Ladefoged, 2001:22).

(5) Catford (2001)
Catford (2001) has a similar opinion to Ladefoged (2001):

A strongly stressed syllable (or, simply, a 'stressed syllable') is one produced with high pulmonic pressure initiator power. A weakly stressed syllable (or, simply, an 'unstressed syllable') is one produced with low pulmonic pressure initiator power. Stress is one of the so-called prosodic features of speech... (Catford, 2001:33).

...you will probably find that you pronounce the stressed syllables – particularly if you stress them strongly- on a higher pitch than the unstressed syllables, and you may also make them longer. There is a natural, physical, connection between stress and pitch... Consequently stressed syllables are often pronounced on a different pitch from neighbouring unstressed syllables (Catford, 2001:166).

...stress is associated with pitch and duration had led to some confusion. 'Is stress really pitch, duration, or energy, or what?' is the kind of muddled question that has often been asked. The answer is that all of these features, pitch, duration and energy of utterance, as well as the inherent sonority of a sound, may contribute to the perceptual prominence of a sound or syllable – that is, the degree to which it appears to stand out from its neighbours. However, from a general phonetic point of view, to prevent confusion, it is best to confine the application of the term stress to initiator power as we have defined it here (Catford, 2001:167-8).

(6) Cruttenden (2001)
In *Gimson's Pronunciation of English, Sixth Edition, rev. by Alan Cruttenden* (2001), the use of the term 'stress' was avoided.

Throughout this book we will avoid use of the term 'stress' altogether, using PROMINENCE as the general term referring to segments or syllables, SONORITY as the particular term referring to the carrying power of individual sounds, and ACCENT as referring to those syllables which stand out above others, either in individual words or in longer utterances (Cruttenden, 2001:24-25).

> Accented syllables are often assumed to be louder than unaccented syllables.... Greater loudness is carried principally by voiced sounds, in which greater amplitude of vibration of the vocal folds, together with the reinforcing resonance of the supraglottal cavities, results in acoustic terms in relatively greater intensity. This strong intensity and the perceived loudness on the part of the listener results from the relatively greater breath effort and muscular energy expended on the articulation of a sound by the speaker. This effort and energy is [*sic*] frequently referred to as 'stress', although, because of the many different ways in which it has been used, this word is avoided here. Loudness is not by itself an efficient device for signalling the location of the accent in English (Cruttenden, 2001:223).

Cruttenden states that "Any of four factors, pitch, loudness, quality, and quantity may help to render a syllable more prominent than its neighbours. But it is principally pitch change which marks an accented syllable.... The principal cue to accent is pitch prominence, which depends as much upon pitch change as pitch height" (Cruttenden, 2001:222).

(7) Cruttenden (1997)

Cruttenden (1997) states as follows:

> ...no systematic difference was made in the use of the three terms 'prominence', 'stress' and 'accent'. In the past the word 'stress' has been used in different and confusing ways. It has sometimes been used simply to refer to syllables (or vowels) made prominent for linguistic purposes, either in words or in sentences. But stress has also often been used to mean 'breath-force or loudness' the implication being that this is the principal means whereby syllables are made prominent. This second type of usage is misguided since ... loudness generally plays a minor role in producing prominences (Cruttenden, 1997:13).

> In this book I shall use the term STRESS to mean 'prominence', however such prominence is achieved. The term ACCENT will be limited to prominences where pitch is involved (hence it is equivalent to PITCH ACCENT). 'Stress' is therefore being used in the more general, less specified, way. In particular I will continue the traditional use of the word 'stress' in two areas. Firstly, the term 'word-stress' will be used to refer to those syllables which would be marked as stressed if stress were marked in a lexicon or dictionary and which therefore have

a potential for 'accent' in utterances. Secondly, it has been suggested that the rhythm of certain languages (the so-called 'stress-timed' ones) is dependent upon the regular occurrence of stressed syllables in connected speech. In my account of this theory I shall continue to make use of the term 'stress' (Cruttenden, 1997:13-14).

(8) Clark and Yallop (1995)
Clark and Yallop (1995:332,335,340,341) state that "Pitch is widely regarded, at least in English, as the most salient determinant of prominence. In other words, when a syllable or word is perceived as 'stressed' or 'emphasized', it is pitch height or a change of pitch, more than length or loudness...." "In fact, although it is clear that stressed syllables often have greater overall acoustic intensity than more weakly stressed ones, loudness seems to be the least salient and least consistent of the three parameters of pitch, duration and loudness – at least for linguistic purposes such as signaling stress". He also states that "stress does not correlate simply with loudness, but represents the total effect of factors such as pitch, loudness and duration." "The term ACCENT is sometimes used loosely to mean stress, referring either to prominence in a general way or more specifically to the emphasis placed on certain syllables."

(9) Denes and Pinson (1993)
Denes and Pinson (1993) state as follows:

> Stress and intonation are linguistic features. Their most important acoustic correlates are the vocal cord (or fundamental) frequency, the duration, and the intensity of the speech sound wave. Stress is associated with vocal cord frequency, as well as with duration and intensity. Intonation is principally related to vocal cord frequency patterns. Also, sentence- and phrase- final words are spoken with longer duration and a characteristic vocal cord frequency pattern. It should be remembered therefore that vocal cord frequency and duration patterns in an utterance are influenced by several factors, such as intonation, stress, and sentence boundaries (Denes and Pinson, 1993:175).

(10) Lieberman (1967)
The American Phonetician Lieberman (1967) states as follows:

> We shall use the term "prominence" for the occurrences of the distinctive feature.... Perceptually, prominence is therefore the perceived

"loudness" of a vowel relative to its environment. The acoustic correlates of prominence are duration, fundamental frequency, and sound pressure level (or amplitude) (Lieberman, 1967:144).

We shall reserve the term "stress" for the abstract entities that are generated by the phonologic rules of the "stress cycle." Most studies of English agree that the vowels of words, short phrases, and sentences are differentiated by relative degrees of stress or "loudness" (Lieberman, 1967:145).

We shall use the term "emphasis" to identify instances where the distinctive feature produces extra prominence on the vowel or vowels of a word (and its consonants), apart from the stress that the vowels of the word would have received from the phonologic stress rules. In other words, emphasis is prominence that is not predicted by the stress cycle (Lieberman, 1967:146).

The term "contrastive stress" could have been used for emphasis, but it might cause some confusion. We want to preserve the distinction between the distinctive feature... and its underlying source. The phonologic feature... in the phonetic output can be the manifestation of either emphasis in the underlying phrase marker or, in certain circumstances, the "stronger" stresses generated by the phonologic feature (Lieberman, 1967:147).

In the next section, previous research on English stress will be introduced.

1.3 Previous research on English stress

As stressed syllables seem to be uttered strongly, 'stress' was defined as 'force' before the experimental research of the 1950s. Most early phoneticians (Sweet, 1906; Bloomfield, 1933) assumed that stress is produced by the degree of force and perceived as degrees of loudness. Sweet (1906:47) explains that "Force .... Physically it is synonymous with the effort by which breath is expelled from the lungs.... Acoustically it produces the effect known as 'loudness', which is dependent on the size of the vibration-waves which produce the sensation of sound." From a speaker's point of view, Bloomfield (1933) states as follows:

> Stress – that is, intensity or loudness – consists in greater amplitude of sound-waves, and is produced by means of more energetic movements, such as pumping more breath, bringing the vocal chords closer together for voicing, and using the muscles more vigorously for oral articulation (Bloomfield, 1933:110-111).

Pike (1943:119), an American phonetician, states that "the stressed syllable has a much stronger initiator pressure than do the others". Kingdom (1959:1) states that "Stress is the relative degree of force used by a speaker on the various syllables he is uttering. It gives a certain basic prominence to the syllables, and hence to the words, on which it is used, and incidentally assists in avoiding monotony. There are two types of stress: Word (or Lexical) Stress and Sentence (or Syntactical) Stress. Word Stress is the relative degree of force used in pronouncing the different syllables of a word of more than one syllable.... Sentence Stress is the relative degree of force given to the different words in a sentence."

In the 1950's, the sound spectrograph was commercialized and practical speech synthesis equipment (e.g., the Pattern Playback at Haskins) was developed (Beckman, 1986). The British phoneticians who suspected that stress was not simple began to undertake instrumental investigations of stress acoustically using several speech synthesis techniques. The series of experiments undertaken by D. B. Fry (1955, 1958, 1965) were influential experimental research undertaken on word stress.

(1) Dennis Butler Fry (1955)
 The leading British experimental phonetician D. B. Fry (1955) undertook research using pattern-playback equipment to examine the influence of certain physical cues on the perception of word stress. English noun/verb word-pairs such as ˈobject / obˈject, ˈsubject / subˈject, ˈdigest / diˈgest, ˈcontract / conˈtract and ˈpermit / perˈmit were synthesized in which the duration and intensity ratios of vowel 1 to vowel 2 were varied over the critical range. The results of this experiment indicate that (a) duration and intensity ratios are both cues for judgments of word stress and (b) duration ratio is a more effective cue than intensity ratio.

(2) Dennis Butler Fry (1958)
 D. B. Fry (1958) undertook research using pattern-playback equipment to examine three physical dimensions which appear to be important in determining word stress judgments in English: duration, intensity and fundamental frequency. The research content was noun / verb word-pairs; ˈobject / obˈject, ˈsubject / subˈject, ˈdigest / diˈgest, ˈcontract / conˈtract and ˈpermit / perˈmit. Subjects were asked to listen to the synthesized words and judge whether stress was placed on the first syllable or on the second syllable.
  The results of the experiments indicate the following:

20   Fundamental concepts

(i) Intensity ratio has a similar influence as duration ratio but it is somewhat less marked.
(ii) "Change in fundamental frequency differs from change of duration and intensity in that it tends to produce an all-or-none effect." That is to say, "the magnitude of the frequency change seems to be relatively unimportant" for English stress judgments on words of two syllables.
(iii) "The experiments with a step-change of frequency show that a higher syllable is more likely to be perceived as stressed." "The fundamental frequency cue may outweigh the duration cue."

D. B. Fry concludes that "all judgments of stress in natural speech depend on the complicated interaction of a number of cues."

(3) Dennis Butler Fry (1965)

D. B. Fry (1965) undertook experiments to examine the part played by vowel quality in word stress judgments obtained from English listeners. The research content was noun/verb word-pairs; ˈobject / obˈject, ˈsubject / subˈject, ˈdigest / diˈgest, and ˈcontract / conˈtract. The result of this experiment shows that "the weight of the duration cue is very considerably greater than that of the formant structure cue". He stated that "the formant structure cue for stress may in fact be less effective than the intensity cue".

These three experiments undertaken by D. B. Fry (1955, 1958, 1965) indicate that fundamental frequency is the most influential cue, longer duration is the second most important cue, greater intensity is the third most important cue and formant structure is the least important cue in perceiving word stress.

Other similar experiments on word stress were undertaken by other phoneticians to confirm D.B.Fry's results (1955, 1958, 1965). The pitch accent theory of Bolinger (1958) is well-known.

(4) Bolinger (1958)

Arguing from the results of D. B. Fry's experiments and from other similar experiments of his own, Bolinger (1958) concludes that the primary cue for stress judgement is pitch prominence and that intensity is not an important factor in stress judgement. He explains that the essential of stress identification is not 'pitch rise' which is only one form of pitch prominence, but rather 'pitch prominence'. He replaces the term 'stress' with the term 'pitch accent' to avoid confusion of stress with intensity.

1.3 Previous research on English stress

(5) Lieberman (1960)

Using twenty-five noun-verb stress pairs, Lieberman (1960) undertook an experiment on word stress in American English. Twenty-five pairs were recorded by six female and ten male native speakers of American English. Two observers listened to the tape recordings and judged which was the stressed syllable of each utterance. The result shows that higher F_0 and amplitude are the most relevant of the acoustic correlates of stressed syllables. The F_0 parameter seems to be the most relevant, which concurs with the results of D. B. Fry for synthetic stress pairs (1955, 1958). However, the data obtained from this experiment indicates that amplitude seems more important than duration. This result does not concur with the results reported by D. B. Fry (1955, 1958).

(6) Morton and Jassem (1965)

Morton and Jassem (1965) undertook research using synthetic nonsense syllables of the forms to examine three physical dimensions which appear to be important in determining word stress judgments in English: duration, intensity and fundamental frequency. Native speakers of British English were asked to listen to the synthesized words and judge whether stress was placed on the first syllable, on the second syllable, or on neither syllable. The results of the experiments indicated that fundamental frequency changes were by far the most effective in producing universally accepted stress-marking. They also indicated that a "raised fundamental frequency is more effective than a lowered one", and changes of 58% in the fundamental frequency "are no more effective than changes of 25% in producing consistent stress marking".

(7) Brown and McGlone (1974)

Brown and McGlone (1974) examined the aero-dynamic and acoustic nature of stress by obtaining intraoral air-pressure and air-flow recordings from sentence productions. The results show that fundamental frequency is a dominant parameter and other parameters may be utilized to denote stress by English speakers.

The major experimental research on word stress undertaken by D. B. Fry (1955, 1958), Bolinger (1958), Lieberman (1960) and Brown and McGlone (1974) shows that fundamental frequency seems to be the most important parameter in perceiving stress. Tiffany and Carrell (1977:151) state that "There appears to be general agreement among phoneticians that while stress is a composite of several features, including pitch, duration, and loudness, the most salient factor is pitch, and nearly always a *rise* in pitch."

However, the experimental research on word stress undertaken by Medress, *et al.* (1972) and Nakatani and Aston (1978) shows that duration is the main parameter for word stress judgements.

(8) Nakatani and Aston (1978)

Nakatani and Aston (1978) undertook an experiment with bisyllabic nonsense words which were embedded in meaningful sentences to assess which acoustic feature is of relative importance as a cue for stress perception between duration, F_0, amplitude and spectral features, using the LPC analysis-synthesis technique. They insist that "the relative importance of the cues depends upon where the word occurs in the sentence". They also state that "contrary to Fry's classic results with words in isolation, the pitch contour was useless as a cue for perceiving the stress pattern of a noun preceded by an accented adjective. The word's duration pattern proved a more robust cue than pitch for stress pattern perception; the word's amplitude contour was useless as a cue."

(9) Beckman (1986)

In *Stress and Non-stress Accent*, Beckman reports two experiments on word stress using minimal word pairs of English and Japanese (Beckman, 1986:145-200). First, "a production experiment" was undertaken "to discover the acoustic correlates of accent in English, an archetypal stress-accent language, and Japanese, an archetypal non-stress-accent language". The English word pairs consisted of the same five minimal pairs used by D. B. Fry (1955, 1958); ˈobject / obˈject, ˈsubject / subˈject, ˈdigest / diˈgest, ˈcontract / conˈtract and ˈpermit / perˈmit. The Japanese word pairs consisted of the six minimal pairs. In the three pairs, the first-syllable was accented versus unaccented patterns; ˈiken (opinion) / iken (differing view), ˈikken (one house) / ikken (glance) and ˈkabu (lower part) / kabu (stocks). In the other three pairs, the first-syllable was accented versus second-syllable accented patterns; ˈkame (turtle) / kaˈme (jug), ˈkami (god) / kaˈmi (paper) and ˈkata (shoulder) / kaˈta (form). The subjects who read the Japanese words in the frame sentence were one female and four male native speakers of Standard Japanese. The subjects who read the English words in the frame sentence were two male and two female native speakers of American English. In order to cue the intended accent pattern, the words were presented to the subjects in appropriate context sentences. The duration and the amplitude measurements were taken from wide-band spectrograms and F₀ measurements from narrow-band spectrograms.

The results showed that the pitch patterns could be a sufficient and robust cue in English word stress perception, but the duration and amplitude patterns could also be a cue. On the other hand, the Japanese word contrasts might be cued solely by the pitch pattern. The amplitude and duration patterns cannot be important as cues to word accent pattern. Beckman concluded that "English and Japanese differ greatly in the extent to which accent is associated with acoustic patterns other than F₀ contours. "Stress-accent patterns in English have a consistent and substantial influence on duration and amplitude patterns, whereas pitch-accent patterns in Japanese do not".

Second, Beckman undertook a perception experiment to discover the relative perceptual salience of the acoustic correlates measured in the production test. Synthetic word pairs: ⎮subject / sub⎮ject, ⎮digest / di ⎮gest, ⎮contract /con⎮tract, ⎮permit / per⎮mit (English), ⎮kame / ka⎮me, ⎮kami / ka⎮mi and ⎮kata / ka⎮ta (Japanese) were prepared. Subjects were 15 native speakers of Japanese, 8 native speakers of American English who had some knowledge of Japanese, and 8 native speakers of English who had no knowledge of Japanese. Subjects listened to the tapes in which the synthetic words were recorded and judged in each word pair whether stress was placed on the first syllable or second syllable. Result showed that all of the Japanese subjects used pitch as the predominate cue to the English accent patterns. The Japanese subjects did not use the vowel quality parameter in judging word stress in English. Word stress of Japanese and English differs greatly as to the relative importance of the 'total amplitude' (duration and amplitude) pattern as a perceptual cue.

(10) Ohyama, Suzuki, and Kiritani (1989)

Ohyama, Suzuki, and Kiritani undertook research using the PARCOR analysis and synthesis technique to discover which factor plays the major role in making Japanese utterance closer to natural English. Various combinations of 1) duration, 2) F₀ and 3) intensity in an English sentence uttered by the three Japanese learners of English were replaced with the same combinations of the same sentence uttered by a native speaker of English. A group of American speakers listened to the re-synthesized utterances and judged their acceptability level as English. The results showed that F₀ seems to play a more important role than duration and intensity in such judgements.

(11) Yabuuchi and Satoi (2000)

Yabuuchi and Satoi undertook research to examine the English prosody of Japanese learners of English through comparing Japanese good English speakers with poor English speakers. The results showed that the F_0 range of good speakers was broader and varied and that of poor speakers was narrow and unchanged.

1.4 Comparison of English prosodic features and Japanese prosodic Features

In this section, English prosodic features and Japanese prosodic features are compared.

1.4.1 Stress accent languages and pitch accent languages

Both English and Japanese employ word stress (accent). Languages that employ word stress (accent) are divided into 'stress accent languages' and 'pitch accent languages'. In English, pitch variation, intensity, and vowel duration may be used to distinguish words. English has an aspect of 'stress accent language' (Kubozono and Ohta, 1998:11).

On the other hand, Japanese is not generally considered to have a stress system. Japanese words are 'characterized by pitch accent'. Some words are distinguished not by intensity or duration but by variations in pitch. For example, *SHIro* means white and *shiRO* means castle, or *HAshi* means chopsticks and *haSHI* means bridge. (Capitalized syllables are uttered higher in pitch, not stressed.)

In Japanese, there is an accent type which is called 'monotone accent' or 'no accent word.' Even when a particle is followed by a word, pitch does not fall and the whole word is uttered in a monotone. This is perceived by native speakers of English as lacking interest. This accent type includes words which have no falling tones, such as *saKANA* (fish) or *aKAI* (red). Which word belongs to this monotone accent type is unpredictable. For example, the word "*watashi*" (I) is a monotone accent and the word "*aN-Ata*" (you) is a pitch accent. The word "*amerika*" (America) is a monotone accent and the word "*KAnada*" (Canada) is a pitch accent (Kubozono and Ohta, 1998:204).

Watanabe (1994:3) states that it is considered that there is some difference in perceiving strength between native speakers of English and Japanese. Native speakers of English may perceive strength by pitch variation, duration and intensity. Japanese learners of English may perceive strength by pitch variation.

As mentioned on page 22 to 23, Beckman (1986) undertook an acoustic experiment on word stress using both American and Japanese informants and strongly suggested that "the perception of the English contrasts cannot be due to pitch-contour contrasts alone, whereas the Japanese contrasts might be cued solely by the F_0 pattern" (Beckman, 1986:170).

1.4.2 Intonation languages and word-pitch languages
When language is analyzed in terms of pitch level which distinguishes meaning, it is classified into 'tone languages', 'word-pitch languages' and 'intonation languages'. English is classified as an 'intonation language'. Japanese is classified as a 'word-pitch language'. Certain languages in southeastern Asia such as Chinese, Vietnamese, Burmese, and some African languages are classified as 'tone languages' (Pike, 1948).

In terms of sentence stress and intonation, English and Japanese are different. In English, the place of word accent may shift in the sentence. Stress works functionally. Word accent is sometimes absent in sentences, owing to the grammatical role or the degree of grammatical importance. Intonation patterns always tend to achieve a consensus on the meaning within a context. When the focus is placed in a sentence, a focused word is uttered higher in pitch and a following tone group is uttered flat so that only the focused word comes into prominence and makes a noticeable impression in English (Sugito, 1990).

On the other hand, in Japanese, accent placement does not change in different sentences (Mizutani, 1990). Every word accent receives the same level in pitch wherever it appears in a sentence. When most Japanese learners of English speak English, they often produce each accent in a sentence so that even when the emphasis is added to a word, the difference in pitch is not noticeable or effective (Sugito, 1990). Their pitch pattern is similar to the Japanese and is quite different from the English pitch pattern spoken by native speakers of English. The reason is that some Japanese speakers produce each accent faithfully whatever the sentence. The result is that a repetitive rise and fall in pitch occurs in an utterance. It is said that "in Japanese, the range of possible intonational variation is considerably smaller than in the English intonation system" (Beckman and Pierrehumbert, 1986:306). The Japanese language tends to be uttered at a higher pitch at the beginning of both a sentence and a phrase (Sugito, 1990). That is, the Japanese language falls in pitch after the beginning of a sentence until the next pause. After a pause, pitch level is slightly higher again but then decreases at the end of a sentence. The difference between the end of a sentence and the end of a phrase is not absolutely clear, although the end of the sentence tends to be lower in pitch (Mizutani, 1990).

In English, the beginning of a sentence is generally not higher in pitch. At the end of a phrase, the voice is a little higher in pitch, which means that the sentence is continuous, and is then lower at the end of the sentence. In English, new information is emphasized; in Japanese, modified words, such as adjectives, adverbs, and particles are often higher in pitch than is new information (Sugito, 1990).

1.4.3 Stress-timed rhythm and mora-timed rhythm

There is a large difference in rhythm between English and Japanese. English rhythm is called 'stress-timed rhythm'. Japanese rhythm is called 'syllable-timed rhythm' or, strictly, 'mora-timed rhythm' (Kubozono and Ohta, 1998:205-206).

English is said to have 'isochronous' stress. The stressed syllables tend to occur at regular time-intervals, regardless of the number of intervening unstressed syllables. This characteristic is referred to as 'isochronism' or 'isochrony'. There is a close relationship between rhythm and word stress or sentence stress. That is to say, rhythm is produced by word stress or sentence stress. From a converse viewpoint, sentence stress may occur in order to carry out the rhythmic structure. Secondary stress in word and stress shift (thir׀teen → ׀thirteen men) also occurred in order to keep the English rhythm.

On the other hand, the rhythm of Japanese is often called 'syllable-timed rhythm' or, strictly, 'mora-timed rhythm'. The syllables are said to occur at regular time-intervals. Japanese is said not to have weak syllables. There is no relationship between rhythm and word accent. A great number of Japanese sentences in which all words are without accent are heard.

Speakers of syllable-timed languages, such as French, Hindi, Finnish, Italian, Spanish, Cantonese, Vietnamese and Japanese often experience particular difficulty in mastering the rhythm of stress-timed languages, such as English, German, Swedish, Persian and Mandarin Chinese. The "imposition of syllable-timed rhythm on English is probably far more detrimental to intelligibility than any distortion of vowel or consonant pronunciation" (Fudge, 1984:3). Fudge (1984) states as follows:

> Because English rhythm is stress-timed, a wrong stressing will lead to a wrong and misleading rhythm, even if the *principle* of stress-timing is correctly handled by the speaker. Comprehensibility depends on rhythm, and therefore the placing of stress within words can play a large part in determining how well a native English hearer will understand the foreign speaker. (Fudge, 1984:4)

Sugito (1990) notes that in Japanese schools, English word accent is not compared with Japanese accent. Word accent is generally taught visually using an accent mark to show the place that is uttered strongly. Japanese teachers tend to try to distinguish the accented syllables by intensity and strain. That English accent is produced by intensity is a common Japanese idea and conventionally it is explained that Japanese is completely different from English. However, experimental research shows that pitch also seems to be bound up with English stress.

1.5 Relationship between music and language

Although relatively few studies have examined the relationship between language and music, Patel (2008), Pastuszek-Lipinska (2007), Magne, *et al.* (2006), Schön, *et al.* (2004), Thompson, *et al.* (2003) and Deutsch (1991) examined this relationship.

Deutsch (1990, 1991, 1994) considers the relationship between music perception and speech production by Californian subjects and southern England subjects. She concludes that there is a significant difference in music perception between Californian and southern England subjects. Deutsch (1991:344) states that "for Californians, the agreed upon orientation of the pitch-class circle is such that the highest position occurs around C# and D. However, for people from southern England, the agreed upon orientation is such that the highest position occurs around G instead. It is assumed that such a template is employed both in the production of speech and in the interpretation of speech produced by others."

Thompson, *et al.* (2003:531) conducted two experiments and concluded as follows:

> In both experiments, musically trained participants were better than untrained participants at extracting prosodic information from speech.... Other evidence suggests that music lessons not only improve the ability to extract prosodic cues, but also improve the ability to interpret speech prosody.

In an experiment conducted by Schön, *et al.* (2004), nine musicians (15 years of musical training on average) and nine non-musicians were asked to listen to 120 French spoken declarative sentences and 120 melodies. All subjects were native speakers of French whose mean age was 31 years. As Schön, *et al.* (2004: 341) noted, "these results are taken as evidence that extensive musician training influences the perception of pitch contour in spoken language." Schön, *et al.* (2004: 347) also noted as follows:

> First and most importantly, behavioral measures in both language and music revealed that musicians were not only more accurate in detecting pitch violations in music ... but they were also more accurate in detecting pitch violations in language.

Pastuszek-Lipinska (2007:824) examined the relationship between music education and foreign language acquisition and noted that the results of the study provide evidence that "music expertise indeed matters in second language acquisition". In her research, 106 native speakers of Polish, some with and some without musical education and training were asked to listen to 82 word sequences in six foreign languages (English, Belgian-Dutch, French, Italian, Spanish, and Japanese) and to repeat them as accurately as they could. The result of this research was as follows (Pastuszek-Lipinska 2007:823):

> The group of musicians encountered fewer difficulties in shadowing speech repetition and produced 56.53% of correct responses to all the provided stimuli.... the group of nonmusicians [sic] performed significantly worse than the group of musicians and produced 39.91% of correct repetitions. Moreover, most musicians performed better in all languages and all word sequences.

Experiment by Wong, *et al.* (2007) involved the ability of seventeen American English learners of Mandarin to recognize Mandarin tonal patterns. They found that "musical training started at an early age contributed to more successful spoken foreign-language learning. The study participants with musical experience also were found to be better at identifying pitch patterns before training."

Recent research undertaken by Mok, *et al.* (2012) investigated the relationship between music and speech. Their findings suggest that "the linguistic and musical mechanisms belong to separate but overlapping domains".

In Chapter 2, pitch movements and sentence stress in English will be investigated whether large pitch movements are produced on the stressed syllables. In Chapters 3—5, whether pitch movement is a key factor in perceiving sentence stress in English will be discussed. In Chapters 6—7, the relationship between ability in music and ability in English will be discussed.

2 Pitch contour of sentence stress in American English

2.1 Purpose

The purpose of this experiment is twofold. Firstly, to examine acoustically the pitch (fundamental frequency, abbreviated as F_0) movements of sentence stress in English uttered by native speakers of American English (AEs). Secondly, to compare the pitch (F_0) contours of AEs with the pitch (F_0) contours of Japanese learners of English (Js) who are not accustomed to speaking English well, in order to make good use of them in English teaching. Although some other parameters (relative duration and intensity) are related to stress, this experiment focuses only on pitch (F_0).

2.2 Method

Three AEs and three Js were asked to utter three kinds of sentences, with emphasis placed each time on a different word. Pitch (F_0) parameters of each sentence are analyzed and shown visually.

2.2.1 Informants

Three of the speakers were male AEs with no hearing and speaking disorder, their ages between 30 and 69. The other three speakers were male Js with no hearing and speaking disorder, their ages between 20 and 22. The six informants who participated in this experiment are shown in Table 2.1.

2.2.2 Materials

Six informants were asked to utter 25 short simple sentences (see Table 2.2). Stressed syllables are shown in capital and bold letters. The sentences contain only the voiced phonemes because voiceless phonemes interrupt the smooth pitch (F_0) contours on the time axis. Each sentence was uttered in different ways depending on where the emphasis was placed in a sentence.

Table 2.1 Background of the six informants

Informants	Nationality	The place lived longest	Educational Background	Status	Age
A1	American	Yokohama	Graduate School	Professor	60's
A2	American	California	Graduate School	Professor	40's
A3	American	New York	Graduate School	English teacher	30's
J1	Japanese	Japan		College student	20's
J2	Japanese	Japan		College student	20's
J3	Japanese	Japan		College student	20's

2.2.3 Recording method

The following sentences were recorded on audio magnetic tapes. All of the speech signals were digitized (16 bits; speed: 11.025 KHz) and stored.

For the analysis of the recorded speeches, speech processing software (Hirasaka, 2000) was used. Figure 2.1 shows the sentence, "Ignore the gloom and **DOOM**" (Table 2.2, (2), (d)) emphasized the word "**DOOM**" uttered by informant A1. Capitalized and bold letters show the emphatic syllables. Figure 2.2 shows the same sentence uttered by informant A2 and Figure 2.3 shows the same sentence uttered by informant A3.

Figures 2.4 to 2.6 show the same sentences uttered by informants J1, J2 and J3. Figures 2.1 to 2.6 are drawn using Hirasaka 2000 (Hirasaka, 2000).

Table 2.2 Change of emphasis in test sentences

(1)	(a)	Avoid every kind of evil.
	(b)	**AVOID** every kind of evil.
	(c)	Avoid **EVery** kind of evil.
	(d)	Avoid every kind of **Evil**.
	(e)	Avoid every kind of evil?
	(f)	**AVOID** every kind of evil?
	(g)	Avoid **EVery** kind of evil?
	(h)	Avoid every kind of **Evil**?
(2)	(a)	Ignore the gloom and doom.
	(b)	Ig**NORE** the gloom and doom.
	(c)	Ignore the **GLOOM** and doom.
	(d)	Ignore the gloom and **DOOM**.
	(e)	Ignore the gloom and doom?
	(f)	Ig**NORE** the gloom and doom?
	(g)	Ignore the **GLOOM** and doom?
	(h)	Ignore the gloom and **DOOM**?

(3)	(a)	But you love me!
	(b)	But **YOU** love me!
	(c)	But you **LOVE** me!
	(d)	But you love **ME**!
	(e)	But you love me?
	(f)	Do you love me?
	(g)	Do **YOU** love me?
	(h)	Do you **LOVE** me?
	(i)	Do you love **ME**?

Notes: These sentences are cited from:
(1) "The first letter of Paul to the Thessalonians", Chapter 5, *The New Testament* (New International Version, 1978) 610.
(2) *The Daily Yomiuri* (Friday, May 5, 2000) 10.
(3) Margaret Mitchell, *Gone with the Wind* (Tokyo: Movie Bunko, Vol.1, 1994) 92.

Capitalized and bold letters show the emphatic syllables.

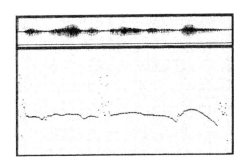

Figure 2.1 F_0 contour and waveform of "Ignore the gloom and **DOOM**" by A1

Figure 2.2 F_0 contour and waveform of "Ignore the gloom and **DOOM**" by A2

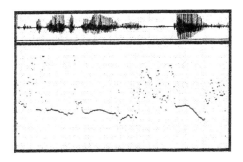
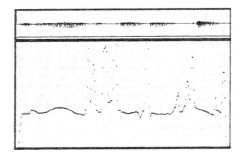

Figure 2.3 F_0 contour and waveform of "Ignore the gloom and **DOOM**" by A3

Figure 2.4 F_0 contour and waveform of "Ignore the gloom and **DOOM**" by J1

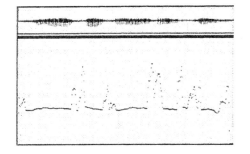
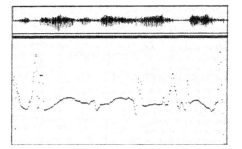

Figure 2.5 F_0 contour and waveform of "Ignore the gloom and **DOOM**" by J2

Figure 2.6 F_0 contour and waveform of "Ignore the gloom and **DOOM**" by J3

2.3 New F_0 contour

F_0 of utterances differs and each word takes a different duration one by one so that the pitch movements of each word are not able to be compared exactly with others. Therefore, the author developed a new "F_0 Contour S" where the F_0 movement of each word and the stressed word could be vis-

32 Pitch contour of sentence stress in American English

ually compared with others. All utterances were set to start at 100 Hz. Logarithm was used to normalize the time of every word, the same all of them keeping the original shape of F_0 movement. Furthermore, the averaged pitch movements of three informants were calculated and shown visually. Figures 2.7 to 2.9 and Figures 2.13 to 2.41 are drawn using "F_0 Contour S".

F_0 was obtained by 4.54 msec (0.00454 sec) from the beginning to the end of the twenty-five kinds of sentences uttered by the six informants.

Table 2.3 shows the F_0 of "Ignore the gloom and **DOOM**" (Table 2.2, (2), (d)) uttered by the three American informants. The first row indicates the normalized duration of utterance of each word, "ignore", "the", "gloom", "and", and "**DOOM**". The left-hand column indicates the F_0 of the informants and their average.

The beginning of this sentence was uttered at 111 Hz and the end of the word "ignore" was uttered at 103 Hz by the informant A1. The value of 111.45 Hz indicates the average F_0 of the word "ignore". The beginning of the next word "the" was uttered at 102 Hz and the end of this word was uttered at 105 Hz and the average F_0 was 106.9 Hz. The beginning of "gloom" was 112 Hz and the end of this word was 113 Hz and the average was 115.96 Hz.

The average F_0 of informant A1, A2 and A3 at the beginning of this sentence was 109.67 Hz. The average of the three informants at the end of "ignore" was 103 Hz. The average F_0 of "ignore" of the three American informants was 109.96 Hz.

Table 2.3 F_0 of "Ignore the gloom and **DOOM**" by three American informants and their average F_0

		Ignore			the			gloom		
Time		0.00	0.33	0.67	1.00	1.33	1.67	2.00	2.33	2.67
F0 (Hz)	A1	111.00	111.45	103.00	102.00	106.90	105.00	112.00	115.96	113.00
	A2	104.00	108.18	105.00	103.00	106.18	107.00	109.00	110.61	110.00
	A3	114.00	110.23	101.00	102.00	102.77	102.00	105.00	106.89	95.00
	Average	109.67	109.96	103.00	102.33	105.28	104.67	108.67	111.15	106.00

and			DOOM		
3.00	3.33	3.67	4.00	4.33	4.67
111.00	108.93	102.00	112.00	112.93	83.00
87.00	98.59	99.00	139.00	154.79	123.00
85.00	91.55	90.00	121.00	109.13	81.00
94.33	99.69	97.00	124.00	125.62	95.67

Next, all utterances were set to start at 100 Hz. In Table 2.4, the beginning of the sentence was set at 100 Hz. The end of the word "ignore" uttered by informant A1 was 92.79 Hz. The average F_0 of the word "ignore"

2.3 New F₀ contour   33

was 100.41 Hz. The beginning of the next word was 91.89 Hz and the end of this word was 94.59 Hz and the average F₀ was 96.31 Hz.

Table 2.4 F₀ of "Ignore the gloom and **DOOM**" by three American informants where the beginning of each sentence was set at 100 Hz

		Ignore			the			gloom		
Time		0.00	0.33	0.67	1.00	1.33	1.67	2.00	2.33	2.67
F0 (Hz)	A1	100.00	100.41	92.79	91.89	96.31	94.59	100.90	104.47	101.80
	A2	100.00	104.02	100.96	99.04	102.09	102.88	104.81	106.35	105.77
	A3	100.00	96.70	88.60	89.47	90.15	89.47	92.11	93.76	83.33
	Average	100.00	100.38	94.12	93.47	96.18	95.65	99.27	101.53	96.97

	and			DOOM		
	3.00	3.33	3.67	4.00	4.33	4.67
	100.00	98.14	91.89	100.90	101.74	74.77
	83.65	94.80	95.19	133.65	148.84	118.27
	74.56	80.30	78.95	106.14	95.73	71.05
	86.07	91.08	88.68	113.57	115.43	88.03

Figure 2.7 is one of the new "F₀ Contour S", which is drawn from Table 2.4. The three F₀ contours from Figures 2.1, 2.2, and 2.3 and their average F₀ are shown in one coordinate. The F₀ is shown on the vertical axis and the normalized duration of utterance on the horizontal axis.

Table 2.5 F₀ of "Ignore the gloom and **DOOM**" by three Japanese informants and their average F₀

		Ignore			the			gloom		
Time		0.00	0.33	0.67	1.00	1.33	1.67	2.00	2.33	2.67
F0 (Hz)	J1	96.00	102.74	91.00	100.00	100.00	100.00	102.00	97.83	86.00
	J2	96.00	100.97	100.00	107.00	102.93	98.00	96.00	100.64	101.00
	J3	108.00	117.36	127.00	125.00	120.81	117.00	113.00	124.95	121.00
	Average	100.00	107.02	106.00	110.67	107.92	105.00	103.67	107.81	102.67

	and			DOOM		
	3.00	3.33	3.67	4.00	4.33	4.67
	96.00	93.49	93.00	109.00	101.32	92.00
	101.00	99.30	97.00	97.00	95.70	87.00
	113.00	112.19	110.00	116.00	113.50	98.00
	103.33	101.66	100.00	107.33	103.51	92.33

Table 2.5 indicates the F₀ of the three Japanese informants (J1, J2, J3) and their average F₀. All the values are obtained as in Table 2.3. In Table 2.6, the beginning of the sentence was set at 100 Hz as in Table 2.4.

Figure 2.8 shows the F₀ contour of the same sentence as Figure 2.7 uttered by the three Japanese informants severally and averaged. In Figure 2.9, only the averages from Figures 2.7 and 2.8 are shown to compare American informants with Japanese informants.

Table 2.6 F₀ of "Ignore the gloom and **DOOM**" by three Japanese informants where the beginning of each sentence was set at 100 Hz

		Ignore			the			gloom		
Time		0.00	0.33	0.67	1.00	1.33	1.67	2.00	2.33	2.67
F0 (Hz)	J1	100.00	107.02	94.79	104.17	104.17	104.17	106.25	101.91	89.58
	J2	100.00	105.17	104.17	111.46	107.22	102.08	100.00	104.83	105.21
	J3	100.00	108.67	117.59	115.74	111.87	108.33	104.63	115.70	112.04
	Average	100.00	106.95	105.52	110.46	107.75	104.86	103.63	107.48	102.28

and			DOOM		
3.00	3.33	3.67	4.00	4.33	4.67
100.00	97.38	96.88	113.54	105.55	95.83
105.21	103.44	101.04	101.04	99.68	90.63
104.63	103.88	101.85	107.41	105.09	90.74
103.28	101.57	99.92	107.33	103.44	92.40

Concerning how the stressed words change in F₀, the changes in F₀ between the stressed words and the preceding words by the three American informants are shown in Table 2.7. In order to show the changes more clearly, all the ends of the word "and" were set to 100 Hz in Table 2.8. "B/A" in Table 2.8 shows that the emphasized word was uttered 1.24 times higher than the preceding word by informant A1 and 1.77 times higher than the preceding word by informant A2.

Table 2.7 The changes in F₀ between the stressed syllable and the preceding syllable by three American informants

Informant	F₀(Hz)	
	F₀ at the end of the word "and"	The highest F₀ of the word "DOOM"
A1	91.89	113.51
A2	95.19	168.27
A3	78.95	109.65
Average	88.68	130.48

Table 2.8 The changes in F₀ between the stressed syllable and the preceding syllable by three American informants where the beginning of each sentence was set at 100 Hz

Informant	F₀(Hz)		B/A
	(A) F₀ at the end of the word "and"	(B) The highest F₀ of the word "DOOM"	
A1	100.00	123.53	1.24
A2	100.00	176.77	1.77
A3	100.00	138.89	1.39
Average	100.00	147.14	1.47

2.3 New F₀ contour 35

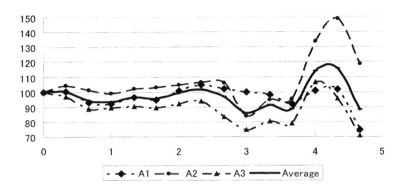

Figure 2.7 F₀ contours of "Ignore the gloom and **DOOM**" by three American informants severally and averaged

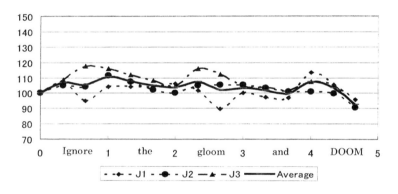

Figure 2.8 F₀ contours of "Ignore the gloom and **DOOM**" by three Japanese informants severally and averaged

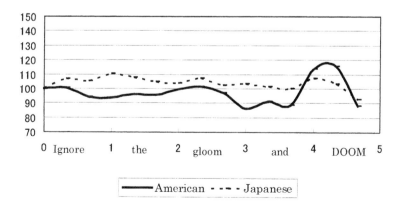

Figure 2.9 The average F₀ contours by American and Japanese informants uttering "Ignore the gloom and **DOOM**"

The change in F₀ between the stressed word and the preceding word by the three Japanese informants is shown in Tables 2.9 and 2.10. "B/A" in Table 2.10 shows that the emphasized word was uttered 1.17 times higher than the preceding word by informant J1 and 1.02 times higher than the preceding word by informant J2.

Table 2.9 The changes in F₀ between the stressed syllable and the preceding syllable by three Japanese informants

Informant	Fo(Hz)	
	Fo at the end of the word "and"	The highest Fo of the word "DOOM"
J1	96.88	113.54
J2	101.04	103.13
J3	101.85	115.74
Average	99.92	110.80

Table 2.10 The changes in F₀ between the stressed syllable and the preceding syllable by three Japanese informants where the beginning of each sentence was set at 100 Hz

Informant	Fo(Hz)		B/A
	(A) Fo at the end of the word "and"	(B) The highest Fo of the word "DOOM"	
J1	100.00	117.20	1.17
J2	100.00	102.06	1.02
J3	100.00	113.64	1.14
Average	100.00	110.89	1.11

Table 2.8 is shown on a bar chart as Figure 2.10. Table 2.10 is shown on a bar chart as Figure 2.11.

In Figure 2.10, the horizontal axis indicates the three American informants and the average is shown at the far right. The vertical axis indicates the change in F₀ between the stressed word, "**DOOM**" and the preceding word, "and". Figure 2.11 shows the F₀ change between the stressed word, "**DOOM**" and the preceding word, "and" by the three Japanese informants.

Figure 2.12 shows only the averages from Figures 2.10 and 2.11 to compare the change in F₀ on the stressed word between American informants and Japanese informants. The average of American informants is shown to the left and the average of Japanese informants is shown to the right.

2.3 New F₀ contour   37

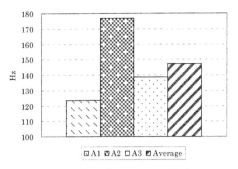

Figure 2.10 The changes in F_0 between the stressed syllable "**DOOM**" and the preceding syllable "and" by three American informants severally and averaged

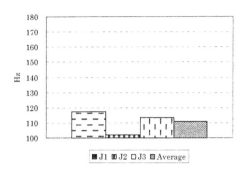

Figure 2.11 The changes in F_0 between the stressed syllable "**DOOM**" and the preceding syllable "and" by three Japanese informants severally and averaged

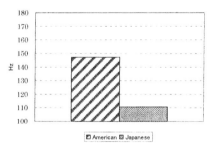

Figure 2.12 Comparison of the changes in F_0 of the stressed syllable between American informants and Japanese informants

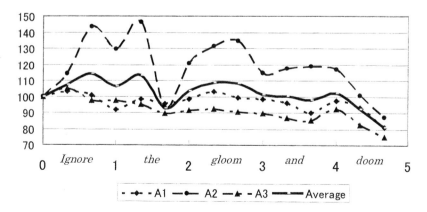

Figure 2.13 F_0 contours of "Ignore the gloom and doom" by three American informants severally and averaged

Figure 2.13 shows the command, "Ignore the gloom and doom", normally uttered by the three American informants.

Figure 2.14 shows the sentence "Ignore the **GLOOM** and doom" by the three American informants. Stress is placed on the word "**GLOOM**". Figure 2.15 shows the same sentence as Figure 2.14 uttered by the three Japanese informants.

Figure 2.16 shows the averages of F_0 patterns by the three American informants and the three Japanese informants who uttered the sentence "Ig**NORE** the gloom and doom", stress is placed on the word "Ig**NORE**".

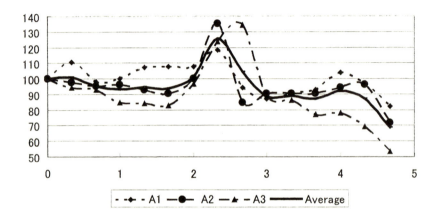

Figure 2.14 F_0 contours of "Ignore the **GLOOM** and doom" by three American informants severally and averaged

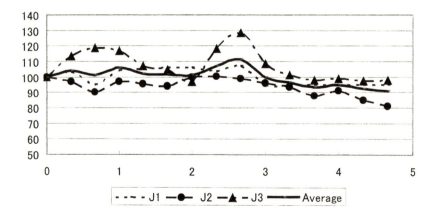

Figure 2.15 F_0 contours of "Ignore the **GLOOM** and doom" by three Japanese informants severally and averaged

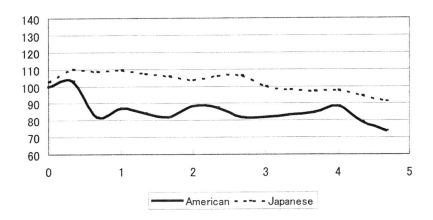

Figure 2.16 The average F_0 contours of "IgNORE the gloom and doom" by American and Japanese informants

2.4 Discussion

With native speakers of American English (AEs), large variations in the fundamental frequency (F_0) were found on the stressed words. On the other hand, with Japanese learners of English (Js) who were not accustomed to speaking English well, small variations in F_0 were found on the stressed words. In Table 2.8, the stressed words uttered by AEs were 1.24 to 1.77 times higher in F_0 than the preceding words. In Table 2.10, on the other hand, the stressed words by Js were only 1.02 to 1.17 times higher in F_0.

In Figure 2.7, a similar tendency is seen among the three American informants. It is found that every word stress ("ignore" and "gloom") except the focused word (**"DOOM"**) is reduced so that prominence is shown on the focused word, **"DOOM"**. In Figure 2.13, though the variations in F_0 are different among the three, the tendency of F_0 patterns is similar.

In Figure 2.8, a different tendency from Figure 2.7 is found. Informant J2 produced the sentence in a monotone and there were no variations in F_0. On the other hand, informant J3 produced the three words, "Ignore", "gloom", and **"DOOM"** on a higher F_0. It seems that informant J3 produced every word with equal stress. The reason the stressed word: **"DOOM"** is not so prominent is that informant J3 did not reduce other stressed syllables of words. The big difference is seen on the vertical axis between Figures 2.10 and 2.11.

Figure 2.9 shows the difference in F_0 patterns between the American informants and the Japanese informants. American informants utter the word "and" at the lowest in F_0 and "**DOOM**" at the highest. That is, the F_0 is lowest before the stressed word and then sharply increases, so that there are F_0 changes between the stressed word and the preceding word. It shows that Japanese informants should utter the word "and" at a much lower in F_0 and the stressed word "**DOOM**" at a much higher in F_0.

Figure 2.12 shows that the great difference in F_0 changes between American informants and Japanese informants. American informants show a great variation in F_0 and the Japanese informants show a small variation in F_0.

In Figure 2.14, word stress of "ignore" and "doom" is reduced in F_0 by informants A2 and A3 so that prominence is only shown on the focused word "**GLOOM**". The informant A1 uttered every word stress relatively higher in F_0, but the difference in F_0 between the word "**GLOOM**" and the following word "and" was very great, so that the prominence was found on "**GLOOM**". In Figure 2.15, though informant J3 succeeded comparatively in achieving prominence, informant J2 spoke with no variations in F_0. In Figure 2.16, the interesting difference between American informants and Japanese informants was seen. Concerning American informants, a great F_0 change was found only on the stressed syllable "Ig**NORE**". Other word stresses on "gloom" and "doom" were reduced in F_0 so that the stress on "Ig**NORE**" was emphasized effectively.

2.5 Summary

In this chapter, the F_0 of three native speakers of American English (AEs) and three Japanese learners of English (Js) were analyzed in order to study the relationship between sentence stress and F_0. The results of AEs are shown as follows:

(1) A large variation in F_0 uttered by AEs was found on the emphasized word in a sentence.
(2) Large variations were not found except on the emphasized word in a sentence. That is, lexical (potential) stresses except on the emphasized word were reduced and almost unchanged in F_0.

The result of (1) and (2) shows that sentence stress is produced effectively and made prominent by AEs. This means that F_0 has a close relationship to sentence stress production in English.

The research undertaken by Nakatani and Aston (1978) seems to support the writer's result from (2). They undertook an experiment on word stress in English, which was covered in section 1.3 (see p.22). They stated that pitch was a useless cue for perceiving the stress of a noun preceded by an accented adjective.

On the other hand, Japanese learners of English who were not accustomed to speaking English well were significantly different from American subjects in pitch patterns. That is, sentence stress was not produced effectively by Japanese subjects. Two types of pitch patterns were seen in the utterance by Japanese subjects as follows:

(a) There were no variations in F_0 in a sentence, so that no word was emphasized in a sentence.
(b) Though variation in F_0 was produced on the emphasized word, variations in F_0 were also produced on all other lexical (potential) stresses as well. Therefore, the emphasized word was not prominent in a sentence.

This result indicates that Japanese learners of English should produce a larger variation in F_0 on the emphasized word and should not produce large variations in F_0 on other lexical (potential) stresses, so that sentence stress stands out effectively.

Japanese do not have a 'weak form' so that it is difficult for Japanese learners of English to use the weak form, which is one of the features of English. They need to be instructed that weak syllables should be uttered lower in F_0 and a stressed syllable is uttered higher in F_0. They also should be instructed to compare contours of native speakers of English with those of Js in order to understand the difference both aurally and visually.

2.6 Devised F_0 contours

In this section, the F_0 contours of 25 sentences as listed in Table 2.2 uttered by three American informants and three Japanese informants are visually shown in from Figures 2.17 to 2.41. The F_0 of 25 utterances were obtained word by word. The F_0's average of the three American informants and that of the three Japanese informants were calculated. The F_0 (Hz) is shown on the vertical axis and the duration of utterance (msec) is shown on the horizontal axis. All 25 "F_0 Contour S" were devised in the same way as Figure 2.7.

(1)-(a) Avoid every kind of evil.

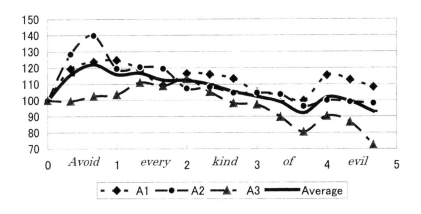

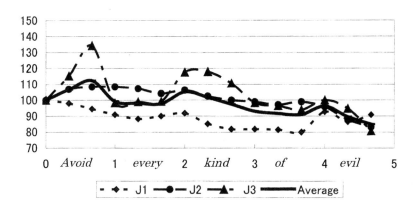

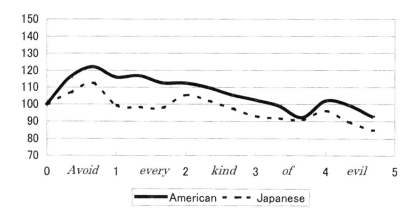

Figure 2.17 F_0 contours of "Avoid every kind of evil." by three American, three Japanese and averaged

2.6 Devised F₀ contours 43

(1)-(b) **AVOID** every kind of evil.

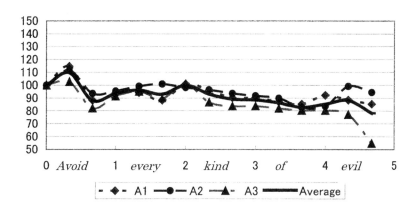

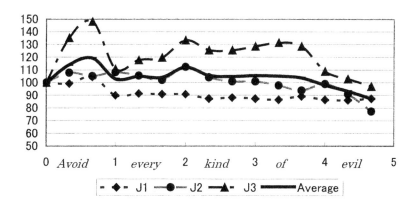

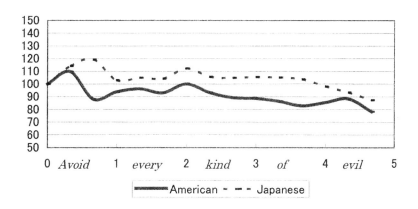

Figure 2.18 F_0 contours of "AVOID every kind of evil." by three American, three Japanese and averaged

44 Pitch contour of sentence stress in American English

(1)-(c) Avoid **EV**ery kind of evil.

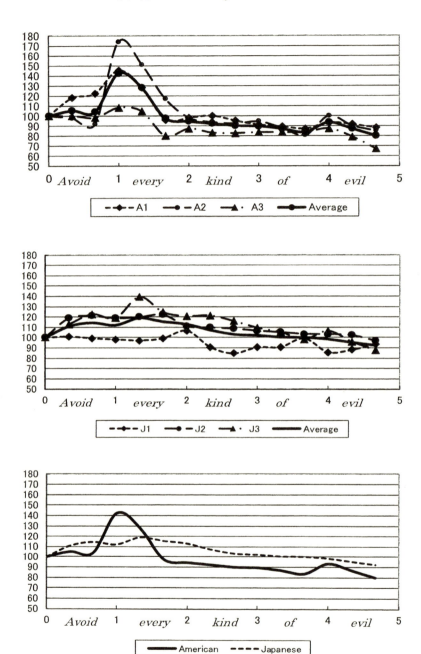

Figure 2.19 F_0 contours of "Avoid **EV**ery kind of evil." by three American, three Japanese and averaged

2.6 Devised F₀ contours   45

(1)-(d) Avoid every kind of Evil.

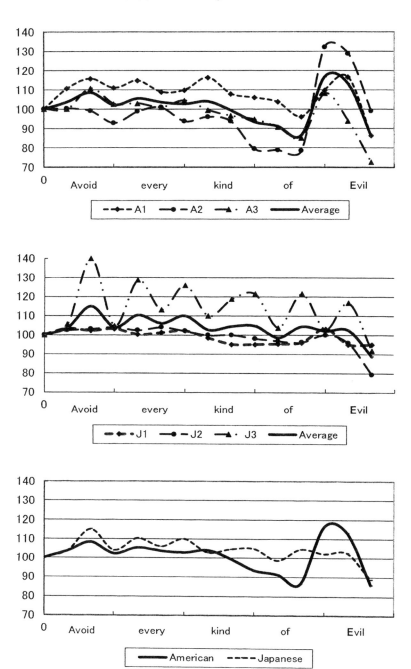

Figure 2.20 F₀ contours of "Avoid every kind of Evil." by three American, three Japanese and averaged

46 Pitch contour of sentence stress in American English

(1)-(e) Avoid every kind of evil?

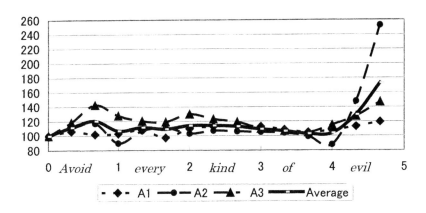

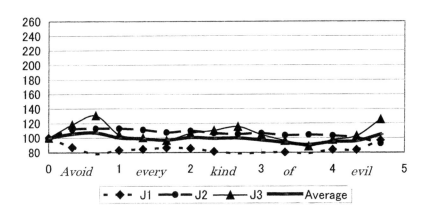

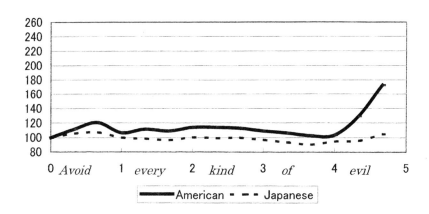

Figure 2.21 F₀ contours of "Avoid every kind of evil?" by three American, three Japanese and averaged

2.6 Devised F₀ contours   47

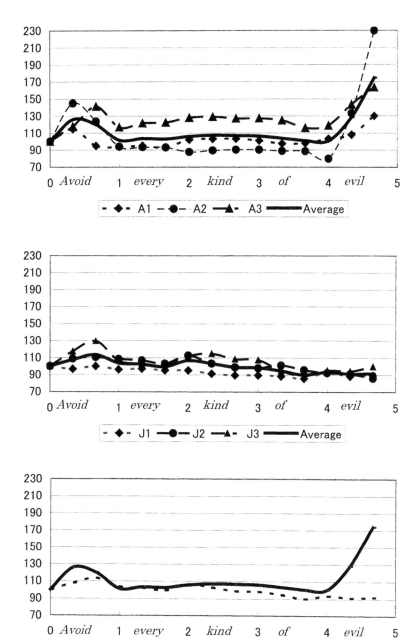

Figure 2.22 F₀ contours of "AVOID every kind of evil?" by three American, three Japanese and averaged

48 Pitch contour of sentence stress in American English

(1)-(g) Avoid **EV**ery kind of evil?

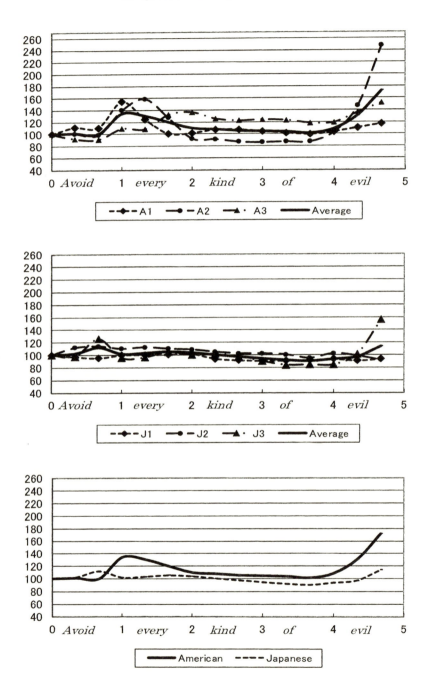

Figure 2.23 F₀ contours of "Avoid **EV**ery kind of evil?" by three American, three Japanese and averaged

2.6 Devised F₀ contours   49

(1)-(h) Avoid every kind of Evil?

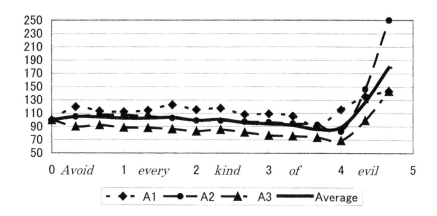

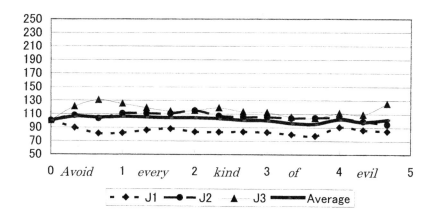

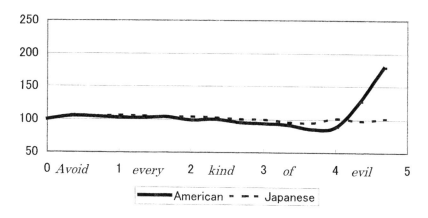

Figure 2.24 F₀ contours of "Avoid every kind of Evil?" by three American, three Japanese and averaged

50   Pitch contour of sentence stress in American English

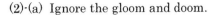
(2)-(a) Ignore the gloom and doom.

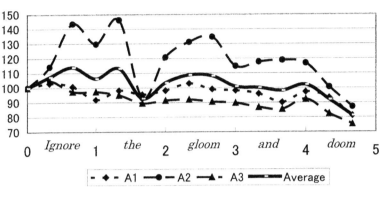

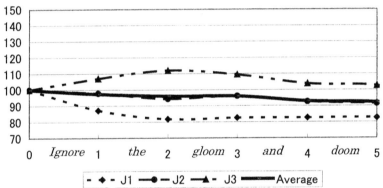

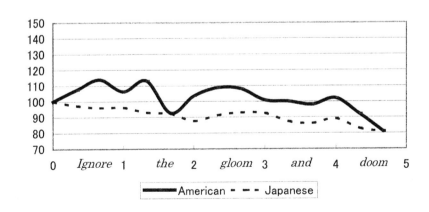

Figure 2.25 F_0 contours of "Ignore the gloom and doom." by three American, three Japanese and averaged

2.6 Devised F_0 contours 51

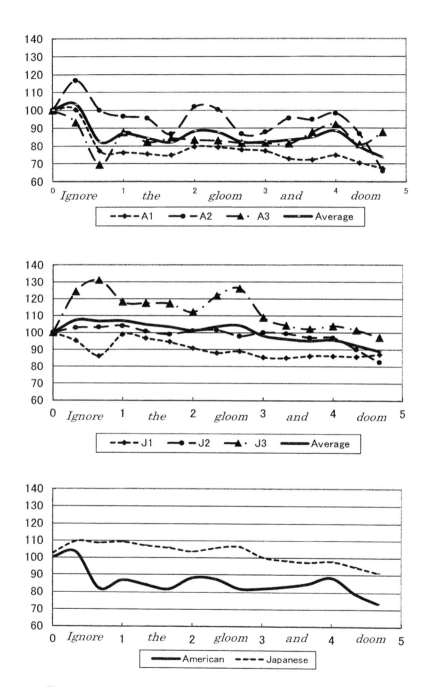

Figure 2.26 F_0 contours of "IgNORE the gloom and doom." by three American, three Japanese and averaged

52 Pitch contour of sentence stress in American English

(2)-(c) Ignore the **GLOOM** and doom.

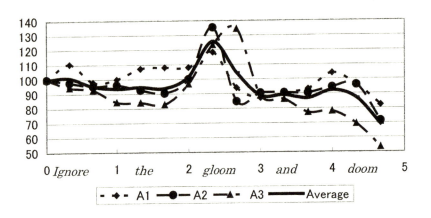

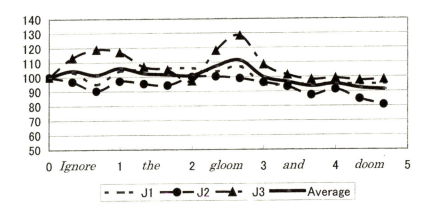

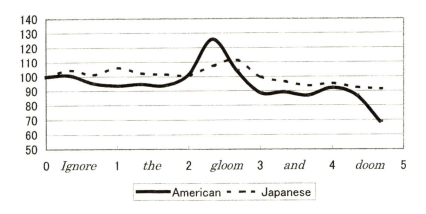

Figure 2.27 F_0 contours of "Ignore the **GLOOM** and doom." by three American, three Japanese and averaged

2.6 Devised F₀ contours 53

(2)-(d) Ignore the gloom and **DOOM**.

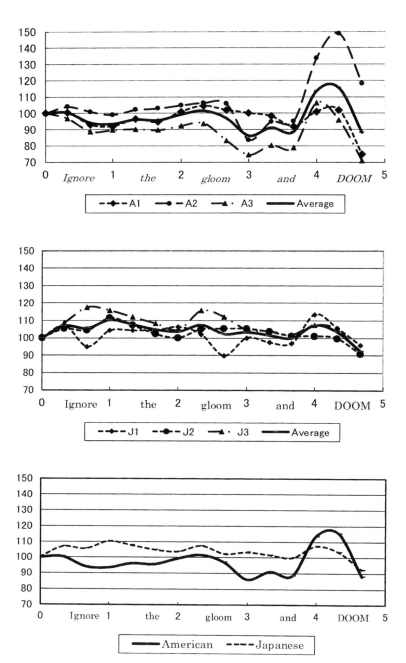

Figure 2.28 F₀ contours of "Ignore the gloom and **DOOM**." by three American, three Japanese and averaged

54 Pitch contour of sentence stress in American English

(2)-(e) Ignore the gloom and doom?

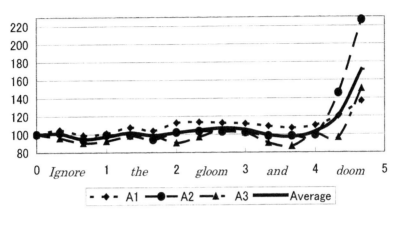

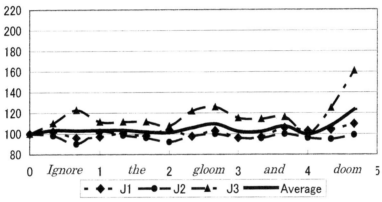

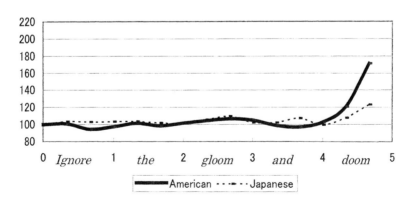

Figure 2.29 F₀ contours of "Ignore the gloom and doom?" by three American, three Japanese and averaged

2.6 Devised F₀ contours 55

(2)-(f) IgNORE the gloom and doom?

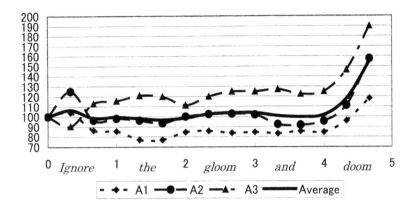

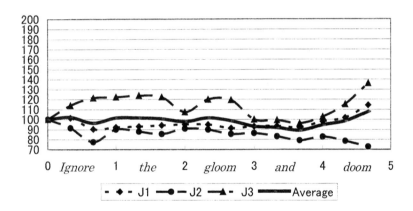

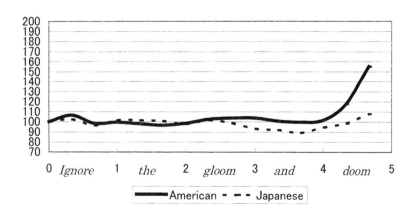

Figure 2.30 F$_0$ contours of "IgNORE the gloom and doom?" by three American, three Japanese and averaged

56 Pitch contour of sentence stress in American English

(2)-(g) Ignore the **GLOOM** and doom?

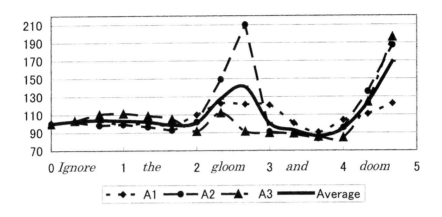

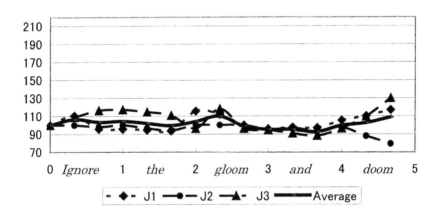

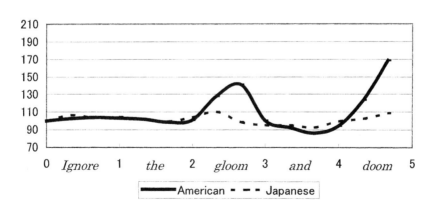

Figure 2.31 F₀ contours of "Ignore the **GLOOM** and doom?" by three American, three Japanese and averaged

2.6 Devised F₀ contours 57

(2)-(h) Ignore the gloom and **DOOM**?

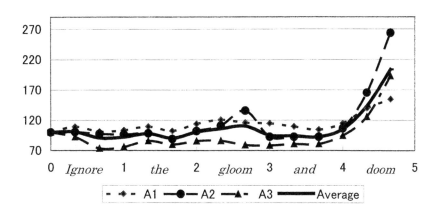

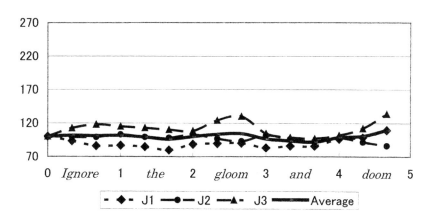

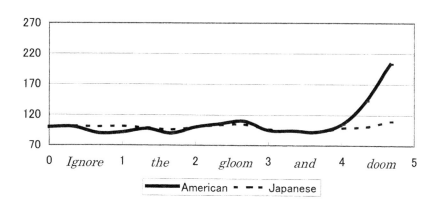

Figure 2.32 F₀ contours of "Ignore the gloom and **DOOM**?" by three American, three Japanese and averaged

58 Pitch contour of sentence stress in American English

(3)-(a) But you love me!

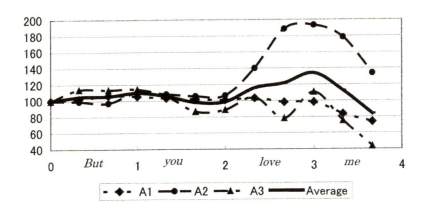

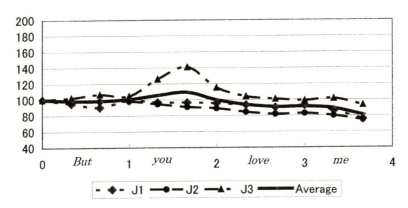

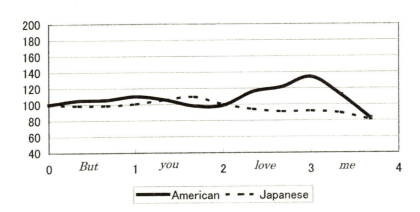

Figure 2.33 F_0 contours of "But you love me!" by three American, three Japanese and averaged

2.6 Devised F₀ contours 59

(3)-(b) But **YOU** love me!

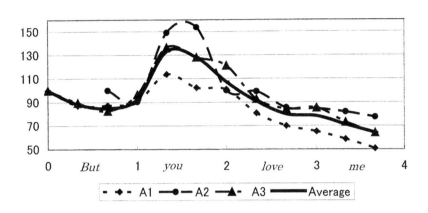

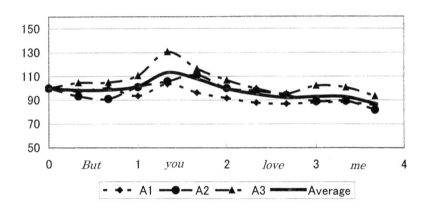

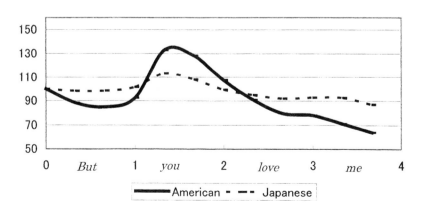

Figure 2.34 F₀ contours of "But **YOU** love me!" by three American, three Japanese and averaged

60 Pitch contour of sentence stress in American English

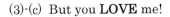

(3)-(c) But you **LOVE** me!

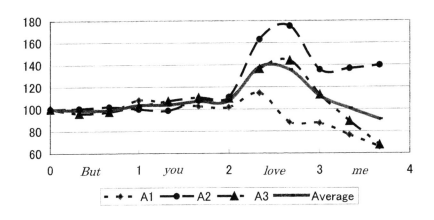

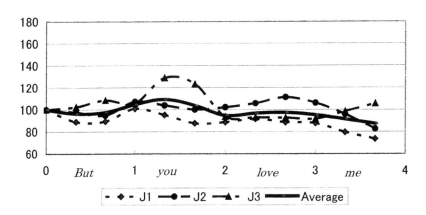

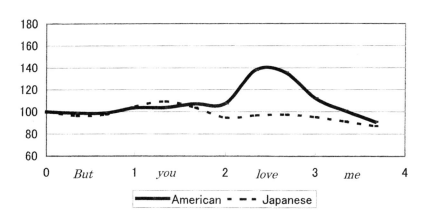

Figure 2.35 F_0 contours of "But you **LOVE** me!" by three American, three Japanese and averaged

2.6 Devised F₀ contours   61

(3)-(d) But you love **ME**!

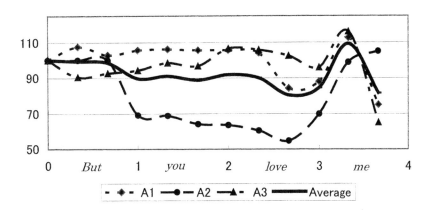

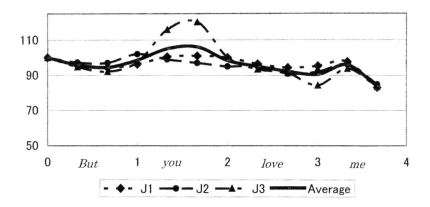

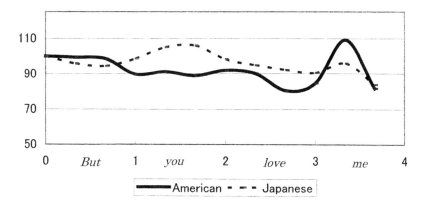

Figure 2.36 F$_0$ contours of "But you love **ME**!" by three American, three Japanese and averaged

62 Pitch contour of sentence stress in American English

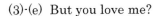

(3)-(e) But you love me?

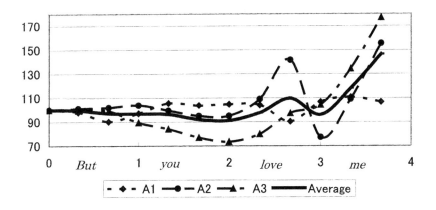

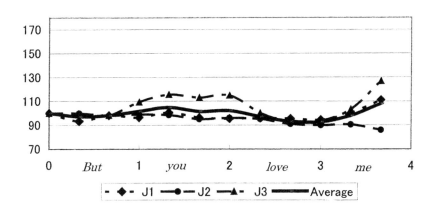

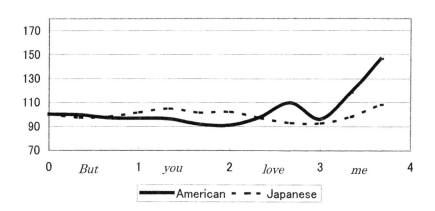

Figure 2.37 F₀ contours of "But you love me?" by three American, three Japanese and averaged

2.6 Devised F₀ contours 63

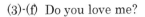

(3)-(f) Do you love me?

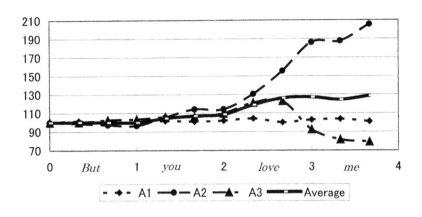

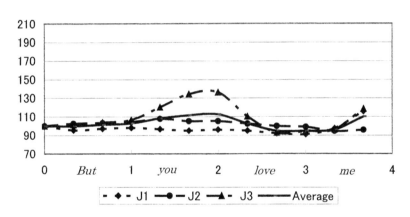

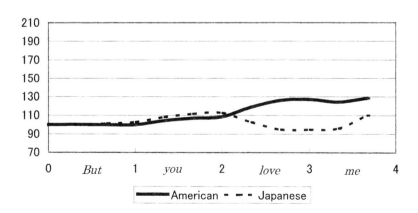

Figure 2.38 F₀ contours of "Do you love me?" by three American, three Japanese and averaged

64 Pitch contour of sentence stress in American English

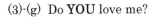

(3)-(g) Do **YOU** love me?

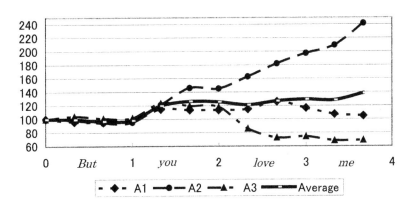

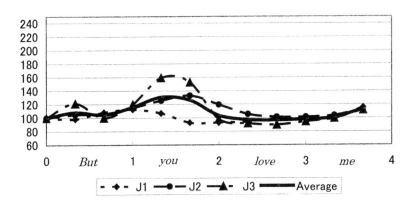

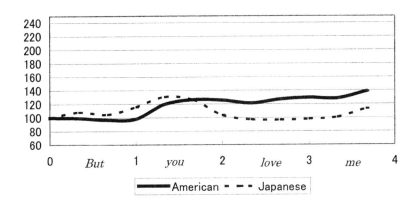

Figure 2.39 F_0 contours of "Do **YOU** love me?" by three American, three Japanese and averaged

2.6 Devised F_0 contours   65

(3)-(h) Do you **LOVE** me?

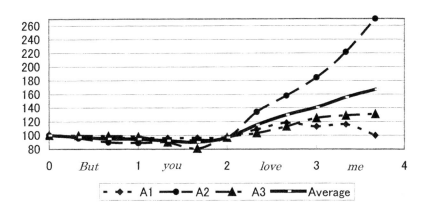

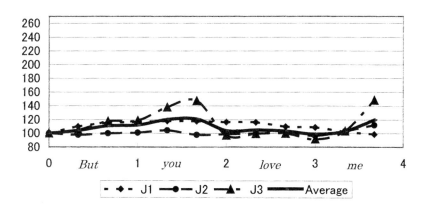

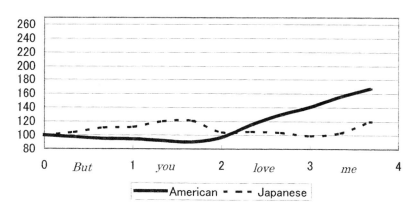

Figure 2.40 F_0 contours of "Do you **LOVE** me?" by three American, three Japanese and averaged

66   Pitch contour of sentence stress in American English

(3)-(i)   Do you love **ME**?

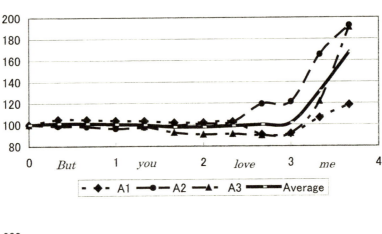

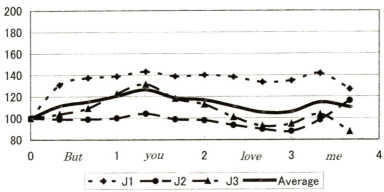

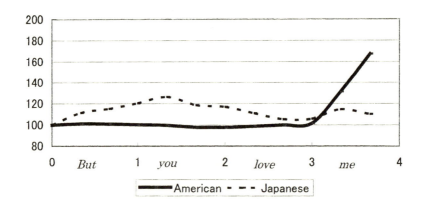

Figure 2.41 F₀ contours of "Do you love **ME**?" by three American, three Japanese and averaged

3 Perception of sentence stress and pitch change by native speakers of American English

3.1 Introduction

When the stressed syllables of native speakers of English are analyzed by speech processing software, it is found that the intensity is higher, the fundamental frequency (F_0, pitch) is changed, the duration is longer, and the vowel quality is changed. The result of the experiment in Chapter 2 shows that F_0 (pitch) movement is one of the major factors in producing sentence stress in American English. The purpose of this chapter is to demonstrate that F_0 movement is also one of the major parameters in perceiving sentence stress. For this purpose, forty native speakers of American English (AEs) listened to synthesized utterances, in which only the F_0 parameter was changed. After the experiment, the result was statistically analyzed.

3.2 Experiment

3.2.1 Purpose
The purpose of the experiment reported in this chapter is to examine acoustically whether F_0 movement is perceived as sentence stress by AEs.

3.2.2 Method
First, one male native speaker of American English, informant A1, was asked to utter two sentences, which were recorded on a micro disk (MD). The utterances were synthesized in different ways depending on where the higher F_0 (pitch) syllable was placed. Synthesized utterances were recorded in random order on a micro disk. Forty American subjects were asked to listen to the synthesized utterances and then to indicate which word was stressed in the utterance.

3.2.3 Materials
One male native speaker of American English, informant A1, was asked to

utter two sentences, "**AVOID** every kind of evil" (This sentence is abbreviated as Sentence 1) and "Ig**NORE** the gloom and doom" (This sentence is abbreviated as Sentence 2). Capitalized and bold letters show the stressed syllables. The speaker's utterances were recorded on a micro disk. All of the speech signals were digitized (16 bits; speed: 11.025 KHz) and stored.

Figure 3.1 shows the F_0 contour of Sentence 1 stressed on the syllable "-**VOID**" by informant A1. F_0 (pitch) is shown on the vertical axis, and the duration of the utterance (msec) on the horizontal axis. The stressed syllable, "-**VOID**" was uttered at a frequency 52 Hz higher than the preceding syllable, "A-". Figure 3.2 shows the F_0 contour of Sentence 2 stressed on the syllable, "-**NORE**" by informant A1. The stressed syllable, "-**NORE**" was uttered at a frequency 35 Hz higher than the preceding syllable, "Ig-".

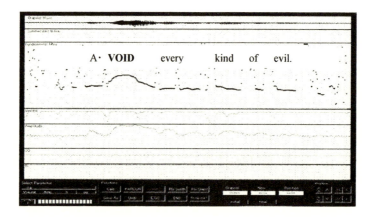

Figure 3.1 F_0 contour of "A**VOID** every kind of evil" by A1

Figure 3.2 F_0 contour of "Ig**NORE** the gloom and doom" by A1

3.2 Experiment

3.2.4 Method of synthesis

Using the partial auto-correlation (PARCOR) (Itakura 1971:1-12) method, two recorded speeches (Figures 3.1 and 3.2) were synthesized in different ways depending on where the higher F_0 syllable was placed with speech processing software (Hirasaka, 2000). All of the speech signals were digitized (16 bits; speed: 11.025 KHz) and stored. The output of the synthesized utterances maintained the same precision by using a D/A converter and recorded on a magnetic disk.

Figures 3.3 to 3.7 show the synthesized F_0 contours using the utterance of Figure 3.1. Underlined and italic letters show the syllables which were set to higher in F_0. The utterance time was not changed, only the F_0 was changed, respectively. In order to mimic the natural human utterance, F_0 was decreased gradually from the start to the end of the utterance. (Ohman 1967: 20-54).

In order to remove the effect of intensity in stress, the highest value of intensity of all words was set to almost the same intensity. Figures 3.8 to 3.12 show graphed outlines of F_0 in Figures 3.3 to 3.7, respectively, in which the value of F_0 is added.

The utterance of Sentence 1 (Figure 3.1) by the Informant A1 begins at 102 Hz and ends at 82 Hz, so that the beginnings of five contours in Sentence 1 (Figures 3.8 to 3.12) were set to 102 Hz and the ends of them were set to 82 Hz. In Figure 3.8, F_0 was decreased uniformly from the beginning to the end. Stressed syllable, "-**VOID**" was uttered at a frequency 52 Hz higher than the preceding syllable, "A-", so that the higher syllables in Figures 3.9 to 3.12 were set to 52 Hz higher than the preceding syllables, respectively. For example, in Figure 3.9, the syllable "A-" was 101 Hz so that the higher syllable "-*void*" was set to 153 Hz (101 Hz + 52 Hz = 153 Hz). In Figure 3.10, the end of "Avoid" which is the preceding word to "*ev*ery" was 96 Hz so that the higher syllable "*ev* -" was set to 148 Hz (96 Hz + 52 Hz = 148 Hz). In the same way, "*kind*" in Figure 3.11 and syllable "*e* -" in Figure 3.12 were set to 52 Hz higher than the end of the preceding word.

Figures 3.13 to 3.16 show the synthesized F_0 contours using the utterance of Figure 3.2. Underlined and italic letters show the higher F_0 syllables. The utterance time was not changed, only the F_0 was changed in each case. The highest value of intensity of all words was made almost the same. Figures 3.17 to 3.20 show graphed outlines of F_0 in Figures 3.13 to 3.16, respectively, in which the value of F_0 is added.

The utterance of Sentence 2 (Figure 3.2) by the Informant A1 begins at 113 Hz and ends at 78 Hz, so that the beginnings of four stimulus types of contours in Sentence 2 (Figures 3.17 to 3.20) were set to 113 Hz and the end of each contour was set to 78 Hz. In Figure 3.17, F_0 was decreased uniformly from the beginning to the end of the utterance. Stressed syllable, "-**NORE**" was uttered at a frequency 35 Hz higher than the preceding syllable, "Ig-", so that the higher syllables in Figures 3.18 to 3.20 were set to 35 Hz higher than the preceding syllables. For example, in Figure 3.18, the syllable "Ig-" was 107 Hz so that the higher syllable "-_nore_" was set to 142 Hz (107 Hz + 35 Hz = 142 Hz). In Figure 3.19, the end of "the" which is the preceding word to "_gloom_" was 96 Hz so that the higher syllable "_gloom_" was set to 131 Hz (96 Hz + 35 Hz = 131 Hz). In the same way, the syllable "_doom_" in Figure 3.20 was set to 35 Hz higher than the end of the preceding word, "and".

The output for the nine synthesized digitized speech signals (Figures 3.3 to 3.7 and Figures 3.13 to 3.16) maintained the same precision using a D/A converter (16bits; speed: 11.025 KHz). They were recorded 5 times each in random order on an audio magnetic disk. Table 3.1 shows the synthesized utterances for the perception test. In this book, the contours of the synthesized utterances in which F_0 was decreased uniformly from the beginning to the end, are defined as 'steady'.

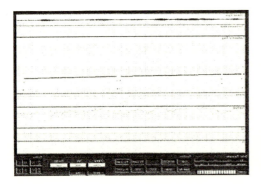

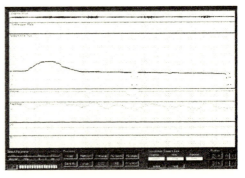

Figure 3.3 Synthesized F_0 contour of "Avoid every kind of evil" ('steady')

Figure 3.4 Synthesized F_0 contour of "A_void_ every kind of evil"

3.2 Experiment 71

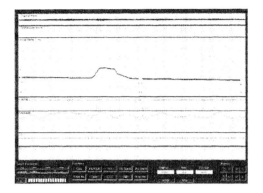

Figure 3.5 Synthesized F_0 contour of "Avoid e_ve_ry kind of evil"

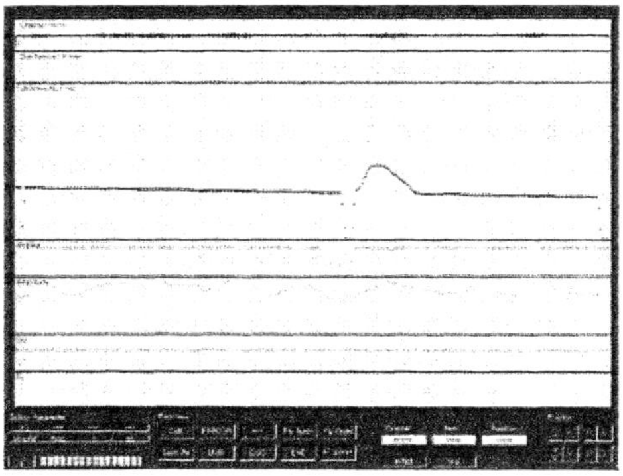

Figure 3.6 Synthesized F_0 contour of "Avoid every _kind_ of evil"

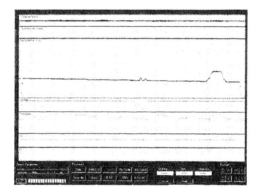

Figure 3.7 Synthesized F_0 contour of "Avoid every kind of _e_vil"

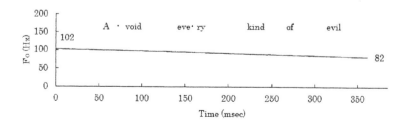

Figure 3.8 Illustration of Figure 3.3, "Avoid every kind of evil" ('steady')

72 Perception of sentence stress and pitch change by AEs

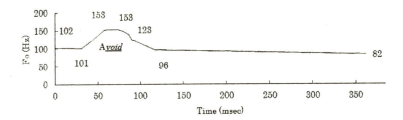

Figure 3.9 Illustration of Figure 3.4, "A*void* every kind of evil"

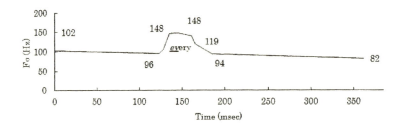

Figure 3.10 Illustration of Figure 3.5, "Avoid *ev*ery kind of evil"

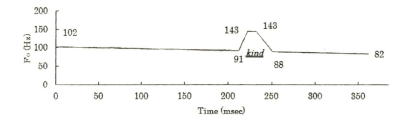

Figure 3.11 Illustration of Figure 3.6, "Avoid every *kind* of evil"

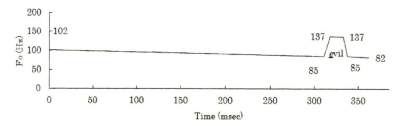

Figure 3.12 Illustration of Figure 3.7, "Avoid every kind of *e*vil"

3.2 Experiment 73

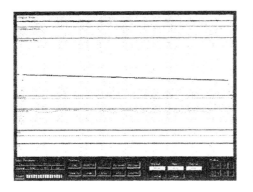

Figure 3.13 Synthesized F_0 contour of "Ignore the gloom and doom" ('steady')

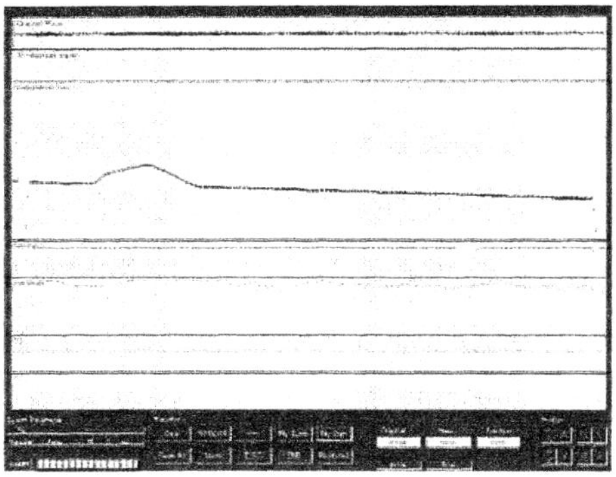

Figure 3.14 Synthesized F_0 contour of "Ig_nore_ the gloom and doom"

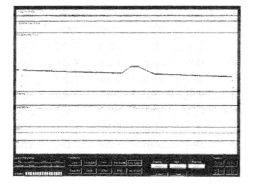 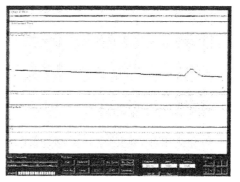

Figure 3.15 Synthesized F_0 contour of "Ignore the _gloom_ and doom"

Figure 3.16 Synthesized F_0 contour of "Ignore the gloom and _doom_"

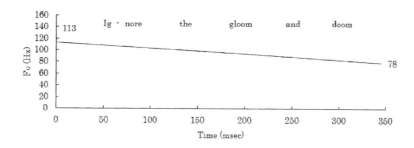

Figure 3.17 Illustration of Figure 3.13, "Ignore the gloom and doom" ('steady')

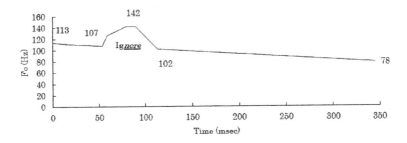

Figure 3.18 Illustration of Figure 3.14, "Ig*nore* the gloom and doom"

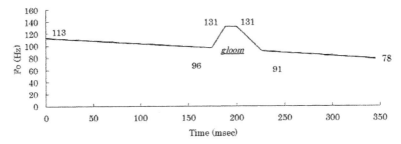

Figure 3.19 Illustration of Figure 3.15, "Ignore the *gloom* and doom"

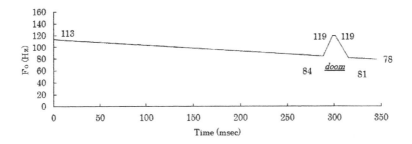

Figure 3.20 Illustration of Figure 3.16, "Ignore the gloom and *doom*"

3.2.5 Method of perception test

The subjects were forty well-educated native speakers of American English (AEs) (10 professors, 19 English teachers, 9 university students, and 2 business persons) with no hearing and speaking disorder, their ages between 19 and 69. The forty subjects who participated in the experiment are listed in Table 3.2. They were asked to listen to the forty-five synthesized utterances (Table 3.1) once and to choose either one stressed word or if there was no stressed word to choose 'monotone (no stressed words)'. The following sheet of Table 3.3 was given to the forty subjects.

Table 3.1 List of change in stress in synthesized utterances

(1)	Avoid every kind of *e*vil.	
(2)	Ignore the *gloom* and doom.	
(3)	Ig*nore* the gloom and doom.	
(4)	Avoid *ev*ery kind of evil.	
(5)	Avoid every kind of evil.	(steady)
(6)	Ig*nore* the gloom and doom.	
(7)	Avoid every *kind* of evil.	
(8)	Avoid every kind of *e*vil.	
(9)	Avoid every kind of evil.	(steady)
(10)	Ignore the *gloom* and doom.	
(11)	A*void* every kind of evil.	
(12)	Ignore the gloom and doom.	(steady)
(13)	Ignore the gloom and *doom*.	
(14)	Ignore the gloom and doom.	(steady)
(15)	Avoid every *kind* of evil.	
(16)	Ignore the gloom and *doom*.	
(17)	A*void* every kind of evil.	
(18)	Avoid *ev*ery kind of evil.	
(19)	Avoid every *kind* of evil.	
(20)	Ignore the *gloom* and doom.	
(21)	Ig*nore* the gloom and doom.	
(22)	Avoid *ev*ery kind of evil.	
(23)	Ignore the gloom and *doom*.	
(24)	Ig*nore* the gloom and doom.	
(25)	Avoid every kind of *e*vil.	
(26)	Avoid every *kind* of evil.	
(27)	Avoid every kind of evil.	(steady)
(28)	Ignore the *gloom* and doom.	
(29)	A*void* every kind of evil.	
(30)	Ignore the gloom and doom.	(steady)
(31)	Avoid every kind of evil.	(steady)
(32)	Ignore the gloom and doom.	(steady)
(33)	Avoid every kind of *e*vil.	
(34)	Ignore the gloom and doom.	(steady)
(35)	A*void* every kind of evil.	
(36)	Avoid *ev*ery kind of evil.	
(37)	Ignore the gloom and *doom*.	
(38)	Avoid every *kind* of evil.	
(39)	Avoid every kind of evil.	(steady)
(40)	Ignore the gloom and *doom*.	
(41)	Avoid *ev*ery kind of evil.	
(42)	Avoid every kind of *e*vil.	
(43)	Ig*nore* the gloom and doom.	
(44)	A*void* every kind of evil.	
(45)	Ignore the *gloom* and doom.	

Note: Underlined and italic letters show the syllables set to higher. Also 'steady' shows the synthesized utterances that F_0 was decreased uniformly.

Table 3.2 Background of the forty subjects

Subjects	Nationality	The place lived longest	Educational background	Status	Age
A1	U.S.A.	Yokohama	Graduate School	Professor	60's
A2	U.S.A.	Yokohama	Graduate School	Professor	60's
A3	U.S.A.	Monterey, California	College	Professor	50's
A4	U.S.A.	Los Angeles	College	Professor	40's
A5	U.S.A.	Texas	College	Professor	20's
A6	U.S.A.	New York	Graduate School	Professor	60's
A7	U.S.A.	Japan	Graduate School	Professor	60's
A8	U.S.A.	Oklahoma	Graduate School	Professor	50's
A9	Canada	Vancouver, Canada	Graduate School	Professor	40's
A10	Canada	Canada (East Side)	Graduate School	Professor	30's
A11	U.S.A.	Georgia	Graduate School	English teacher	40's
A12	U.S.A.	Denver, Colorado	College	English teacher	40's
A13	U.S.A.	Portsmouth, Virginia	College	English teacher	40's
A14	U.S.A.	Bellingham, Washington	College	English teacher	40's
A15	U.S.A.	Colorado	College	English teacher	30's
A16	U.S.A.	California	College	English teacher	30's
A17	U.S.A.	Mishigan	College	English teacher	30's
A18	U.S.A.	California	High School	English teacher	30's
A19	U.S.A.	Witchita, Kansas/ Pensacok, Florida	College	English teacher	30's
A20	U.S.A.	San Diego, California	Graduate School	English teacher	40's
A21	U.S.A.	New York	Graduate School	English teacher	40's
A22	U.S.A.	California	Graduate School	English teacher	30's
A23	U.S.A.	Detroit, Michigan	College	English teacher	50's
A24	U.S.A.	California	College	English teacher	40's
A25	U.S.A.	Germany	College	English teacher	30's
A26	U.S.A.	Waxahachie, Texas	College	English teacher	30's
A27	U.S.A.	California	College	English teacher	30's
A28	U.S.A.	Ohio	High School	English teacher	30's
A29	Canada	Calgary, Alberta	Graduate School	English teacher	30's
A30	U.S.A.	Seattle	College	University Student	20's
A31	U.S.A.	Milwarkie, Oregon	College	University Student	20's
A32	U.S.A.	Oregon	College	University Student	20's
A33	U.S.A.	Salem, Oregon	College	University Student	20's
A34	U.S.A.	Hillsboro, Oregon	College	University Student	20's
A35	U.S.A.	Portland, Oregon	College	University Student	20's
A36	U.S.A.	San Diego, California	College	University Student	20's
A37	U.S.A.	Kaneohe, Hawaii	College	University Student	20's
A38	U.S.A.	Hawaii	College	University Student	20's
A39	U.S.A.	Philadelphia	Graduate School	Business Person	50's
A40	U.S.A.	Washington State	Graduate School	Business Person	50's

Table 3.3 Perception test sheet

Please circle one stressed word in each sentence, "Avoid every kind of evil" or "Ignore the gloom and doom". If there is no stressed word in a sentence, please circle "monotone (no stressed words)".

Nationality	
The place you've lived longest (e.g. Chicago)	
Age	20's 30's 40's 50's 60's
Educational Background	High School College Graduate School

1   Avoid / every / kind / evil / monotone (no stressed words)
2   Ignore / gloom / doom / monotone (no stressed words)
3   Ignore / gloom / doom / monotone (no stressed words)
4   Avoid / every / kind / evil / monotone (no stressed words)
5   Avoid / every / kind / evil / monotone (no stressed words)
6   Ignore / gloom / doom / monotone (no stressed words)
7   Avoid / every / kind / evil / monotone (no stressed words)
8   Avoid / every / kind / evil / monotone (no stressed words)
9   Avoid / every / kind / evil / monotone (no stressed words)
10 Ignore / gloom / doom / monotone (no stressed words)

40 Ignore / gloom / doom / monotone (no stressed words)
41 Avoid / every / kind / evil / monotone (no stressed words)
42 Avoid / every / kind / evil / monotone (no stressed words)
43 Ignore / gloom / doom / monotone (no stressed words)
44 Avoid / every / kind / evil / monotone (no stressed words)
45 Ignore / gloom / doom / monotone (no stressed words)

3.3 Stress perception by native speakers of American English (Group A)

3.3.1 Background theory
(A) Assuming that an event happens k times in a series of n tests, the sample ratio p is:
$$p = k / n \qquad (3.1)$$ (Inagaki, et al., 1996: 138.)
(B) Generally, the probability p in which an event happens x times in n tests is calculated by the binominal distribution.
(C) When the mean np is large in a binominal distribution, the probability is calculated from the fact that the binominal distribution approximates to a normal distribution (np>5 approximately).
$$Z = \{(x/n)-p\} / \{p(1-p)/n\}^{1/2} \qquad (3.2)$$ (Inagaki, et al., 1996: 138.)
This approximates to a standard normal distribution. Using this, a test was carried out after setting a critical region of Z.

N (people) random samples were drawn from native speakers of American English (AEs). These are labeled as Group A. A ratio test was carried out to examine whether the incorrect answer rate p_0 is considered as the incorrect answer rate of Group A. The hypothesis was set as follows:

Null hypothesis $\quad H_0 : p=p_0 \quad$ (The incorrect answer rate of Group A is considered as p_0.)
Alternative hypothesis $\quad H_1 : p \neq p_0 \quad$ (The incorrect answer rate of Group A differs from p_0.)
(Inagaki, et al 1996: 138.)

From the normal distribution table, the critical region $Z_{0.01}=2.58$, $Z_{0.05}=1.96$, and $Z_{0.1}=1.64$ were used (Inagaki, et al., 1996: 65). That is to say; when the level of significance was 0.01 (confidence level is 0.99), $Z_{0.01}=2.58$; when the level of significance is 0.05 (confidence level is 0.95), $Z_{0.05}=1.96$; and when level of significance is 0.1 (confidence level is 0.9), $Z_{0.1}=1.64$. The confidence level means the probability that the conclusion is determined to be right (Inagaki, et al., 1996: 117).

3.3.2 Test of incorrect answer rate
In this book, the incorrect answers are defined as follows:
(1) when subjects listened to the synthesized utterances with a higher F_0 syllable, but did not answer that there was a stressed syllable on a higher F_0 syllable, and
(2) when subjects listened to the synthesized utterances in which F_0 was decreased uniformly from the beginning to the end ('steady'), but did not answer that there were no stressed words ('monotone') in a sen-

tence.

Tables 3.4 and 3.5 show the results in which 40 AEs listened to the nine stimulus types of synthesized utterances five times at random. These are shown graphically in Figures 3.21 and 3.22.

Table 3.4 The incorrect answer rate of each word by AEs (Group A) <Sentence 1> (The total test number is 40 (people) versus 5 (times) =200)

Higher Fo word	Correct answer	Incorrect answer	Total	Incorrect answer rate (p)	Correct answer rate (1-p)
evil	150	50	200	25.0%	75.0%
"steady"	181	19	200	9.5%	90.5%
Avoid	182	18	200	9.0%	91.0%
every	188	12	200	6.0%	94.0%
kind	190	10	200	5.0%	95.0%
Total	891	109	1000	10.9%	89.1%

Table 3.5 The incorrect answer rate of each word by AEs (Group A) <Sentence 2> (The total test number is 40 (people) versus 5 (times) =200)

Higher Fo word	Correct answer	Incorrect answer	Total	Incorrect answer rate (p)	Correct answer rate (1-p)
doom	146	54	200	27.0%	73.0%
"steady"	164	36	200	18.0%	82.0%
gloom	168	32	200	16.0%	84.0%
Ignore	175	25	200	12.5%	87.5%
Total	653	147	800	18.4%	81.6%

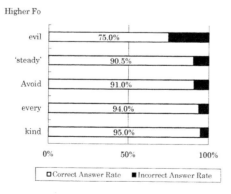

Figure 3.21 The incorrect answer rate of each word by AEs (Group A) <Sentence 1>

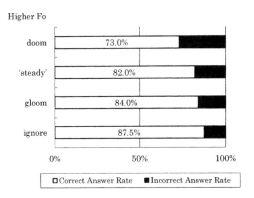

Figure 3.22 The incorrect answer rate of each word by AEs (Group A)
<Sentence 2>

(1) Higher "<u>e</u>vil" in Sentence 1
A test was carried out to determine whether the incorrect answer rate is considered as 0.3 at a significance level of 0.05 when Group A listened to the synthesized utterances where the word "<u>e</u>vil" was set to higher in F₀.

    Null hypothesis H_0 : p=0.3 (The incorrect answer rate of Group A is considered as 0.3.)
    Alternative hypothesis H_1 : p≠0.3 (The incorrect answer rate of Group A differs from 0.3.)

Where $Z_{0.05}$=1.96.
Here n=200, x/n=0.25, p=0.3. Entering these values in formula (3.2), the following result was obtained.
|Z|=1.543.
Then
|Z|<1.96(=$Z_{0.05}$).

    Therefore, H_0 was accepted because Z was not included in the critical region. This means that the incorrect answer rate is considered as 30% at a level of significance = 0.05. That is, the incorrect answer rate is considered as 30% with a 95% probability.

(2) No stressed words ('steady') in Sentence 1
A test was carried out to determine whether the incorrect answer rate is considered as 0.1 at a significance level of 0.05 when Group A listened to the synthesized utterances where F₀ was decreased uniformly ('steady') in Sentence 1.

Null hypothesis H_0 : p=0.1 (The incorrect answer rate of Group A is considered as 0.1.)
Alternative hypothesis H_1 : p≠0.1 (The incorrect answer rate of Group A differs from 0.1.)

Where $Z_{0.05}$=1.96.
Here n=200, x/n=0.095, p=0.1. Entering these values in formula (3.2), the following result was obtained:
|Z|=0.2357.
Then
|Z|<1.96(=$Z_{0.05}$).

Therefore, H_0 was accepted because Z was not included in the critical region. This means that the incorrect answer rate is considered as 10% when the level of significance is 0.05.

(3) Higher "A*void*" in Sentence 1
A test was carried out to determine whether the incorrect answer rate is considered as 0.1 at a significance level of 0.05 when Group A listened to the synthesized utterances where the word "A*void*" was set to higher in F_0.
Null hypothesis H_0 : p=0.1 (The incorrect answer rate of Group A is considered as 0.1.)
Alternative hypothesis H_1 : p≠0.1 (The incorrect answer rate of Group A differs from 0.1)

Where $Z_{0.05}$=1.96.
Here n=200, x/n=0.09, p=0.1. Entering these values in formula (3.2), the following result was obtained:
|Z|=0.4714.
Then
|Z|<1.96 (=$Z_{0.05}$).

Therefore, H_0 was accepted because Z was not included in the critical region. This means that the incorrect answer rate is considered as 10% at a level of significance = 0.05. That is, the incorrect answer rate is considered as 10% with a 95% probability.

(4) Higher "*ev*ery" in Sentence 1
A test was carried out to determine whether the incorrect answer rate is considered as 0.1 at a significance level of 0.05 when Group A listened to the synthesized utterances where the word "*ev*ery" was set to higher in F_0.
Null hypothesis H_0 : p=0.1 (The incorrect answer rate of Group A is considered as 0.1.)
Alternative hypothesis H_1 : p≠0.1 (The incorrect answer rate of Group A differs from 0.1)

Where $Z_{0.05}=1.96$.
Here n=200, x/n=0.06, p=0.1. Entering these values in formula (3.2), the following result was obtained:
$|Z|=1.886$.
Then
$|Z|<1.96(=Z_{0.05})$.

Therefore, H_0 was accepted because Z was not included in the critical region. This means that the incorrect answer rate is considered as 10% at a level of significance = 0.05.

(5) Higher "*kind*" in Sentence 1
A test was carried out to determine whether the incorrect answer rate is considered as 0.1 at a significance level of 0.05 when Group A listened to the synthesized utterances where the word "*kind*" was set to higher in F_0.

    Null hypothesis H_0 : p=0.1 (The incorrect answer rate of Group A is considered as 0.1.)
    Alternative hypothesis H_1 : p≠0.1 (The incorrect answer rate of Group A differs from 0.1)

Where $Z_{0.05}=1.96$.
Here n=200, x/n=0.06, p=0.1. Entering these values in formula (3.2), the following result was obtained:
$|Z|=2.357$.
Then
$|Z|>1.96(=Z_{0.05})$.

Therefore, H_1 was accepted because Z was included in the critical region. This means that the incorrect answer rate is not considered as 10% at a level of significance = 0.05.

When the level of significance was set at 0.01, $|Z|<2.58$ ($=Z_{0.01}$). Therefore, H_0 was accepted. This means that the incorrect answer rate is considered as 10% at a level of significance = 0.01.

Next, a test was also carried out to determine whether the incorrect answer rate is considered as 0.05 at a significance level of 0.05.

    Null hypothesis H_0 : p=0.05 (The incorrect answer rate of Group A is considered as 0.05.)
    Alternative hypothesis H_1 : p≠0.05 (The incorrect answer rate of Group A differs from 0.05.)

Where $Z_{0.05}=1.96$.
Here n=200, x/n=0.05, p=0.05. Entering these values in formula (3.2), the following result was obtained:
Z=0.
Then

Z<1.96 (=$Z_{0.05}$).

Therefore, H_0 was accepted because Z was not included in the critical region. This means that the incorrect answer rate is considered as 5% at a level of significance = 0.05.

(6) Higher "*doom*" in Sentence 2

A test was carried out to determine whether the incorrect answer rate is considered at 0.3 at a significance level of 0.05 when Group A listened to the synthesized utterances where the word "*doom*" was set to higher in F_0.

    Null hypothesis H_0 : p=0.3 (The incorrect answer rate of Group A is considered as 0.3.)

    Alternative hypothesis H_1 : p≠0.3 (The incorrect answer rate of Group A differs from 0.3)

Where $Z_{0.05}$=1.96.

Here n=200, x/n=0.27, p=0.3. Entering these values in formula (3.2), the following result was obtained:

|Z|=0.9258.

Then

|Z|<1.96 (=Z 0.05).

Therefore, H_0 was accepted because Z was not included in the critical region. This means that the incorrect answer rate is considered as 30% at a level of significance = 0.05.

(7) No stressed words ('steady') in Sentence 2

A test was carried out to determine whether the incorrect answer rate is considered as 0.2 at a significance level of 0.05 when Group A listened to the synthesized utterances where F_0 was decreased uniformly ('steady') in Sentence 2.

    Null hypothesis H_0 : p=0.2 (The incorrect answer rate of Group A is considered as 0.2.)

    Alternative hypothesis H_1 : p≠0.2 (The incorrect answer rate of Group A differs from 0.2.)

Where $Z_{0.05}$=1.96.

Here n=200, x/n=0.18, p=0.2. Entering these values in formula (3.2), the following result was obtained:

|Z|=0.7071.

Then

|Z|<1.96 (=$Z_{0.05}$).

Therefore, H_0 was accepted because Z was not included in the critical region. This means that the incorrect answer rate is considered as 20% when the level of significance is 0.05.

(8) Higher "*gloom*" in Sentence 2
A test was carried out to determine whether the incorrect answer rate is considered as 0.2 at a significance level of 0.05 when Group A listened to the synthesized utterances where the word "*gloom*" was set to higher in F_0.

    Null hypothesis $H_0 : p=0.2$ (The incorrect answer rate of Group A is considered as 0.2.)

    Alternative hypothesis $H_1 : p \neq 0.2$ (The incorrect answer rate of Group A differs from 0.2)

Where $Z_{0.05}=1.96$.
Here n=200, x/n=0.16, p=0.2. Entering these values in formula (3.2), the following result was obtained:
$|Z|=1.4142$.
Then
$|Z|<1.96 (=Z_{0.05})$.

  Therefore, H_0 was accepted because Z was not included in the critical region. This means that the incorrect answer rate is considered as 20% at a level of significance = 0.05.

(9) Higher "Ig*nore*" in Sentence 2
A test was carried out to determine whether the incorrect answer rate is considered as 0.1 at a significance level of 0.05 when Group A listened to the synthesized utterances where the word "Ig*nore*" was set to higher in F_0.

    Null hypothesis $H_0 : p=0.1$ (The incorrect answer rate of Group A is considered as 0.1.)

    Alternative hypothesis $H_1 : p \neq 0.1$ (The incorrect answer rate of Group A differs from 0.1)

Where $Z_{0.05}=1.96$.
Here n=200, x/n=0.125, p=0.1. Entering these values in formula (3.2), the following result was obtained:
$|Z|=1.1785$.
Then
$|Z|<1.96 (=Z_{0.05})$.

  Therefore, H_0 was accepted because Z was not included in the critical region. This means that the incorrect answer rate is considered as 10% at a level of significance = 0.05.

(10) Summary of Section 3.3.2
Tables 3.6 and 3.7 show the summary from (1) to (9) represented in the graph in Figures 3.23 and 3.24.

Table 3.6 Estimated value of the incorrect answer rate for each word by AEs (Group A) <Sentence 1>

Higher Fo word	Incorrect Answer Rate (%)	Correct Answer Rate (%)
evil	30	70
'steady', avoid, every	10	90
kind	5	95

(The level of significance is 0.05)

Table 3.7 Estimated value of the incorrect answer rate for each word by AEs (Group A) <Sentence 2>

Higher Fo word	Incorrect Answer Rate (%)	Correct Answer Rate (%)
doom	30	70
'steady', gloom	20	80
ignore	10	90

(The level of significance is 0.05)

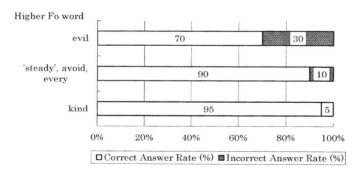

Figure 3.23 Estimated value of the incorrect answer rate for each word by AEs (Group A) <Sentence 1> (The level of significance is 0.05)

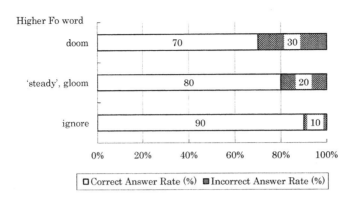

Figure 3.24 Estimated value of the incorrect answer rate for each word by AEs (Group A) <Sentence 2> (The level of significance is 0.05)

3.3.3 Test of difference in incorrect answer rate between words

Next, each test was carried out to determine whether there was a difference in the incorrect answer rate between words. Random samples of n_1 and n_2 were chosen from the two groups of AEs (A_1 and A_2). Data were analyzed statistically whether the incorrect answer rate of words, p_1 was equal to p_2.

Null hypothesis $H_0 : p_1 = p_2$ (There is no difference in the incorrect answer rate between Group A1 and A2)
Alternative hypothesis $H_1 : p_1 \neq p_2$ (There is a difference in the incorrect answer rate between Group A1 and A2)

The difference in the incorrect answer rate between Group A1 and A2 was unknown, so that it was estimated from two sample rates.

$p_1 = x_1 / n_1$ (n_1: a sample number in Group A_1, x_1: a data number) (3.3)
$p_2 = x_2 / n_2$ (n_2: a sample number in Group A_2, x_2: a data number) (3.4)

(Inagaki, *et al.*, 1996: 139.)

A test of Parameter Variance was carried out. Using the fact that the binominal distribution approximates to a normal distribution:

$$Z = (p_1 - p_2) / [\{p_1(1-p_1)/n_1\} + \{p_2(1-p_2)/n_2\}]^{1/2}$$
$$= \{(x_1/n_1) - (x_2/n_2)\} / [\{(x_1/n_1)(1-x_1/n_1)\}/n_1 + \{(x_2/n_2)(1-x_2/n_2)\}/n_2]^{1/2} \quad (3.5)$$

(Inagaki, *et al* 1996: 140.)

This approximates to a standard normal distribution. Using this, a test was carried out after setting a critical region of Z. From the normal distribution table, the critical regions $Z_{0.01} = 2.58$, $Z_{0.05} = 1.96$, and $Z_{0.1} = 1.64$ were used.

3.3 Stress perception by AEs

(1) A test was carried out to determine whether there was a difference in the incorrect answer rate between "_e_vil" and 'steady' in Sentence 1 at a significance level of 0.05.

   Null hypothesis $H_0 : p_1=p_2$ (There is no difference in the incorrect answer rate between Group A1 and A2.)
   Alternative hypothesis $H_1 : p_1 \neq p_2$ (There is a difference in the incorrect answer rate between Group A1 and A2.)

Where $Z_{0.05}=1.96$.
Here $n_1=200$, $x_1/n_1=0.25$, $n_2=200$, $x_2/n_2=0.095$. Entering these values in formula (3.5), the following result was obtained:
$|Z|=4.192$.
Then
$|Z|>1.96 (=Z_{0.05})$.

 Therefore, H_0 was rejected and H_1 was accepted. This means that there was a significant difference in the incorrect answer rate between "_e_vil" and 'steady' at a level of significance = 0.05.

 When the level of significance was set at 0.01, $|Z|=4.192>2.58 (=Z_{0.01})$. Therefore, H_0 was rejected and H_1 was accepted. This means that there was also a significant difference in the incorrect answer rate between them at a level of significance = 0.01.

(2) A test was carried out to determine whether there was a difference in the incorrect answer rate between 'steady' and "A_void_" in Sentence 1 at a significance level of 0.05.

   Null hypothesis $H_0 : p_1=p_2$ (There is no difference in the incorrect answer rate between Group A1 and A2.)
   Alternative hypothesis $H_1 : p_1 \neq p_2$ (There is a difference in the incorrect answer rate between Group A1 and A2.)

Where $Z_{0.05}=1.96$.
Here $n_1=200$, $x_1/n_1=0.095$, $n_2=200$, $x_2/n_2=0.09$. Entering these values in formula (3.5), the following result was obtained:
$|Z|=0.1726$.
Then
$|Z|<1.96 (=Z_{0.05})$.

 Therefore, H_0 was accepted because Z was not included in the critical region. This means that there was no significant difference in the incorrect answer rate between 'steady' and "A_void_" at a level of significance = 0.05.

(3) A test was carried out to determine whether there was a difference in the incorrect answer rate between "A_void_" and "_e_very" in Sentence 1 at a

significance level of 0.05.

    Null hypothesis $H_0 : p_1=p_2$ (There is no difference in the incorrect answer rate between Group A1 and A2.)

    Alternative hypothesis $H_1 : p_1 \neq p_2$ (There is a difference in the incorrect answer rate between Group A1 and A2.)

Where $Z_{0.05}=1.96$.

Here $n_1=200$, $x_1/n_1=0.09$, $n_2=200$, $x_2/n_2=0.06$. Entering these values in formula (3.5), the following result was obtained:

$|Z|=1.1408$.

Then

$|Z|<1.96 \ (=Z_{0.05})$.

    Therefore, H_0 was accepted because Z was not included in the critical region. This means that there was no significant difference in the incorrect answer rate between "A_void_" and "_ev_ery" at a level of significance = 0.05.

(4) A test was carried out to determine whether there was a difference in the incorrect answer rate between "_ev_ery" and "_kind_" in Sentence 1 at a significance level of 0.05.

    Null hypothesis $H_0 : p_1=p_2$ (There is no difference in the incorrect answer rate between Group A1 and A2.)

    Alternative hypothesis $H_1 : p_1 \neq p_2$ (There is a difference in the incorrect answer rate between Group A1 and A2.)

Where $Z_{0.05}=1.96$.

Here $n_1=200$, $x_1/n_1=0.06$, $n_2=200$, $x_2/n_2=0.05$. Entering these values in formula (3.5), the following result was obtained:

$|Z|=0.4387$.

Then

$|Z|<1.96 \ (=Z_{0.05})$.

    Therefore, H_0 was accepted because Z was not included in the critical region. This means that there was no significant difference in the incorrect answer rate between "_ev_ery" and "_kind_" at a level of significance = 0.05.

(5) A test was carried out to determine whether there was a difference in the incorrect answer rate between 'steady' and "_kind_" in Sentence 1 at a significance level of 0.05.

    Null hypothesis $H_0 : p_1=p_2$ (There is no difference in the incorrect answer rate between Group A1 and A2.)

    Alternative hypothesis $H_1 : p_1 \neq p_2$ (There is a difference in the incorrect answer rate between Group A1 and A2.)

Where $Z_{0.05}=1.96$.

Here $n_1=200$, $x_1/n_1=0.095$, $n_2=200$, $x_2/n_2=0.05$. Entering these values in

3.3 Stress perception by AEs

formula (3.5), the following result was obtained:
$|Z|=1.7419$.
Then
$|Z|<1.96\ (=Z_{0.05})$.

Therefore, H_0 was accepted because Z was not included in the critical region. This means that there was no significant difference in the incorrect answer rate between 'steady' and "*kind*" at a level of significance = 0.05.

(6) A test was carried out to determine whether there was a difference in the incorrect answer rate between "*doom*" and 'steady' in Sentence 2 at a significance level of 0.05.

    Null hypothesis $H_0 : p_1=p_2$ (There is no difference in the incorrect answer rate between Group A1 and A2.)
    Alternative hypothesis $H_1 : p_1 \neq p_2$ (There is a difference in the incorrect answer rate between Group A1 and A2.)

Where $Z_{0.05}=1.96$.
Here $n_1=200$, $x_1/n_1=0.27$, $n_2=200$, $x_2/n_2=0.18$. Entering these values in formula (3.5), the following result was obtained:
$|Z|=2.1687$.
Then
$|Z|>1.96\ (=Z_{0.05})$.

Therefore, H_0 was rejected and H_1 was accepted. This means that there was a significant difference in the incorrect answer rate between "*doom*" and 'steady' at a level of significance = 0.05.

When the level of significance was 0.01, $|Z|=2.1687<2.58\ (=Z_{0.01})$. Therefore, H_0 was accepted. This means that there was no significant difference in the incorrect answer rate between them at a level of significance = 0.01. That is, though there was a significant difference in the incorrect answer rate between them with a 95% probability, there was no significant difference in the incorrect answer rate between them with a 99% probability.

(7) A test was carried out to determine whether there was a difference in the incorrect answer rate between 'steady' and "*gloom*" in Sentence 2 at a significance level of 0.05.

    Null hypothesis $H_0 : p_1=p_2$ (There is no difference in the incorrect answer rate between Group A1 and A2.)
    Alternative hypothesis $H_1 : p_1 \neq p_2$ (There is a difference in the incorrect answer rate between Group A1 and A2.)

Where $Z_{0.05}=1.96$.
Here $n_1=200$, $x_1/n_1=0.18$, $n_2=200$, $x_2/n_2=0.16$. Entering these values in

formula (3.5), the following result was obtained:
$|Z|=0.5326$.
Then
$|Z|<1.96 (=Z_{0.05})$.

Therefore, H_0 was accepted. This means that there was no significant difference in the incorrect answer rate between 'steady' and "*gloom*" at a level of significance = 0.05.

(8) A test was carried out to determine whether there was a difference in the incorrect answer rate between "*gloom*" and "Ig*nore*" in Sentence 2 at a significance level of 0.05.

      Null hypothesis $H_0 : p_1=p_2$ There is no difference in the incorrect answer rate between Group A1 and A2.)

      Alternative hypothesis $H_1 : p_1 \neq p_2$ (There is a difference in the incorrect answer rate between Group A1 and A2.)

Where $Z_{0.05}=1.96$.
Here $n_1=200$, $x_1/n_1=0.16$, $n_2=200$, $x_2/n_2=0.125$. Entering these values in formula (3.5), the following result was obtained:
$|Z|=1.002$.
Then
$|Z|<1.96 (=Z_{0.05})$.

Therefore, H_0 was accepted. This means that there was no significant difference in the incorrect answer rate between "*gloom*" and "Ig*nore*" at a level of significance = 0.05.

(9) A test was carried out to determine whether there was a difference in the incorrect answer rate between 'steady' and "Ig*nore*" in Sentence 2 at a significance level of 0.05.

      Null hypothesis $H_0 : p_1=p_2$ (There is no difference in the incorrect answer rate between Group A1 and A2.)

      Alternative hypothesis $H_1 : p_1 \neq p_2$ (There is a difference in the incorrect answer rate between Group A1 and A2.)

Where $Z_{0.05}=1.96$.
Here $n_1=200$, $x_1/n_1=0.18$, $n_2=200$, $x_2/n_2=0.125$. Entering these values in formula (3.5), the following result was obtained:
$|Z|=1.5343$.
Then
$|Z|<1.96 (=Z_{0.05})$.

Therefore, H_0 was accepted. This means that there was no significant difference in the incorrect answer rate between 'steady' and "Ig*nore*" at a level of significance = 0.05.

(10) Summary of Section 3.3.3

For Sentence 1, the incorrect answer rate was high (30%) only when "*e̱vil*" was set to higher in F₀ at a level of significance = 0.05. There was no significant difference in the incorrect answer rate (5% to 10%) between words when "A*void*", "*ev*ery" and "*kind*" were set to higher in F₀ and 'steady' at a level of significance = 0.05. For Sentence 2, the incorrect answer rate was only high (30%) when "*doom*" was set to higher in F₀ at a level of significance = 0.05. There was no significant difference in the incorrect answer rate (10% to 20%) between words when "Ig*nore*" and "*gloom*" were set to higher in F₀ and 'steady' at a level of significance = 0.05. An approximant graphs are shown in Figures 3.25 and 3.26.

To discover why the incorrect answer rate was only high when the last word of the sentence was set to higher in F₀, the contents of the answers will be examined in the next section.

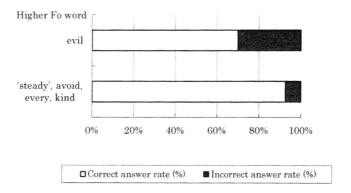

Figure 3.25 Comparison of the incorrect answer rates <Sentence 1>

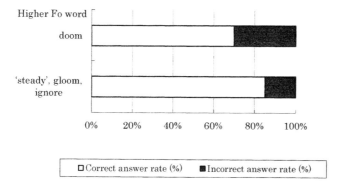

Figure 3.26 Comparison of the incorrect answer rates <Sentence 2>

3.4 Details of answers

(1) Higher "evil" in Sentence 1
Why was the incorrect answer rate only high when "evil" was set to higher in F_0, though the F_0 difference was the same? How did the synthesized utterances differ from natural utterance when AEs uttered the Sentence 1 with the stress on "Evil"?

The F_0 contour of the synthesized utterance in Figure 3.12 and the F_0 contour of the natural utterance in Figure 3.27 were compared. Figure 3.27 shows the F_0 contour when American informant A1 uttered the Sentence 1 with the stress on "Evil". The top value of "E" was 41 Hz higher than the preceding word, but 71 Hz higher than the end of "–vil". This means that not only the stressed syllable was higher in F_0 than the preceding syllable, but also the following syllable greatly decreased in F_0, so that "Evil" was emphasized.

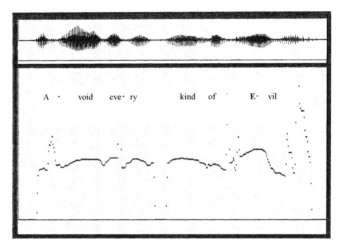

Figure 3.27 F_0 contour of "Avoid every kind of Evil" by informant A1

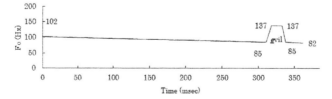

(**Figure 3.12** Illustration of synthesized F_0 contour of "Avoid every kind of evil")

Was the reason that the incorrect answer rate of "evil" was high because the difference (52 Hz) in pitch was too small? The differences in pitch on

other stressed words uttered by informant A1 were as follows:
- When stress was placed on "AVOID" (Figure 3.1): The top value of –VOID" was 52 Hz higher than the preceding word, and 65 Hz higher than the following syllable.
- When stress was placed on "EVery" (Figure 3.33): The top value of "EVery" was 61 Hz higher than the preceding word, and 74 Hz higher than "kind".
- When stress was placed on "KIND" (Figure 3.35): The top value of "KIND" was 59 Hz higher than the preceding word, and 76 Hz higher than the following syllable.

When stress was placed on other words, the following syllable decreased significantly, the same as when stress was placed on "Evil". Therefore, the writer must find another cause for the incorrect answer rate being highest when "evil" was set to higher in F0. In the synthesized utterances, "evil" differed from other words in that the utterance time of "evil" was short.

The top bar of Figure 3.28 shows the utterance time when informant A1 placed stress on "AVOID in Sentence 1. The F0 contour of this speech was shown in Figure 3.1. If the utterance time of a whole sentence was 100%, then the utterance time of "AVOID" was 43%, "every" was 26%, "kind" was 16% and "evil" was 11%. The utterance time of "AVOID" was the longest (481 msec). The length of "every" (290 msec), "kind" (181 msec) and "evil" (118 msec) gradually decreased. The utterance time of all the synthesized utterances in Figures 3.3 to 3.7 is equal to the top bar.

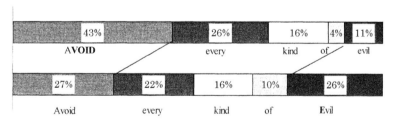

Time of Utterance

Figure 3.28 The comparison of the utterance time between when A1 places stress on "AVOID" (the top bar) and when A1 places stress on "Evil" (the bottom bar)

The bottom bar in Figure 3.28 shows the utterance time when informant A1 placed stress on "Evil". If the utterance time of a whole sentence was 100%, then the utterance time of "Avoid" was 27%, "every" was 22%, "kind" was 16% and "Evil" was 26%. The utterance time of "Evil" (344 msec, 26%) was 226 msec longer than the utterance time of unstressed word "evil" (118 msec, 11%) in the top bar. "Evil" (344 msec, 26%) was almost the same length as "Avoid" (363 msec, 27%).

For the synthesized utterance in Figure 3.7, even though "<u>e</u>vil" was set to higher in F₀, the utterance time of "<u>e</u>vil" was very short (11%) as in the top bar in Figure 3.28. When stress was placed on "Evil" in a natural utterance, the utterance time of "Evil" was much longer and "Avoid" was much shorter as in the bottom bar in Figure 3.28. In this way, when stress was placed on a word, the utterance time of the word generally increased in length. It was considered that "<u>e</u>vil" was too short in the synthesized utterance to perceive stress on "<u>e</u>vil".

What kinds of answers did the subjects give in detail?

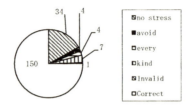

Figure 3.29 Answers of Higher "<u>e</u>vil"

Figure 3.29 shows the contents of the answers when forty subjects each listened to the synthesized utterances, where "<u>e</u>vil" was set to higher in F₀, five times at random. An invalid answer is when subjects did not answer or chose more than two words.

The correct answer, stress on "<u>e</u>vil", was chosen 150 out of 200 times. The incorrect answers were chosen as follows; "no stressed words" ('monotone') was chosen 34 times, stress on "Avoid" was chosen 4 times, stress on "every" was chosen 4 times, and stress on "kind" was chosen 7 times. An invalid answer occurred once. For synthesized utterance, "Avoid" was the longest so that it was expected that the greatest number of incorrect answers would occur by subjects thinking that stress was placed on "Avoid". However, the results of this experiment show that this incorrect answer only occurred 4 times. The most common incorrect answer was made by subjects responding that "no stressed words" were perceived in the sentence.

When forty subjects listened to the synthesized utterances of "<u>e</u>vil" with the F₀ set higher five times, two subjects answered incorrectly all five times. Of these two subjects, the most common incorrect answer was made by stating there were "no stressed words". This number of incorrect answers occurred eight out of ten times.

It is surmised that the reason there were a large number of incorrect answers made by stating that there was no stress placed on "_e_vil" was that even though "_e_vil" was set to higher in F₀, "_e_vil" was too short to be easily heard.

Therefore, it can be assumed that the length of the utterance time was also one of the key elements of stress.

(2) No stressed words ('steady') in Sentence 1

Figure 3.30 shows the F₀ contour when Informant A1 uttered Sentence 1 with no stressed words. Figure 3.31 shows the contents of the answers when forty subjects each listened to the synthesized utterances in Figure 3.8 five times at random. The correct answer "no stressed words" was chosen 181 out of 200 times. The incorrect answers were chosen as follows; stress on "Avoid" was chosen 5 times, stress on "every" was chosen 3 times, stress on "kind" was chosen 9 times, and stress on "evil" was chosen twice.

For synthesized utterance, "Avoid" was the longest in duration and the highest in F₀ in Sentence 1. Therefore, it was expected that the greatest number of incorrect answers would occur by subjects thinking that stress was placed on "Avoid". However, there were more incorrect answers where stress was placed on "kind" than on "Avoid".

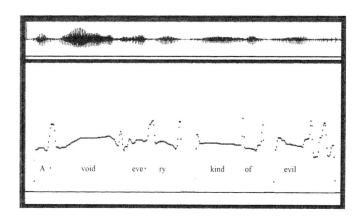

Figure 3.30 F₀ contour of Sentence 1 with no stressed words by informant A1

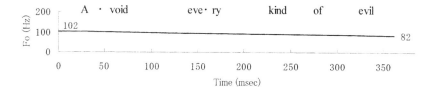

(**Figure 3.8** Illustration of synthesized F₀ contour of "Avoid every kind of evil" ('steady')

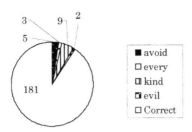

Figure 3.31 Answers of 'steady' <Sentence 1>

(3) Higher "A*void*" in Sentence 1
Figure 3.9 shows the top of "– *void*" was set to 52 Hz higher in F_0 than the preceding syllable, "A –". Figure 3.32 shows the contents of the answers when forty American subjects each listened to the synthesized utterances in Figure 3.9 five times. This synthesized utterances was perceived as having "no stressed words" 11 out of 200 times.

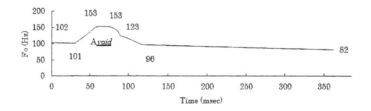

(**Figure 3.9** Illustration of synthesized F_0 contour of "A*void* every kind of evil")

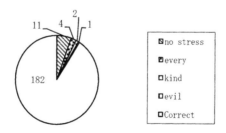

Figure 3.32 Answers of Higher "A*void*"

(4) Higher "*ev*ery" in Sentence 1
Figure 3.33 shows the F_0 contour when Informant A1 utters the Sentence 1 with the stress on "**EV**ery". Figure 3.34 shows the contents of the an-

swers when forty subjects each listened to the synthesized utterances in Figure 3.10 five times. The correct answer "ev̱ery" was chosen 188 out of 200 times. The incorrect answers were chosen as follows; "no stressed words" was chosen 3 times, stress on "Avoid" was chosen 4 times, stress on "kind" was chosen 5 times, and stress on "evil" was not chosen.

Figure 3.33 F₀ contour of "Avoid **EV**ery kind of evil" by informant A1

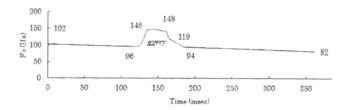

(**Figure 3.10** Illustration of synthesized F₀ contour of "Avoid ev̱ery kind of evil")

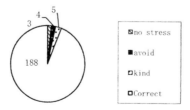

Figure 3.34 Answers of Higher "ev̱ery"

(5) Higher "*kind*" in Sentence 1

Figure 3.35 shows the F_0 contour when Informant A1 uttered Sentence 1 with the stress on "**KIND**". Figure 3.36 shows the contents of the answers when forty subjects each listened to the synthesized utternces in Figure 3.11 five times. The correct answer "*kind*" was chosen 190 out of 200 times. The incorrect answers were chosen as follows; "no stressed words" was chosen 5 times, and stress on "Avoid", "every", "evil", was chosen once each. Invalid answers occurred twice.

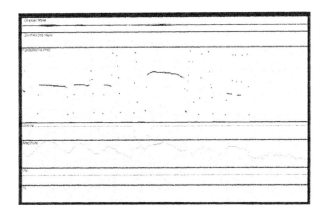

Figure 3.35 F_0 contour of "Avoid every **KIND** of evil" by informant A1

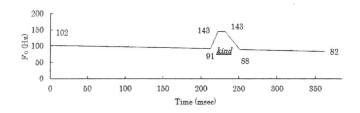

(**Figure 3.11** Illustration of synthesized F_0 contour of "Avoid every *kind* of evil")

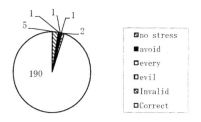

Figure 3.36 Answers of Higher "*kind*"

(6) Higher "*doom*" in Sentence 2

Why was the number of incorrect answers the greatest when "*doom*" was set to higher in F_0? How did the synthesized utterances differ from natural utterance when AEs uttered the Sentence 2 with the stress on "**DOOM**"?

Figure 3.37 shows the F_0 contour when Informant A1 uttered Sentence 2 with the stress on "**DOOM**". The top value of "**DOOM**" was 31 Hz higher than the preceding word, but 43 Hz higher than the end of "**DOOM**". The same as "**E**vil" in Sentence 1, the stressed syllable was higher in F_0 than the preceding syllable, and the following syllable decreased in F_0 to emphasize the stressed syllable. The increase in F_0 was maintained at the same Hz in each synthesized utterance, so that there must be another cause for the highest rate of incorrect perception of "*doom*". In the synthesized utterances, "*doom*" differed from the other words in that the utterance time of "*doom*" was short.

The top bar of Figure 3.38 shows the utterance time when informant A1 placed stress on "Ig**NORE**" in Sentence 2. The F_0 contour of this speech was shown in Figure 3.2. If the length of a whole sentence was 100%, then "Ig**NORE**" was 47%, "gloom" was 20% and "doom" was 13%. The length of "Ig**NORE**" was the longest (517 msec) and "gloom" (217 msec) and "doom" (140 msec) gradually decreased. This utterance was used to synthesize the utterances so that "Ig*nore*" was the longest word in all the synthesized utterances in Figures 3.13 to 3.16.

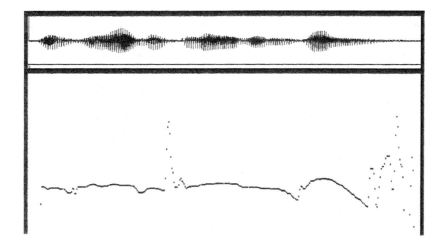

Figure 3.37 F_0 contour of Sentence 2 with the stress on "**DOOM**" by Informant A1

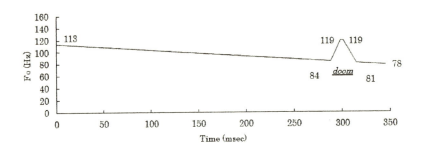

(**Figure 3.20** Illustration of synthesized F₀ contour of "Ignore the gloom and *doom*")

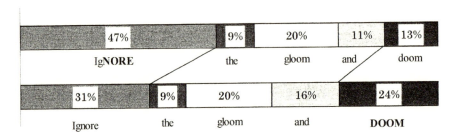

Time of Utterance

Figure 3.38 The comparison of the utterance time between when A1 places stress on "Ig**NORE**" (the top bar) and when A1 places stress on "**DOOM**" (the bottom bar)

The bottom bar in Figure 3.38 shows the utterance time when informant A1 placed stress on "**DOOM**". If the length of a whole sentence was 100%, then the length of "Ignore" was 31%, "gloom" was 20% and "**DOOM**" was 24%. The length of "gloom" in both sentences (the top and the bottom bars) was 20%. The stressed word "**DOOM**" (295 msec, 24%) in the bottom bar was 155 msec longer than the unstressed word "doom" in the top bar. The unstressed word "Ignore" (386 msec, 31%) in the bottom bar was 131 msec shorter than the stressed word "Ig**NORE**" in the top bar.

It was considered that the reason there were fewer subjects who perceived that stress was placed on "*doom*" was that the length of "*doom*" (the top bar) was too short in the synthesized utterance to perceive stress on "doom", even though "doom" was set to 35 Hz higher in F₀ in Figure 3.20. In natural utterance, the length of the stressed word generally increased in length. The same as "Evil" in Sentence 1, it could be also considered

3.4 Details of answers 101

that the shortness of the utterance time of "*doom*" was one of the reasons why the incorrect answer rate was high.

"Figure 3.39 shows the contents of the answers when forty American subjects each listened to the synthesized utterances, where "*doom*" was set to higher in F_0, five times at random. The correct answer, stress on "*doom*", was chosen 146 out of 200 times. The incorrect answers were chosen as follows; "no stressed words" was chosen 42 times, stress on "Ignore" was chosen 8 times, and stress on "gloom" was chosen 3 times. An invalid answer occurred once.

For synthesized utterances, "Ignore" was the longest in duration so that it was expected that the greatest number of incorrect answers would occur by subjects thinking that stress was placed on "Ignore". However, the results of this experiment show that this incorrect answer only occurred 8 times. The most common incorrect answer was given by subjects responding that "no stressed words" were perceived in the sentence.

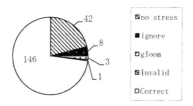

Figure 3.39 Answers of Higher "*doom*"

(7) No stressed words ('steady') in Sentence 2

Figure 3.40 shows the F_0 contour when Informant A1 uttered Sentence 2 with no stressed words. Figure 3.41 shows the contents of the answers when forty subjects each listened to the synthesized utterances in Figure 3.17 five times at random. The correct answer "no stressed words" was chosen 164 times out of 200 times. Although F_0 was decreased uniformly from the beginning to the end in the synthesized utterance, subjects perceived stress on "Ignore" 24 times. Stress on "gloom" was chosen 3 times and stress on "doom" was chosen 9 times.

102　Perception of sentence stress and pitch change by AEs

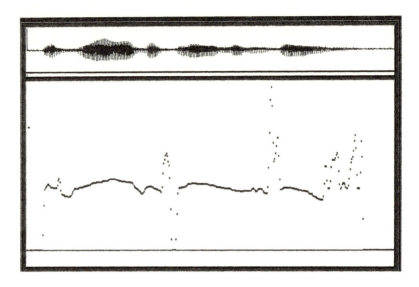

Figure 3.40 F₀ contour of Sentence 2 with no stressed words by Informant A1

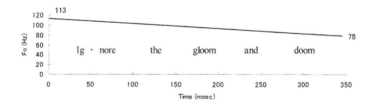

(**Figure 3.17** Illustration of synthesized F₀ contour of "Ignore the gloom and doom" ('steady'))

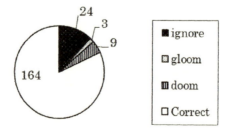

Figure 3.41 Answers of 'steady' <Sentence 2>

(8) Higher "*gloom*" in Sentence 2

Figure 3.42 shows the F_0 contour when Informant A1 uttered the Sentence 2 with the stress on "**GLOOM**". Figure 3.43 shows the contents of the answers when forty subjects each listened to the synthesized utterance in Figure 3.19 five times. In the synthesized utterance, the top of "*gloom*" was set to 35 Hz higher in F_0 than the preceding syllable, but 15 times out of 200 times the sentences were perceived by subjects as having "no stressed words". The correct answer, stress on "gloom", was chosen 168 times out of 200 times. Stress on "ignore" was chosen 10 times and stress on "doom" was chosen 6 times. An invalid answer occurred once.

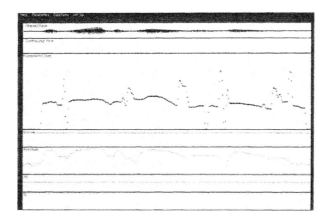

Figure 3.42 F_0 contour of Sentence 2 with the stress on "**GLOOM**" by Informant A1

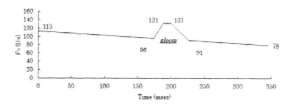

(**Figure 3.19** Illustration of synthesized F_0 contour of "Ignore the *gloom* and doom")

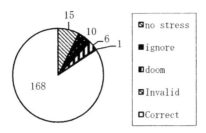

Figure 3.43 Answers of Higher "*gloom*"

(9) Higher "Ig*nore*" in Sentence 2
Figure 3.44 shows the contents of the answers when forty subjects each listened to the synthesized utterance shown in Figure 3.18 five times. In the synthesized utterance, the top of "Ig*nore*" was set to 35 Hz higher in F_0 than in the preceding syllable, but 18 out of 200 times subjects perceived "no stressed words". The correct answer, stress on "Ig*nore*", was chosen 175 out of 200 times. Stress on "gloom" was chosen 5 times and stress on "doom" was chosen once. An invalid answer occurred once.

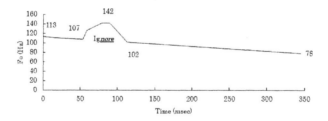

(**Figure 3.18** Illustration of synthesized F_0 contour of "Ig*nore* the gloom and doom")

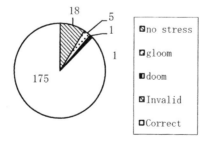

Figure 3.44 Answers of Higher "Ig*nore*"

3.4 Details of answers

(10) Summary of Section 3.4

Table 3.8 shows the summary of answers in Sentence 1. Table 3.9 shows the relationship as a percentage in Table 3.8. Table 3.8 is shown as pie charts in Figures 3.29, 3.31, 3.32, 3.34 and 3.36.

When "_e_vil", "A_void_" and "_kind_" were set to higher in F_0, although "Avoid" was the longest word, the greatest number of incorrect answers was made by subjects responding that there were "no stressed words" in the sentence. When F_0 was decreased uniformly ('steady'), although "Avoid" was also the longest word, the largest number of incorrect answers was made by subjects choosing "kind" as the stressed word.

Table 3.10 shows the summary of answers in Sentence 2. Table 3.11 shows the relationship as a percentage in Table 3.10. Table 3.10 is shown as pie charts in Figures 3.39, 3.41, 3.43 and 3.44.

When "_doom_", "_gloom_" and "Ig_nore_" were set to higher in F_0, although "Ignore" was the longest word, the greatest number of incorrect answers was made by subjects responding that there were "no stressed words" in the sentence. When F_0 was decreased uniformly ('steady'), "Ignore" was the longest word, and the largest number of incorrect answers was made by subjects choosing "ignore" as the stressed word.

Table 3.8 Details of answers in Sentence 1

Higher F_0 Words	'steady'	avoid	every	kind	evil	invalid	Total others	Total incorrect answers	Total correct answers	Total utterances
evil	34	4	4	7		1	16	50	150	200
'steady'		5	3	9	2	0	19	19	181	200
Avoid	11		4	2	1	0	7	18	182	200
every	3	4		5	0	0	9	12	188	200
kind	5	1	1		1	2	5	10	190	200

Table 3.9 Details of answers in Sentence 1 (%)

Higher F_0 Words	'steady'	avoid	every	kind	evil	invalid	Total others	Incorrect answer rate	Correct answer rate	Total utterances
evil	17.0%	2.0%	2.0%	3.5%		0.5%	8.0%	25.0%	75.0%	100%
'steady'		2.5%	1.5%	4.5%	1.0%	0.0%	9.5%	9.5%	90.5%	100%
Avoid	5.5%		2.0%	1.0%	0.5%	0.0%	3.5%	9.0%	91.0%	100%
every	1.5%	2.0%		2.5%	0.0%	0.0%	4.5%	6.0%	94.0%	100%
kind	2.5%	0.5%	0.5%		0.5%	1.0%	2.5%	5.0%	95.0%	100%

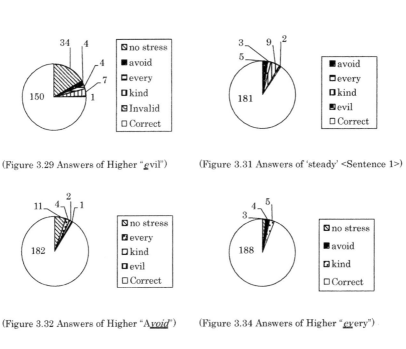

(Figure 3.29 Answers of Higher "_e_vil")

(Figure 3.31 Answers of 'steady' <Sentence 1>)

(Figure 3.32 Answers of Higher "A_void_")

(Figure 3.34 Answers of Higher "_ev_ery")

(Figure 3.36 Answers of Higher "_kind_")

Why did a large number of subjects incorrectly respond that there was "no stressed words"? When someone placed stress on any syllable, the stressed portion has a higher intensity, the F_0 is moved, and the duration is longer. However, with some synthesized utterances, the longest word and the higher F_0 word are separate. Therefore, it can be surmised that the reason for these incorrect responses is either of the two:
(1) the synthesized utterances was perceived to have two words that were stressed, or
(2) the synthesized utterances was perceived to have "no stress", as no one word was clearly perceived to be prominent.

3.4 Details of Answers

Table 3.10 Details of answers in Sentence 2

Higher Fo Words	'steady'	ignore	gloom	doom	invalid	Total others	Total incorrect answers	Total correct answers	Total utterances
doom	42	8	3		1	12	54	146	200
'steady'		24	3	9	0	36	36	164	200
gloom	15	10		6	1	17	32	168	200
Ignore	18		5	1	1	7	25	175	200

Table 3.11 Details of answers in Sentence 2 (%)

Higher Fo Words	'steady'	ignore	gloom	doom	invalid	Total others	Incorrect answer rate	Correct answer rate	Total utterances
doom	21.0%	4.0%	1.5%		0.5%	6.0%	27.0%	73.0%	100%
'steady'		12.0%	1.5%	4.5%	0.0%	18.0%	18.0%	82.0%	100%
gloom	7.5%	5.0%		3.0%	0.5%	8.5%	16.0%	84.0%	100%
Ignore	9.0%	0.0%	2.5%	0.5%	0.5%	3.5%	12.5%	87.5%	100%

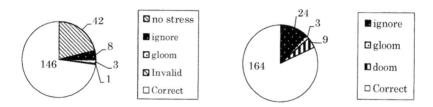

(Figure 3.39 Answers of Higher "*doom*")　　(Figure 3.41 Answers of 'steady' <Sentence 2>)

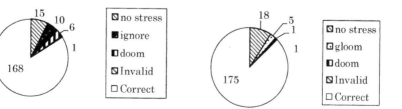

(Figure 3.43 Answers of Higher "*gloom*")　　(Figure 3.44 Answers of Higher "Ig*nore*")

3.5 Test of difference in incorrect answer rate between Sentence 1 and Sentence 2

A test was carried out to determine whether there was a difference in the incorrect answer rate between Sentence 1 and Sentence 2. Table 3.12 and Figure 3.45 show the result of tallying up the incorrect answer rate of each sentence.

From the result of Table 3.12, the following result was obtained:
$P_{A1}=0.108$.
$P_{A2}=0.184$.

Null hypothesis $H_0 : P_{A1}=P_{A2}$ (There is no difference in the incorrect answer rate between Group A_1 and Group A_2.)
Alternative hypothesis $H_1 : P_{A1} \neq P_{A2}$ (There is a difference in the incorrect answer rate between Group A_1 and Group A_2.)

Where $Z_{0.05}=1.96$.
Here $n_1=200$, $x_1/n_1=0.108$, $n_2=200$, $x_2/n_2=0.184$. Entering these values in formula (3.5), the following result was obtained:
$|Z|=4.4964$.
Then
$|Z|>1.96 (=Z_{0.05})$.

Therefore, H_0 was rejected and H_1 was accepted. This means that there was a significant difference in the incorrect answer rate between Sentence 1 and Sentence 2 at a level of significance = 0.05. The perception rate of Sentence 1 (89.2%) was higher than Sentence 2 (81.6%).

Sentence 1 was quoted from the bible and Sentence 2 was from a newspaper title. When informant A1 placed stress in Sentence 1, the variation in F_0 was 52 Hz. When informant A1 placed stress in Sentence 2, the variation in F_0 was 35 Hz. Therefore, the variation in F_0 of synthesized utterances in Sentence 1 was set at 52 Hz and in Sentence 2 set at 35 Hz to be the same as informant A1. It was considered that a possible reason for the larger number of incorrect answers in Sentence 2 was that Sentence 2 was 17 Hz smaller than Sentence 1 in F_0 variation.

Table 3.12 Comparison of the incorrect answer rates between Sentence 1 and Sentence 2

	Correct answers	Incorrect answers	Total	Incorrect answer rate (p)	Correct answer rate (1-p)
Sentence 1	892	108	1000	0.108	0.892
Sentence 2	653	147	800	0.184	0.816

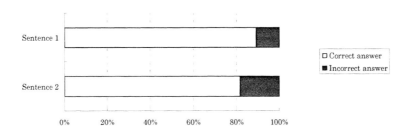

Figure 3.45 Comparison of the incorrect answer rates between Sentence 1 and Sentence 2

3.6 Total perception rate of Sentence 1 and Sentence 2

Table 3.13 and Figure 3.46 show the results of the perception rate of Sentence 1 and Sentence 2. When 40 AEs listened to the synthesized utterances where only the F_0 parameter was changed (5 types of Sentence 1 and 4 types of Sentence 2), an average of 85.8% of subjects perceived stress on the word which was set to higher in F_0.

Table 3.13 The perception rate of Sentence 1 and Sentence 2

	Correct answers	Incorrect answers	Total	Incorrect answer rate (p)	Correct answer rate (1-p)
Sentence 1 + Sentence 2	1545	255	1800	0.142	0.858

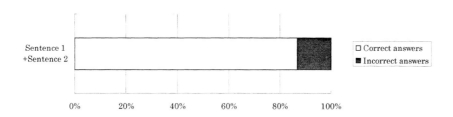

Figure 3.46 The perception rate of Sentence 1 and Sentence 2

3.7 Summary

One native speaker of American English (informant A1) was asked to utter two sentences "**AVOID** every kind of evil" and "Ig**NORE** the gloom and doom". The utterances were synthesized in nine ways depending on where the higher F_0 syllable was placed. Then forty native speakers of American English (AEs) listened to nine stimulus types of synthesized utterances five times ordered at random (40 listeners versus 5 repetitions = 200 times). The forty subjects were then asked to indicate which word was stressed in the utterance. The result of this experiment shows that an average of 85.8% of subjects perceived stress on the higher syllable in F_0. This indicates that the variation in F_0 is a key factor in perceiving sentence stress.

In Chapter 2, the production of sentence stress and variation in F_0 were observed. The result of the experiments in Chapter 2 and Chapter 3 shows that the variation in F_0 is an important factor both in producing and perceiving sentence stress. However, it is possible that the utterance time is also an important factor because the perception rate was low (70%) when the utterance time was short even when the F_0 was higher.

Generally in English classes in Japan, students are taught that stress should be uttered more strongly. However, from this research it can be surmised that students also need to note the variation in F_0 and the length as well as the intensity of the stressed syllable.

4 Perception of pitch change with a comparison of native speakers of American English and Japanese

4.1 Introduction

In Chapter 2, the pitch (F_0) movements on a stressed word in each sentence uttered by Japanese learners of English (Js) and native speakers of American English (AEs) were observed. Emphasized words uttered by AEs were marked by a higher pitch than preceding syllables. There was a large pitch variation only on a focused word and small pitch variations on other word stresses, so that the focused word was remarkably prominent in a sentence. On the other hand, variations in pitch on emphasized words uttered by Js were small. Some Js moved F_0 on all word stresses to be the same as an emphasized word, so that the focused word was not prominent. Js differed from AEs in producing sentence stress in English.

In Chapter 3, utterances of a native speaker of American English (informant A1) were separated into sound source information (F_0 and amplitude) and track resonance information by PARCOR analysis; and F_0 only was controlled using the speech processing software. Forty AEs were asked to listen to nine stimulus types of synthesized utterances five times in random order to examine whether they could perceive stress on the higher F_0. The result showed that an average of 85.8% of AEs perceived stress on the syllable with higher F_0. This was interpreted to mean that F_0 was a parameter in perceiving stress in a sentence.

In this chapter, 116 Js were asked to listen to the same nine stimulus types of synthesized utterances played five times at random and the results were compared with the results of 40 AEs. In this study, 40 AEs which are referred to as Group A and 116 Js are referred to as Group B.

4.2 Experiment

4.2.1 Purpose
The purpose of this experiment is twofold. Firstly, it aims to examine whether Js perceive stress on the higher syllable in F_0. Secondly, it aims to compare the results of 116 Js and 40 AEs statistically.

4.2.2 Method
One hundred and sixteen Js (Group B) were asked to listen to the nine stimulus types of synthesized utterances used in Chapter 3 five times at random (see p.75). The synthesized utterances were five stimulus types of "**AVOID** every kind of evil" (Sentence 1) and four stimulus types of "**Ig-NORE** the gloom and doom" (Sentence 2). Capitalized and bold letters show the stressed syllables. The variation in F_0 of synthesized utterances in Sentence 1 was set 52Hz higher than the preceding syllable and the variation in F_0 of synthesized utterances in Sentence 2 was set 35Hz higher than the preceding syllable. One hundred and sixteen Js were university students with no hearing and speaking disorder, their ages were between 19 and 29. They were asked to listen to forty-five synthesized utterances once which were recorded on a micro disk and to choose either one stressed word or if there was no stressed word to choose 'monotone' (no stressed words).

4.3 Stress perception by Japanese learners of English (Group B)

4.3.1 Background theory
(A) Assuming that an event happens k times in a series of n tests, the sample ratio p is:
$$p = k / n \qquad (4.1) \quad \text{(Inagaki, }et\ al.,\text{ 1996: 138.)}$$
(B) Generally, the probability p in which an event happens x times in n tests is calculated by the binominal distribution.
(C) When the mean np is large in a binominal distribution, the probability is calculated from the fact that the binominal distribution approximates to a normal distribution (np>5 approximately).
$$Z = \{(x/n) - p\} / \{p(1-p)/n\}^{1/2} \qquad (4.2) \quad \text{(Inagaki, }et\ al.,\text{ 1996: 138.)}$$
This approximates to a standard normal distribution. Using this, a test was carried out after setting a critical region of Z.

N (people) random samples were drawn from Js. A ratio test was carried out to determine whether the incorrect answer rate p_0 is considered as the incorrect answer rate of Group B. The hypothesis was set as follows:

4.3 Stress perception by Js

Null hypothesis $H_0 : p = p_0$ (The incorrect answer rate of Group B is considered as p_0.)

Alternative hypothesis $H_1 : p \neq p_0$ (The incorrect answer rate of Group B differs from p_0.)

(Inagaki, et al., 1996: 138.)

From the normal distribution table, the critical region $Z_{0.01}=2.58$, $Z_{0.05}=1.96$, and $Z_{0.1}=1.64$ were used (Inagaki, et al., 1996: 65). That is to say, when the level of significance was 0.01, $Z_{0.01}=2.58$; when the level of significance is 0.05, $Z_{0.05}=1.96$; and when level of significance is 0.1, $Z_{0.1}=1.64$.

4.3.2 Test of incorrect answer rates

As stated in Chapter 3, incorrect answers are defined as follows:
(1) when subjects listen to synthesized utterances with a higher F_0 syllable, they do not answer that there is a stressed syllable on a higher F_0 syllable, and
(2) when subjects listen to synthesized utterances in which F_0 was decreased uniformly from the beginning to the end, they do not answer that there are no stressed words.

Tables 4.1 and 4.2 show the results in which 116 Js listened to nine stimulus types of synthesized utterances five times at random. These are shown graphically in Figures 4.1 and 4.2. Underlined and italic letters show the syllables which were set to higher in F_0.

Table 4.1 The incorrect answer rate of each word by Js (Group B) <Sentence 1> (The total of each stimulus is 580 (116 (listeners) × 5 (repetitions))).

Higher F_0 word	Correct answer	Incorrect answer	Total	Incorrect answer rate (p)	Correct answer rate (1-p)
*e*vil	526	54	580	9.3%	90.7%
*ev*ery	542	38	580	6.6%	93.4%
'steady'	549	31	580	5.3%	94.7%
kind	567	13	580	2.2%	97.8%
A*void*	568	12	580	2.1%	97.9%
Total	2752	148	2900	5.1%	94.9%

Note: Underlined and italic letters show the syllables set to higher. Also 'steady' shows the synthesized utterances that F_0 was decreased uniformly.

Table 4.2 The incorrect answer rate of each word by Js (Group B) <Sentence 2> (The total of each stimulus is 580 (116 (listeners) × 5 (repetitions))).

Higher F0 word	Correct answer	Incorrect answer	Total	Incorrect answer rate (p)	Correct answer rate (1-p)
doom	331	249	580	42.9%	57.1%
gloom	410	170	580	29.3%	70.7%
'steady'	511	69	580	11.9%	88.1%
Ig_nore_	519	61	580	10.5%	89.5%
Total	1771	549	2320	23.7%	76.3%

Note: Underlined and italic letters show the syllables set to higher. Also 'steady' shows the synthesized utterances that F0 was decreased uniformly.

A test was carried out to determine whether the incorrect answer rate is considered as 0.09 at a significance level of 0.05 when Group B listened to the synthesized utterances where the word "_e_vil" was set to higher in F0 in Sentence 1.

Null hypothesis $H_0 : p=0.09$ (The incorrect answer rate of Group B is considered as 0.09.)
Alternative hypothesis $H_1 : p \neq 0.09$ (The incorrect answer rate of Group B differs from 0.09.)

Where $Z_{0.05}=1.96$.
Here, n=580, x/n=0.093, p=0.09. Entering these values in formula (4.2), the following result was obtained:
$|Z|=0.153$.
Then
$|Z|<1.96 (=Z_{0.05})$.

Therefore, H_0 was accepted because Z was not included in the critical region. This means that the incorrect answer rate is considered as 9% when the level of significance is 0.05.

The other incorrect answer rates were also tested at a level of significance = 0.05. Tables 4.3 and 4.4 show the results of the test of the incorrect answer rates in Tables 4.1 and 4.2. They were represented in the graph in Figures 4.3 and 4.4.

4.3 Stress perception by Js 115

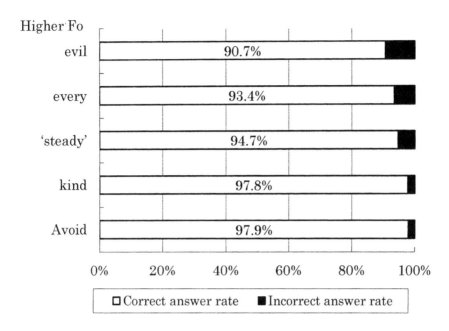

Figure 4.1 The incorrect answer rate of each word by Js (Group B) <Sentence 1>

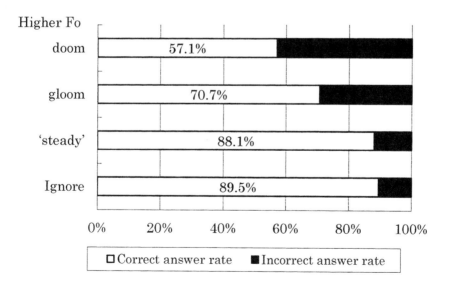

Figure 4.2 The incorrect answer rate of each word by Js (Group B) <Sentence 2>

Table 4.3 Estimated value of the incorrect answer rate for each word by Js (Group B) <Sentence 1>

Higher Fo word	Correct answer rate (%)	Incorrect answer rate (%)
evil	91	9
every	94	6
'steady'	95	5
kind	98	2
Avoid	98	2

(The level of significance is 0.05)

Table 4.4 Estimated value of the incorrect answer rate for each word by Js (Group B) <Sentence 2>

Higher Fo word	Correct answer rate (%)	Incorrect answer rate (%)
doom	60	40
gloom	70	30
'steady'	90	10
Ignore	90	10

(The level of significance is 0.05)

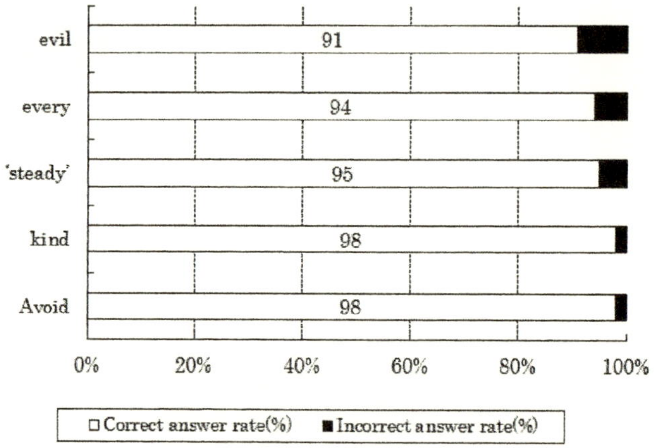

Figure 4.3 Estimated value of the incorrect answer rate for each word by Js (Group B) <Sentence 1>

4.3 Stress perception by Js   117

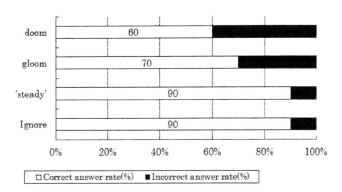

Figure 4.4 Estimated value of the incorrect answer rate for each word by Js (Group B) <Sentence 2>

4.3.3 Test of difference in incorrect answer rate between words

Next, each test was carried out to determine whether there was a difference in the incorrect answer rate between words. Random samples of n_1 and n_2 were chosen from the two groups of Js (B_1 and B_2). Data were analyzed statistically whether the incorrect answer rate of words, p_1 was equal to p_2.

    Null hypothesis $H_0 : p_1 = p_2$ (There is no difference in the incorrect answer rate between Group B_1 and Group B_2.)

    Alternative hypothesis $H_1 : p_1 \neq p_2$ (There is a difference in the incorrect answer rate between Group B_1 and Group B_2.)

The difference in the incorrect answer rate between Group B_1 and Group B_2 was unknown, so that it was estimated from two sample rates.

    $p_1 = x_1 / n_1$ (n_1 : a sample number in Group B_1,
                                   x_1 : a data number) (4.3)

    $p_2 = x_2 / n_2$ (n_2 : a sample number in Group B_2,
                                   x_2 : a data number) (4.4)

                                                     (Inagaki, *et al.*, 1996: 139.)

A test of Parameter Variance was carried out. Using the fact that the binominal distribution approximates to a normal distribution:

$$Z = (p_1 - p_2) / [\{p_1(1-p_1)/n_1\} + \{p_2(1-p_2)/n_2\}]^{1/2}$$
$$= \{(x_1/n_1) - (x_2/n_2)\} / [\{(x_1/n_1)(1-x_1/n_1)\}/n_1 + \{(x_2/n_2)(1-x_2/n_2)\}/n_2]^{1/2} \quad (4.5)$$

                                                     (Inagaki, *et al.*, 1996: 140.)

This approximates to a standard normal distribution. Using this, a test was carried out after setting a critical region of Z. From the normal distribution table, the critical regions $Z_{0.01}=2.58$, $Z_{0.05}=1.96$, and $Z_{0.1}=1.64$ were used.

(1) A test was carried out at a level of significance = 0.05 to determine whether there was a difference in the incorrect answer rate between "<u>e</u>vil" and "<u>e</u>very" in Sentence 1.

        Null hypothesis H_0 : $p_1=p_2$ (There is no difference in the incorrect answer rate between Group B_1 and Group B_2.)

        Alternative hypothesis H_1 : $p_1 \neq p_2$ (There is a difference in the incorrect answer rate between Group B_1 and Group B_2.)

Where $Z_{0.05}=1.96$.
Here $n_1=580$, $x_1/n_1=0.093$, $n_2=580$, $x_2/n_2=0.066$. Entering these values in formula (4.5), the following result was obtained.
$|Z|=1.7407$.
Then
$|Z|<1.96 (=Z_{0.05})$.

    Therefore, H_0 was accepted because Z was not included in the critical region. This means that there was no significant difference in the incorrect answer rate between "<u>e</u>vil" and "<u>e</u>very" at a level of significance = 0.05.

(2) A test was carried out at a level of significance = 0.05 to determine whether there was a difference in the incorrect answer rate between "<u>e</u>very" and 'steady' in Sentence 1.

        Null hypothesis H_0 : $p_1=p_2$ (There is no difference in the incorrect answer rate between Group B_1 and Group B_2.)

        Alternative hypothesis H_1 : $p_1 \neq p_2$ (There is a difference in the incorrect answer rate between Group B_1 and Group B_2.)

Where $Z_{0.05}=1.96$.
Here $n_1=580$, $x_1/n_1=0.066$, $n_2=580$, $x_2/n_2=0.05$. Entering these values in formula (4.5), the following result was obtained:
$|Z|=0.8692$.
Then
$|Z|<1.96 (=Z_{0.05})$.

    Therefore, H_0 was accepted because Z was not included in the critical region. This means that there was no significant difference in the incorrect answer rate between "_ev_ery" and 'steady' at a level of significance = 0.05.

(3) A test was carried out at a level of significance = 0.05 to determine whether there was a difference in the incorrect answer rate between "_e_vil" and 'steady' in Sentence 1.

    Null hypothesis $H_0 : p_1=p_2$ (There is no difference in the incorrect answer rate between Group B_1 and Group B_2.)
    Alternative hypothesis $H_1 : p_1 \neq p_2$ (There is a difference in the incorrect answer rate between Group B_1 and Group B_2.)

Where $Z_{0.05}=1.96$.
Here $n_1=580$, $x_1/n_1=0.093$, $n_2=580$, $x_2/n_2=0.053$. Entering these values in formula (4.5), the following result was obtained:
$|Z|=2.5989$.
Then
$|Z|>1.96 (=Z_{0.05})$.

Therefore, H_0 was rejected and H_1 was accepted. This means that there was a significant difference in the incorrect answer rate between "_e_vil" and 'steady' at a level of significance = 0.05.

When the level of significance was 0.01, $|Z|=2.5989>2.58 (=Z_{0.01})$. Therefore, H_0 was rejected and H_1 was accepted. This means that when the level of significance is 0.01, there was also a significant difference in the incorrect answer rate.

(4) A test was carried out at a level of significance = 0.05 to determine whether there was a difference in the incorrect answer rate between 'steady' and "_kind_" in Sentence 1.

    Null hypothesis $H_0 : p_1=p_2$ (There is no difference in the incorrect answer rate between Group B_1 and Group B_2.)
    Alternative hypothesis $H_1 : p_1 \neq p_2$ (There is a difference in the incorrect answer rate between Group B_1 and Group B_2.)

Where $Z_{0.05}=1.96$.
Here $n_1=580$, $x_1/n_1=0.053$, $n_2=580$, $x_2/n_2=0.022$. Entering these values in formula (4.5), the following result was obtained:
$|Z|=2.7757$.
Then

$|Z|>1.96 \ (=Z_{0.05})$.

Therefore H_0 was rejected and H_1 was accepted. This means that there was a significant difference in the incorrect answer rate between 'steady' and "*kind*" at a level of significance = 0.05.

When the level of significance was 0.01, $|Z|=2.7757>2.58 \ (=Z_{0.01})$, H_0 was rejected and H_1 was accepted. This means that when the level of significance is 0.01, there was also a significant difference in the incorrect answer rate.

(5) A test was carried out at a level of significance = 0.05 to determine whether there was a difference in the incorrect answer rate between "*kind*" and "A*void*" in Sentence 1.

    Null hypothesis $H_0 : p_1=p_2$ (There is no difference in the incorrect answer rate between Group B_1 and Group B_2.)

    Alternative hypothesis $H_1 : p_1 \neq p_2$ (There is a difference in the incorrect answer rate between Group B_1 and Group B_2.)

Where $Z_{0.05}=1.96$.
Here $n_1=580$, $x_1/n_1=0.022$, $n_2=580$, $x_2/n_2=0.021$. Entering these values in formula (4.5), the following result was obtained:
$|Z|=0.2021$.
Then
$|Z|<1.96 \ (=Z_{0.05})$.

Therefore, H_0 was accepted. This means that there was no significant difference in the incorrect answer rate between "*kind*" and "A*void*" when the level of significance is 0.05.

(6) A test was carried out at a level of significance = 0.05 to determine whether there was a difference in the incorrect answer rate between "*doom*" and "*gloom*" in Sentence 2.

    Null hypothesis $H_0 : p_1=p_2$ (There is no difference in the incorrect answer rate between Group B_1 and Group B_2.)

    Alternative hypothesis $H_1 : p_1 \neq p_2$ (There is a difference in the incorrect answer rate between Group B_1 and Group B_2.)

Where $Z_{0.05}=1.96$.
Here $n_1=580$, $x_1/n_1=0.429$, $n_2=580$, $x_2/n_2=0.293$. Entering these values in formula (4.5), the following result was obtained:

$|Z|=4.8781$.
Then
$|Z|>1.96$ $(=Z_{0.05})$.

Therefore, H_0 was rejected and H_1 was accepted. This means that there was a significant difference in the incorrect answer rate between "_doom_" and "_gloom_" at a level of significance = 0.05.

When the level of significance was 0.01, $|Z|=4.8781>2.58$ $(=Z_{0.01})$. H_0 was rejected and H_1 was accepted. This means that there was also a significant difference in the incorrect answer rate at a level of significance = 0.01.

(7) A test was carried out at a level of significance = 0.05 to determine whether there was a difference in the incorrect answer rate between "_gloom_" and 'steady' in Sentence 2.

   Null hypothesis H_0 : $p_1=p_2$ (There is no difference in the incorrect answer rate between Group B_1 and Group B_2.)

   Alternative hypothesis H_1 : $p_1 \neq p_2$ (There is a difference in the incorrect answer rate between Group B_1 and Group B_2.)

Where $Z_{0.05}=1.96$.
Here $n_1=580$, $x_1/n_1=0.293$, $n_2=580$, $x_2/n_2=0.119$. Entering these values in formula (4.5), the following result was obtained:
$|Z|=7.508$.
Then
$|Z|>1.96$ $(=Z_{0.05})$.

Therefore, H_0 was rejected and H_1 was accepted. This means that there was a significant difference in the incorrect answer rate between "_gloom_" and 'steady' at a level of significance = 0.05.

When the level of significance was 0.01, $|Z|=7.508>2.58$ $(=Z_{0.01})$. H_0 was rejected and H_1 was accepted. This means that there was also a significant difference in the incorrect answer rate at a level of significance = 0.01.

(8) A test was carried out at a level of significance = 0.05 to determine whether there was a difference in the incorrect answer rate between 'steady' and "Ig_nore_" in Sentence 2.

   Null hypothesis H_0 : $p_1=p_2$ (There is no difference in the incorrect answer rate between Group B_1 and Group B_2.)

Alternative hypothesis $H_1 : p_1 \neq p_2$ (There is a difference in the incorrect answer rate between Group B_1 and Group B_2.)

Where $Z_{0.05}=1.96$.
Here $n_1=580$, $x_1/n_1=0.119$, $n_2=580$, $x_2/n_2=0.105$. Entering these values in formula (4.5), the following result was obtained:
$|Z|=0.7448$.
Then
$|Z|<1.96 (=Z_{0.05})$.

Therefore, H_0 was accepted. This means that there was no significant difference in the incorrect answer rate between 'steady' and "Ig*nore*" at a level of significance = 0.05.

(9) A test was carried out at a level of significance = 0.05 to determine whether there was a difference in the incorrect answer rate between the last word in Sentence 1, "*e*vil" and the last word in Sentence 2, "*doom*".

Null hypothesis $H_0 : p_1=p_2$ (There is no difference in the incorrect answer rate between Group B_1 and Group B_2.)
Alternative hypothesis $H_1 : p_1 \neq p_2$ (There is a difference in the incorrect answer rate between Group B_1 and Group B_2.)

Where $Z_{0.05}=1.96$.
Here $n_1=580$, $x_1/n_1=0.093$, $n_2=580$, $x_2/n_2=0.429$. Entering these values in formula (4.5), the following result was obtained:
$|Z|=14.107$.
Then
$|Z|>1.96 (=Z_{0.05})$.

Therefore, H_0 was rejected and H_1 was accepted. This means that there was a significant difference in the incorrect answer rate between "*e*vil" and "*doom*" at a level of significance = 0.05. The incorrect answer rate of "*e*vil" was lower than "*doom*".

Although for AEs, there was no significant difference in the incorrect answer rate between "*e*vil" (25%), which was the last word in Sentence 1, and "*doom*" (27%), which was the last word in Sentence 2 (see section 3.3), for Js, there was a significant difference in the incorrect answer rate between "*e*vil" and "*doom*". The incorrect answer rate of "*e*vil" was lower (9.3%) and the incorrect answer rate of "*doom*" was higher (42.9%).

(10) Summary of Section 4.3.3
Figure 4.5 shows the result of testing the difference in the incorrect

4.3 Stress perception by Js

answer rates between words in Sentence 1 by Js at a level of significance = 0.05. Figure 4.6 shows the result of testing the difference in the incorrect answer rates between words in Sentence 1 by AEs (see section 3.3). Figure 4.7 shows the result of testing the difference in the incorrect answer rates between words in Sentence 2 by Js. Figure 4.8 shows the result of testing the difference in the incorrect answer rates between words in Sentence 2 by AEs (see section 3.3).

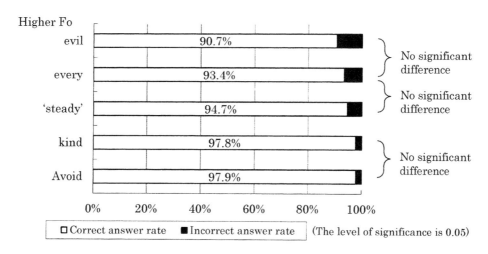

Figure 4.5 Comparison of the incorrect answer rates of words in Sentence 1 by Js

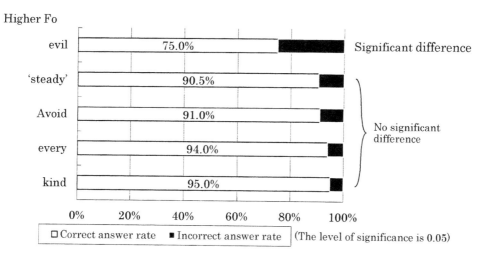

Figure 4.6 Comparison of the incorrect answer rates of words in Sentence 1 by AEs

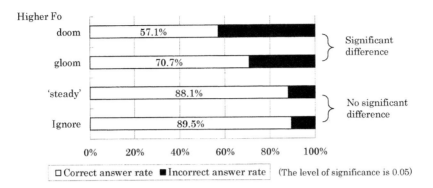

Figure 4.7 Comparison of the incorrect answer rates of words in Sentence 2 by Js

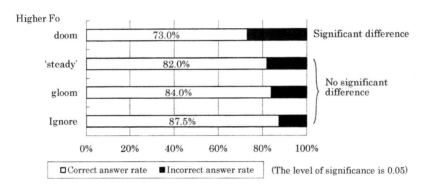

Figure 4.8 Comparison of the incorrect answer rates of words in Sentence 2 by AEs

In Figures 4.5 and 4.6, both of the incorrect answer rates of AEs and Js were the highest when the last word "<u>e</u>vil" was set to higher in Sentence 1. In Figures 4.7 and 4.8, both of the incorrect answer rates of AEs and Js were the highest when the last word "<u>doom</u>" was set to higher in Sentence 2.

For AEs, there was no significant difference between words except when "<u>e</u>vil" was set to higher in Sentence 1 at a level of significance = 0.05 (Figure 4.6). In Sentence 2, there was no significant difference between words except when "<u>doom</u>" was set to higher at a level of significance = 0.05 (Figure 4.8).

On the other hand, for Js, only the incorrect answer rate of the last word "<u>e</u>vil" was not high and there was no significant difference between "<u>e</u>vil" and "<u>ev</u>ery" in Sentence 1 at a level of significance = 0.05 (Figure 4.5).

There were also no significant differences between "*ev*ery" and 'steady' and between "*kind*" and "A*void*". In Sentence 2, there was a significant difference between "*doom*" and "*gloom*" (Figure 4.7). There was no significant difference between 'steady' and "Ig*nore*" at a level of significance = 0.05.

4.3.4 Test of difference in incorrect answer rate between Sentence 1 and Sentence 2

A test was carried out to determine whether there was a difference in the incorrect answer rates between Sentence 1 and Sentence 2. Table 4.5 and Figure 4.9 show the result of tallying up the incorrect answer rate of each sentence when Js listened to the five types of Sentence 1 and four types of Sentence 2.

Table 4.5 The incorrect answer rates of Sentence 1 and Sentence 2 by Js

Js	Correct answer	Incorrect answer	Total	Incorrect answer rate	Correct answer rate
Sentence 1	2752	148	2900	5.1%	94.9%
Sentence 2	1771	549	2320	23.7%	76.3%

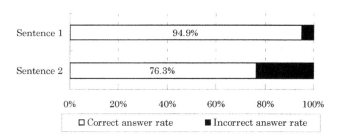

Figure 4.9 The incorrect answer rates of Sentence 1 and Sentence 2 by Js

Entering the result of Table 4.5 in formulae (4.3) and (4.4), the following result was obtained:

$P_{B1} = 0.051$.
$P_{B2} = 0.237$.

Null hypothesis $H_0 : P_{B1} = P_{B2}$ (There is no difference in the incorrect answer rate between Group B_1 and Group B_2.)

Alternative hypothesis $H_1 : P_{B1} \neq P_{B2}$ (There is a difference in the incorrect answer rate between Group B_1 and Group B_2.)

Where $Z_{0.05}=1.96$.
Here $n_1=580$, $x_1/n_1=0.051$, $n_2=580$, $x_2/n_2=0.237$. Entering these values in formula (4.5), the following result was obtained:
$|Z|=19.0865$.
Then
$|Z|>1.96 (=Z_{0.05})$.

Therefore, H_0 was rejected and H_1 was accepted. This means that there was a significant difference in the incorrect answer rate between Sentence 1 and 2 when the level of significance was set at 0.05. The incorrect answer rate of Sentence 1 was lower than Sentence 2.

Concerning both AEs group and Js group, there were significant differences in the incorrect answer rates between Sentence 1 and Sentence 2. The incorrect answer rate of Sentence 1 was higher than Sentence 2 (concerning AEs group, see Chapter 3, p.108).

Synthesized utterances in Sentence 1 were set 52 Hz higher than the preceding syllable and synthesized utterances in Sentence 2 were set 35 Hz higher than the preceding syllable. It was considered that a possible reason for the larger number of incorrect answers in Sentence 2 was that Sentence 2 was 17 Hz smaller than Sentence 1 in F_0 variation.

4.3.5 Total perception rate of Sentence 1 and Sentence 2

Table 4.6 and Figure 4.10 show the total of the perception rate of Sentence 1 and Sentence 2. When 116 Js listened to the synthesized utterances where only the F_0 parameter was changed (5 stimulus types of Sentence 1 and 4 stimulus types of Sentence 2), an average of 86.6% of subjects perceived stress on the word which was set to higher in F_0.

Table 4.6 Total perception rate of Sentence 1 and Sentence 2 by Js

Js	Correct answer	Incorrect answer	Total	Incorrect answer rate	Correct answer rate
Sentence 1 + Sentence 2	4523	697	5220	13.4%	86.6%

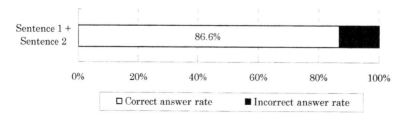

Figure 4.10 Total perception rate of Sentence 1 and Sentence 2 by Js

4.4 Comparison of incorrect answer rate between American subjects and Japanese subjects

4.4.1 Test of difference in incorrect answer rates of words between American subjects and Japanese subjects

Next, the following tests were carried out to determine whether there was a difference in the incorrect answer rate of words between AEs (Group A) and Js (Group B). N_1 and n_2 random samples were chosen from the two groups of A and B. Data were analyzed statistically whether the incorrect answer rate of words, p_1 was equal to p_2.

Null hypothesis $H_0 : p_1 = p_2$ (There is no difference in the incorrect answer rate between Group A and Group B.)

Alternative hypothesis $H_1 : p_1 \neq p_2$ (There is a difference in the incorrect answer rate between Group A and Group B.)

The difference in the incorrect answer rate between Group A and Group B was unknown, so that it was estimated from two sample rates.

$p_1 = x_1 / n_1$ (n_1: a sample number in Group A, x_1: a data number) (4.6)
$p_2 = x_2 / n_2$ (n_2: a sample number in Group B, x_2: a data number) (4.7)

A test of Parameter Variance was carried out. Using the fact that the binominal distribution approximates to a normal distribution:

$$Z = (p_1 - p_2) / [\{p_1(1-p_1)/n_1\} + \{p_2(1-p_2)/n_2\}]^{1/2}$$
$$= \{(x_1/n_1) - (x_2/n_2)\} / [\{(x_1/n_1)(1-x_1/n_1)\}/n_1 + \{(x_2/n_2)(1-x_2/n_2)\}/n_2]^{1/2} \quad (4.8)$$

(Inagaki, *et al* 1996: 140.)

This approximates to a standard normal distribution. Using this, a test was carried out after setting a critical region of Z. From the normal distribution table, the critical regions $Z_{0.01} = 2.58$, $Z_{0.05} = 1.96$, and $Z_{0.1} = 1.64$ were used.

(1) Higher "*e*vil" in Sentence 1
Table 4.7 shows the result of the numbers of correct and incorrect answers by AEs (Group A) and Js (Group B) when Group A and Group B listened to

the synthesized utterances where "_e_vil" was set to higher in F_0.

Table 4.7 The numbers of correct and incorrect answers by AEs (Group A) and Js (Group B) when "_e_vil" was set to higher in F_0

evil	Correct answer	Incorrect answer	Total	Incorrect answer rate	Correct answer rate
AEs (Group A)	150	50	200	25.0%	75.0%
Js (Group B)	526	54	580	9.3%	90.7%

Entering the result of Table 4.7 in formulae (4.6) and (4.7), the following result was obtained:
  P_A=0.25.
  P_B=0.093.

  Null hypothesis $H_0 : p_1 = p_2$ (There is no difference in the incorrect answer rate between Group A and Group B.)

  Alternative hypothesis $H_1 : p_1 \neq p_2$ (There is a difference in the incorrect answer rate between Group A and Group B.)

Where $Z_{0.05}$=1.96.
Here n_1=200, x_1/n_1=0.250, n_2=580, x_2/n_2=0.093. Entering these values in formula (4.8), the following result was obtained:
Z=4.7674.
Then
$|Z|>1.96 (=Z_{0.05})$.

Therefore, H_0 was rejected and H_1 was accepted because Z was included in the critical region. This means that there was a significant difference in the incorrect answer rate between Group A and Group B when the level of significance was set at 0.05. The incorrect answer rate of Js (Group B) was lower than AEs (Group A).

When the level of significance was set at 0.01, there was also a significant difference in the incorrect answer rate between Group A and Group B.

(2) No stressed words ('steady') in Sentence 1
Table 4.8 shows the result of the numbers of correct and incorrect answers by AEs (Group A) and Js (Group B) when they listened to the synthesized utterances where F_0 was decreased uniformly ('steady') in Sentence 1.

Table 4.8 The numbers of correct and incorrect answers by AEs (Group A) and Js (Group B) when F_0 was decreased uniformly ('steady') in Sentence 1

'steady'	Correct answer	Incorrect answer	Total	Incorrect answer rate	Correct answer rate
AEs (Group A)	182	18	200	9.0%	91.0%
Js (Group B)	549	31	580	5.3%	94.7%

Entering the result of Table 4.8 in formulae (4.6) and (4.7), the following result was obtained:
$P_A = 0.09$.
$P_B = 0.053$.

    Null hypothesis $H_0 : p_1 = p_2$ (There is no difference in the incorrect answer rate between Group A and Group B.)

    Alternative hypothesis $H_1 : p_1 \neq p_2$ (There is a difference in the incorrect answer rate between Group A and Group B.)

Where $Z_{0.05} = 1.96$.
Here $n_1 = 200$, $x_1/n_1 = 0.090$, $n_2 = 580$, $x_2/n_2 = 0.053$. Entering these values in formula (4.8), the following result was obtained:
$Z = 1.6400$.
Then
$|Z| < 1.96 \, (= Z_{0.05})$.

Therefore, H_0 was accepted. This means that there was no significant difference in the incorrect answer rate between Group A and Group B when the level of significance was set at 0.05.

When the level of significance was set at 0.01, there was also no significant difference in the incorrect answer rate between Group A and Group B.

(3) Higher "A*void*" in Sentence 1
Table 4.9 shows the result of the numbers of correct and incorrect answers by AEs (Group A) and Js (Group B) when "A*void*" was set to higher in F_0.

Table 4.9 The numbers of correct and incorrect answers by AEs (Group A) and Js (Group B) when "A*void*" was set to higher in F_0

avoid	Correct answer	Incorrect answer	Total	Incorrect answer rate	Correct answer rate
AEs (Group A)	182	18	200	9.0%	91.0%
Js (Group B)	568	12	580	2.1%	97.9%

Entering the result of Table 4.9 in formulae (4.6) and (4.7), the following result was obtained:
P_A=0.09.
P_B=0.021.

Null hypothesis H_0 : p_1=p_2 (There is no difference in the incorrect answer rate between Group A and Group B.)

Alternative hypothesis H_1 : $p_1 \neq p_2$ (There is a difference in the incorrect answer rate between Group A and Group B.)

Where $Z_{0.05}$=1.96.
Here n_1=200, x_1/n_1=0.090, n_2=580, x_2/n_2=0.021. Entering these values in formula (4.8), the following result was obtained:
Z=3.2877.
Then
$|Z|$>1.96 (=$Z_{0.05}$).

Therefore, H_0 was rejected and H_1 was accepted because Z was included in the critical region. This means that there was a significant difference in the incorrect answer rate between Group A and Group B when the level of significance was set at 0.05. The incorrect answer rate of Js (Group B) was lower than AEs (Group A).

When the level of significance was set at 0.01, there was also a significant difference in the incorrect answer rate between them.

(4) Higher "every" in Sentence 1
Table 4.10 shows the result of the numbers of correct and incorrect answers by AEs (Group A) and Js (Group B) when "every" was set to higher in F_0.

4.4 Comparison between American and Japanese subjects

Table 4.10 The numbers of correct and incorrect answers by AEs (Group A) and Js (Group B) when "e$\underline{v}$ery" was set to higher in F$_0$

every	Correct answer	Incorrect answer	Total	Incorrect answer rate	Correct answer rate
AEs (Group A)	188	12	200	6.0%	94.0%
Js (Group B)	542	38	580	6.6%	93.4%

Entering the result of Table 4.10 in formulae (4.6) and (4.7), the following result was obtained:
P_A=0.06.
P_B=0.066.

Null hypothesis H_0 : $p_1=p_2$ (There is no difference in the incorrect answer rate between Group A and Group B.)

Alternative hypothesis H_1 : $p_1 \neq p_2$ (There is a difference in the incorrect answer rate between Group A and Group B.)

Where $Z_{0.05}$=1.96.
Here n_1=200, x_1/n_1=0.060, n_2=580, x_2/n_2=0.066. Entering these values in formula (4.8), the following result was obtained:
$|Z|$=0.2802.
Then
$|Z|$<1.96 (=$Z_{0.05}$).

Therefore, H_0 was accepted. This means that there was no significant difference in the incorrect answer rate between Group A and Group B when the level of significance was set at 0.05.

When the level of significance was set at 0.01, there was also no significant difference in the incorrect answer rate between Group A and Group B.

(5) Higher "*kind*" in Sentence 1
Table 4.11 shows the result of the numbers of correct and incorrect answers by AEs (Group A) and Js (Group B) when "*kind*" was set to higher in F$_0$.

Table 4.11 The numbers of correct and incorrect answers by AEs (Group A) and Js (Group B) when "*kind*" was set to higher in F_0

kind	Correct answer	Incorrect answer	Total	Incorrect answer rate	Correct answer rate
AEs (Group A)	190	10	200	5.0%	95.0%
Js (Group B)	567	13	580	2.2%	97.8%

Entering the result of Table 4.11 in formulae (4.6) and (4.7), the following result was obtained:
P_A=0.05.
P_B=0.022.

    Null hypothesis H_0 : p_1=p_2 (There is no difference in the incorrect answer rate between Group A and Group B.)

    Alternative hypothesis H_1 : $p_1 \neq p_2$ (There is a difference in the incorrect answer rate between Group A and Group B.)

Where $Z_{0.05}$=1.96.
Here n_1=200, x_1/n_1=0.050, n_2=580, x_2/n_2=0.022. Entering these values in formula (4.8), the following result was obtained:
Z=1.6627.
Then
$|Z|<1.96 (=Z_{0.05})$.

Therefore, H_0 was accepted. This means that there was no significant difference in the incorrect answer rate between Group A and Group B when the level of significance was set at 0.05.

When the level of significance was set at 0.01, there was also no significant difference in the incorrect answer rate between Group A and Group B.

(6) Higher "*doom*" in Sentence 2
Table 4.12 shows the result of the numbers of correct and incorrect answers by AEs (Group A) and Js (Group B) when "*doom*" was set to higher in F_0.

Entering the result of Table 4.12 in formulae (4.6) and (4.7), the following result was obtained:
P_A=0.27.
P_B=0.429.

4.4 Comparison between American and Japanese subjects

Null hypothesis $H_0 : p_1 = p_2$ (There is no difference in the incorrect answer rate between Group A and Group B.)

Alternative hypothesis $H_1 : p_1 \neq p_2$ (There is a difference in the incorrect answer rate between Group A and Group B.)

Where $Z_{0.05} = 1.96$.
Here $n_1 = 200$, $x_1/n_1 = 0.270$, $n_2 = 580$, $x_2/n_2 = 0.429$. Entering these values in formula (4.8), the following result was obtained:
$|Z| = 4.2458$.
Then
$|Z| > 1.96 \, (= Z_{0.05})$.

Therefore, H_0 was rejected and H_1 was accepted because Z was included in the critical region. This means that there was a significant difference in the incorrect answer rate between Group A and Group B when the level of significance was set at 0.05. The incorrect answer rate of AEs (Group A) was lower than Js (Group B).

When the level of significance was set at 0.01, there was also a significant difference in the incorrect answer rate between Group A and Group B.

Table 4.12 The numbers of correct and incorrect answers by AEs (Group A) and Js (Group B) when "*doom*" was set to higher in F_0

doom	Correct answer	Incorrect answer	Total	Incorrect answer rate	Correct answer rate
AEs (Group A)	146	54	200	27.0%	73.0%
Js (Group B)	331	249	580	42.9%	57.1%

(7) No stressed words ('steady') in Sentence 2
Table 4.13 shows the result of the numbers of correct and incorrect answers by AEs (Group A) and Js (Group B) when they listened to the synthesized utterances where F_0 was decreased uniformly ('steady') in Sentence 2.

Entering the result of Table 4.13 in formulae (4.6) and (4.7), the following result was obtained:
$P_A = 0.18$.
$P_B = 0.119$.

Null hypothesis $H_0 : p_1 = p_2$ (There is no difference in the incorrect answer rate between Group A and Group B.)

Alternative hypothesis $H_1 : p_1 \neq p_2$ (There is a difference in the incorrect answer rate between Group A and Group B.)

Where $Z_{0.05}=1.96$.
Here $n_1=200$, $x_1/n_1=0.180$, $n_2=580$, $x_2/n_2=0.119$. Entering these values in formula (4.8), the following result was obtained:
$Z=2.0137$.
Then
$|Z|>1.96 (=Z_{0.05})$.

Therefore, H_0 was rejected and H_1 was accepted because Z was included in the critical region. This means that there was a significant difference in the incorrect answer rate between Group A and Group B when the level of significance was set at 0.05. The incorrect answer rate of AEs (Group A) was lower than Js (Group B).

When the level of significance was set at 0.01, $|Z|<2.58(=Z_{0.01})$. Therefore, there was no significant difference in the incorrect answer rate between Group A and Group B.

Table 4.13 The numbers of correct and incorrect answers by AEs (Group A) and Js (Group B) when F_0 was decreased uniformly ('steady') in Sentence 2

'steady'	Correct answer	Incorrect answer	Total	Incorrect answer rate	Correct answer rate
AEs (Group A)	164	36	200	18.0%	82.0%
Js (Group B)	511	69	580	11.9%	88.1%

(8) Higher "*gloom*" in Sentence 2
Table 4.14 shows the result of the numbers of correct and incorrect answers by AEs (Group A) and Js (Group B) when "*gloom*" was set to higher in F_0.

Table 4.14 The numbers of correct and incorrect answers by AEs (Group A) and Js (Group B) when "*gloom*" was set to higher in F_0

gloom	Correct answer	Incorrect answer	Total	Incorrect answer rate	Correct answer rate
AEs (Group A)	168	32	200	16.0%	84.0%
Js (Group B)	410	170	580	29.3%	70.7%

Entering the result of Table 4.14 in formulae (4.6) and (4.7), the following result was obtained:

4.4 Comparison between American and Japanese subjects

$P_A=0.16$.
$P_B=0.293$.

    Null hypothesis $H_0 : p_1=p_2$ (There is no difference in the incorrect answer rate between Group A and Group B.)

    Alternative hypothesis $H_1 : p_1 \neq p_2$ (There is a difference in the incorrect answer rate between Group A and Group B.)

Where $Z_{0.05}=1.96$.
Here $n_1=200$, $x_1/n_1=0.160$, $n_2=580$, $x_2/n_2=0.293$. Entering these values in formula (4.8), the following result was obtained:
$|Z|=4.1489$.
Then
$|Z|>1.96$ $(=Z_{0.05})$.

Therefore, H_0 was rejected and H_1 was accepted because Z was included in the critical region. This means that there was a significant difference in the incorrect answer rate between Group A and Group B when the level of significance was set at 0.05. The incorrect answer rate of AEs (Group A) was lower than Js (Group B).

When the level of significance was set at 0.01, there was also a significant difference in the incorrect answer rate between Group A and Group B.

(9) Higher "Ig*nore*" in Sentence 2
Table 4.15 shows the result of the numbers of correct and incorrect answers by AEs (Group A) and Js (Group B) when "Ig*nore*" was set to higher in F_0.

Table 4.15 The numbers of correct and incorrect answers by AEs (Group A) and Js (Group B) when "Ig*nore*" was set to higher in F_0

ignore	Correct answer	Incorrect answer	Total	Incorrect answer rate	Correct answer rate
AEs (Group A)	175	25	200	12.5%	87.5%
Js (Group B)	519	61	580	10.5%	89.5%

Entering the result of Table 4.15 in formulae (4.6) and (4.7), the following result was obtained:
$P_A=0.125$.
$P_B=0.105$.

Null hypothesis $H_0 : p_1 = p_2$ (There is no difference in the incorrect answer rate between Group A and Group B.)

Alternative hypothesis $H_1 : p_1 \neq p_2$ (There is a difference in the incorrect answer rate between Group A and Group B.)

Where $Z_{0.05}=1.96$.
Here $n_1=200$, $x_1/n_1=0.125$, $n_2=580$, $x_2/n_2=0.105$. Entering these values in formula (4.8), the following result was obtained:
$Z = 0.7446$.
Then
$|Z| < 1.96 \, (=Z_{0.05})$.

Therefore, H_0 was accepted. This means that there was no significant difference in the incorrect answer rate between Group A and Group B when the level of significance was set at 0.05.

When the level of significance was set at 0.01, there was also no significant difference in the incorrect answer rate between Group A and Group B.

(10) Summary of Section 4.4.1
Tables 4.16 and 4.17 and Figures 4.11 and 4.12 show the results of testing whether there was a significant difference in the incorrect answer rates between AEs and Js. There were significant differences in the incorrect answer rates at a level of significance = 0.05 when "A*void*" and "*e*vil" were set to higher in F_0 in Sentence 1. The incorrect answer rate of Js was lower than AEs. There were no significant differences in the incorrect answer rates when "*e*very" and "*kind*" were set to higher in F_0 and 'steady'. In Sentence 2, there were significant differences in the incorrect answer rates when "*gloom*" and "*doom*" were set to higher in F_0 and 'steady'. When "*gloom*" and "*doom*" were set to higher in F_0, the incorrect answer rate of AEs was lower than Js. When there were no words set to higher ('steady'), the incorrect answer rate of Js was lower than AEs. There was no significant difference in the incorrect answer rates when "Ig*nore*" was set to higher in F_0.

4.4 Comparison between American and Japanese subjects

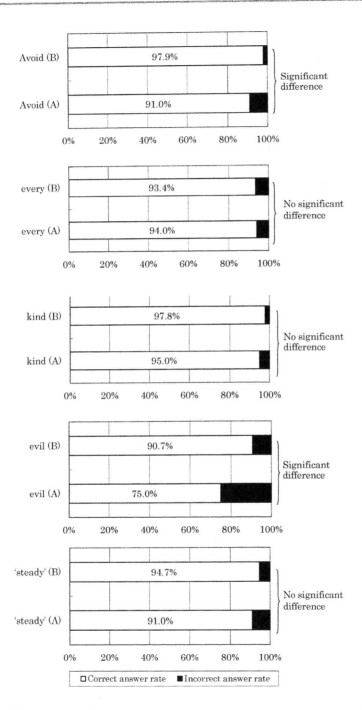

Figure 4.11 Results of testing to determine whether there are significant differences in the incorrect answer rates of words in Sentence 1 between AEs (A) and Js (B) (The level of significance is 0.05)

138   Perception of pitch change with a comparison of AEs and Js

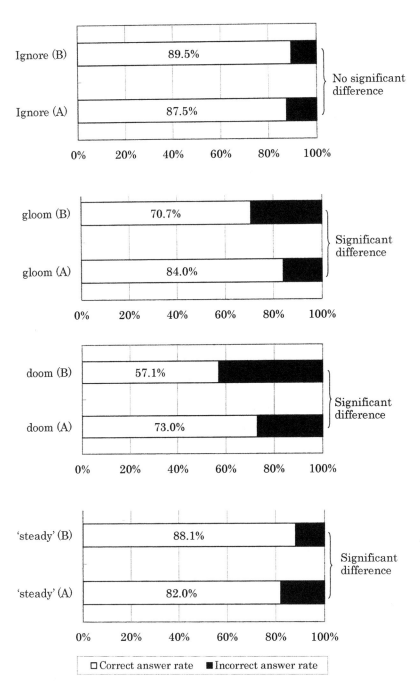

Figure 4.12 Results of testing to determine whether there are significant differences in the incorrect answer rates of words in Sentence 2 between AEs (A) and Js (B) (The level of significance is 0.05)

4.4 Comparison between American and Japanese subjects

Table 4.16 Significant differences in the incorrect answer rates of words in Sentence 1 between AEs (A) and Js (B)

Higher Fo word	Significant difference
avoid	Significant difference
every	No
kind	No
evil	Significant difference
'steady'	No

(The level of significance is 0.05)

Table 4.17 Significant differences in the incorrect answer rates of words in Sentence 2 between AEs (A) and Js (B)

Higher Fo word	Significant difference
ignore	No
gloom	Significant difference
doom	Significant difference
'steady'	Significant difference

(The level of significance is 0.05)

4.4.2 Test of difference in incorrect answer rates of sentences between American subjects and Japanese subjects

Tests were carried out to determine whether there was a difference in the incorrect answer rate of Sentence 1 between AEs and Js and there was a difference in the incorrect answer rate of Sentence 2 between AEs and Js. Table 4.18 and Figure 4.13 show the results of Sentence 1 and Table 4.19 and Figure 4.14 show the results of Sentence 2.

Entering the result of Table 4.18 in formulae (4.6) and (4.7), the following result was obtained:

p_A=0.051.
p_B=0.108.

    Null hypothesis $H_0 : p_1 = p_2$ (There is no difference in the incorrect answer rate between Group A and Group B.)

    Alternative hypothesis $H_1 : p_1 \neq p_2$ (There is a difference in the incorrect answer rate between Group A and Group B.)

Where $Z_{0.05}$=1.96.
Here n_1=1000, x_1/n_1=0.108, n_2=2900, x_2/n_2=0.051. Entering these values in formula (4.8), the following result was obtained:
$|Z|$=5.3580.
Then
$|Z|>1.96 (=Z_{0.05})$.

Therefore, H_0 was rejected and H_1 was accepted. This means that there was a significant difference in the incorrect answer rate of Sentence 1 between AEs and Js when the level of significance was set at 0.05. It was concluded that the number of incorrect answers of Js was fewer than AEs.

Entering the result of Table 4.19 in the formulae (4.6) and (4.7), the following result was obtained:
$p_A=0.184$.
$p_B=0.237$.

Null hypothesis $H_0 : p_1=p_2$ (There is no difference in the incorrect answer rate between Group A and Group B.)

Alternative hypothesis $H_1 : p_1 \neq p_2$ (There is a difference in the incorrect answer rate between Group A and Group B.)

Where $Z_{0.05}=1.96$.
Here $n_1=800$, $x_1/n_1=0.184$, $n_2=2320$, $x_2/n_2=0.237$. Entering these values in formula (4.8), the following result was obtained:
$|Z|=3.2468$.
Then
$|Z|>1.96 (=Z_{0.05})$.

Therefore, H_0 was rejected and H_1 was accepted. This means that there was a significant difference in the incorrect answer rate of Sentence 2 between AEs and Js when the level of significance was set at 0.05. It was concluded that the number of incorrect answers of AEs was fewer than Js.

Table 4.18 The incorrect answer rates of Sentence 1 by AEs and Js

Sentence 1	Correct answer	Incorrect answer	Total	Incorrect answer rate	Correct answer rate
AEs (Group A)	892	108	1000	10.8%	89.2%
Js (Group B)	2752	148	2900	5.1%	94.9%

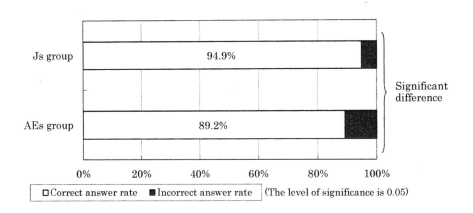

Figure 4.13 The incorrect answer rates of Sentence 1 by AEs and Js

4.5 Details of answers from American and Japanese subjects 141

Table 4.19 The incorrect answer rates of Sentence 2 by AEs and Js

Sentence 2	Correct answer	Incorrect answer	Total	Incorrect answer rate	Correct answer rate
AEs (Group A)	653	147	800	18.4%	81.6%
Js (Group B)	1771	549	2320	23.7%	76.3%

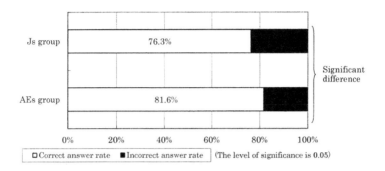

Figure 4.14 The incorrect answer rates of Sentence 2 by AEs and Js

4.5 Details of answers from American subjects and Japanese subjects

In Figures 4.15 to 4.19, the left-hand charts show the answers of Sentence 1 by forty AEs and the right-hand charts show the answers of Sentence 1 by 116 Js.

In Figure 4.15, the left-hand chart shows the answers of AEs who listened to the synthesized utterances where "evil" was set to higher in F_0 five times. Seventy-five percent of AEs answered "there was a stress on "evil", 17.0% answered "there were no stressed words", 2.0% answered "there was a stress on "Avoid", 2.0% answered "there was a stress on "every", 3.5% answered "there was a stress on "kind", and 0.5% was invalid because two words were selected or no words were selected. In Figure 4.15, the right-hand chart shows the answers of Js who listened to the synthesized utterances where "evil" was set to higher in F_0 five times. Ninety point seven percent of Js answered "there was a stress on "evil", 6.7% answered "there was no stress", 1.4% answered "there was a stress on "Avoid", 0.5% answered "there was a stress on "every", and 0.7% answered "there was a stress on "kind".

Before the experiment, the writer expected that the largest incorrect answer made by subjects would be "Avoid", because the utterance time of "Avoid" in synthesized utterance was the longest in Sentence 1. However, only 2.0% of AEs and 1.4% of Js answered "there was a stress on "Avoid". The most common incorrect answer made by subjects was that there were "no stressed words" (AEs: 17.0%, Js: 6.7%).

Figure 4.16 shows the answers of AEs and Js when they listened to the synthesized utterances where F_0 was decreased uniformly ('steady') in Sentence 1. For AEs, the incorrect answer, "there was a stress on "kind", was 4.5%. The number of this incorrect answer was greater than the incorrect answers, "there was a stress on "Avoid" (2.5%). For Js, the incorrect answer, "there was a stress on "Avoid" (3.1%), was a little greater than the number of other incorrect answers. When "A*void*" was set to higher in F_0 in Figure 4.17, the greatest number of incorrect answers was "no stress" (AEs: 5.5%, Js: 1.6%). When "*kind*" was set to higher in F_0 in Figure 4.19, the greatest number of incorrect answers was also "no stress" (AEs: 2.5%, Js: 1.2%).

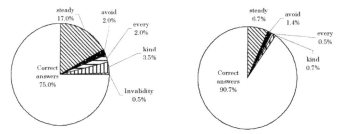

Figure 4.15 Answers by AEs (Left) and Js (Right) when "*e*vil" was set to higher in F_0

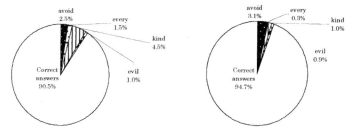

Figure 4.16 Answers by AEs (Left) and Js (Right) in the case of 'steady' in Sentence 1

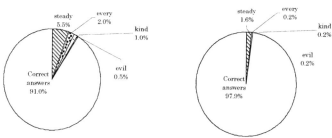

Figure 4.17 Answers by AEs (Left) and Js (Right) when "A*void*" was set to higher in F_0

4.5 Details of Answers from American and Japanese subjects   143

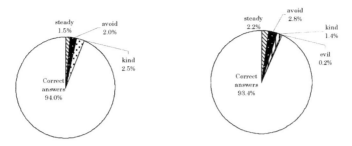

Figure 4.18 Answers by AEs (Left) and Js (Right) when "_every_" was set to higher in F_0

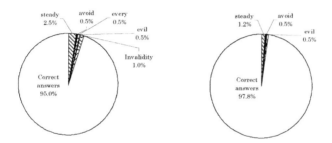

Figure 4.19 Answers by AEs (Left) and Js (Right) when "_kind_" was set to higher in F_0

In figures 4.15 to 4.19, all the perception rates are more than 90% except for the left-hand chart in Figure 4.15. When AEs listened to the synthesized utterances where "_evil_" was set to higher in F_0, the perception rate was especially low (75.0%) and the incorrect answer, "there were no stressed words", was the most frequent (17.0%).

In natural utterance, when stress is placed on "Evil", "Evil" becomes much longer. That is, when informant A1 placed stress on "Evil", the length of "Evil" was 26% if the length of a whole sentence was 100% (see Figure 3.28 in Chapter 3). However, "_evil_" for the synthesized utterance was very short. The length of "_evil_" was 11% if the length of a whole sentence was 100%. It was considered that the utterance time of "_evil_" in the synthesized utterance was too short for AEs to perceive stress on "_evil_" even though "_evil_" was set to higher in F_0 (Chapter 3).

On the other hand, For Js, there was no significant difference in the incorrect answer rate between when "_evil_" was set to higher in F_0 and when "_every_" was set to higher in F_0, of which the incorrect answer rate was the second highest. The shortness of the utterance time of "_evil_" did not seem to influence the perception rate of Js.

In Figures 4.20 to 4.23, the left-hand charts show the answers of Sentence 2 by forty AEs and the right-hand charts show the answers of Sentence 2 by 116 Js.

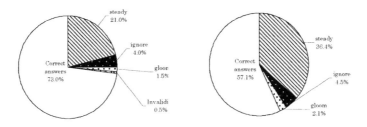

Figure 4.20 Answers by AEs (Left) and Js (Right) when "*doom*" was set to higher in F_0

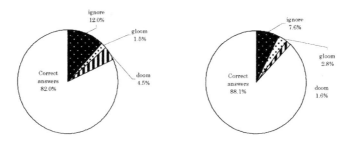

Figure 4.21 Answers by AEs (Left) and Js (Right) in the case of 'steady' in Sentence 2

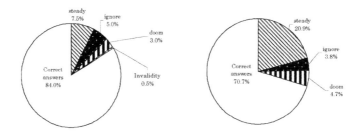

Figure 4.22 Answers by AEs (Left) and Js (Right) when "*gloom*" was set to higher in F_0

4.5 Details of Answers from American and Japanese subjects   145

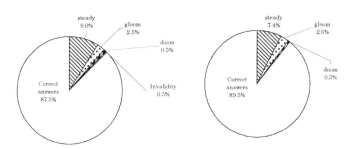

Figure 4.23 Answers by AEs (Left) and Js (Right) when "Ig<u>nore</u>" was set to higher in F$_0$

In Figure 4.20, the left-hand chart shows the answers of AEs who listened to the synthesized utterance where "<u>doom</u>" was set to higher in F$_0$ five times. Seventy-three percent of AEs answered "there was a stress on "<u>doom</u>", 21.0% answered "there was no stress", 4.0% answered "there was a stress on "Ignore", and 1.5% answered "there was a stress on "gloom", and 0.5% was invalid. In Figure 4.20, the right-hand chart shows the answers of Js who listened to the synthesized utterance where "<u>doom</u>" was set to higher in F$_0$ five times. Fifty-seven point one percent of Js answered "there was a stress on "<u>doom</u>", 36.4% answered "there was no stress", 4.5% answered "there was a stress on "Ignore", and 2.1% answered "there was a stress on "gloom".

Before the experiment, the writer expected that the largest incorrect answer made by subjects would be "Ignore", because "Ignore" in synthesized utterances was the longest even though "<u>doom</u>" was set to higher in F$_0$ in Sentence 2. However, only 4.0% of AEs and 4.5% of Js answered "there was a stress on "Ignore". The most common incorrect answer made by subjects was that there was "no stress" (AEs: 21.0%, Js: 36.4%).

When "<u>gloom</u>" was set to higher in F$_0$ in Figure 4.22, the most common incorrect answer made by subjects was also that there was "no stress" (AEs: 7.5%, Js: 20.9%). When "Ig<u>nore</u>" was set to higher in F$_0$ in Figure 4.23, the most common incorrect answer made by subjects was also that there was "no stress" (AEs: 9.0%, Js: 7.4%).

In natural utterance, when stress is placed on "**DOOM**", "**DOOM**" becomes much longer. That is, when informant A1 placed stress on "**DOOM**", the length of "**DOOM**" was 24% if the length of a whole sentence was 100% (see Figure 3.38 in Chapter 3). However, "<u>doom</u>" for the synthesized utterance was very short. The length of "<u>doom</u>" was 13% if the length of a whole sentence was 100%. It was considered that "<u>doom</u>" was too short in the synthesized utterance for subjects to perceive stress on "<u>doom</u>" even though "*doom*" was set to higher in F₀.

The length rate of "*evil*" and "*doom*" in the synthesized utterance was 11% and 13% in each sentence and there was no great difference (2%) in the length rate. On the other hand, concerning the F₀ changes, although "*evil*" was 52 Hz higher than the preceding syllable, "*doom*" was only 35 Hz higher than the preceding syllable. Even though there was a great difference in the F₀ changes (17 Hz), for AEs, there was no significant difference in the incorrect answer rate between "*evil*" (25.0%) and "*doom*" (27.0%). For Js, there was a significant difference in the incorrect answer rates between "*evil*" (9.3%) and "*doom*" (42.9%). The number of incorrect answers of "*doom*" where the utterance time was the shortest and the F₀ change was 17 Hz smaller than "*evil*" was the greatest.

Figure 4.21 shows the answers of subjects who listened to the synthesized utterance 'steady' in Sentence 2. The incorrect answer 'stressed word was "Ignore"' was greater (AEs: 12.0%, Js: 7.6%) than any other incorrect answers. "Ignore" was the longest word in synthesized utterances in Sentence 2.

4.6 Test of difference in incorrect answer rate between American subjects and Japanese subjects (total of Sentence 1 and Sentence 2)

A test was carried out to determine whether there was a significant difference in the incorrect answer rates between 40 AEs and 116 Js. Table 4.20 and Figure 4.24 show the results of tallying up incorrect answer rates and perception rates.

Entering the result of Table 4.20 in the formulae (4.6) and (4.7), the following result was obtained:

$p_A = 0.142$.

$p_B = 0.134$.

Null hypothesis	$H_0 : p_1 = p_2$	(There is no difference in the incorrect answer rate between Group A and Group B.)
Alternative hypothesis	$H_1 : p_1 \neq p_2$	(There is a difference in the incorrect answer rate between Group A and Group B.)

Where $Z_{0.05} = 1.96$.

Here $n_1 = 1800$, $x_1/n_1 = 0.142$, $n_2 = 5220$, $x_2/n_2 = 0.134$. Entering these values in formula (4.8), the following result was obtained:

$|Z| = 0.8596$.

4.6 Test of Difference between American and Japanese Subjects

Then
$|Z| < 1.96 \ (=Z_{0.05})$.

Therefore, H_0 was accepted. This means that there was no significant difference in the incorrect answer rate between AEs and Js when the level of significance was set at 0.05.

Watanabe (1994:3) states that "we have to consider that there is some difference in perceiving the syllable stress between native speakers of English and Japanese. The former perceive English stress by pitch variation, duration and intensity. On the other hand, in Japanese, as the duration of each syllable is almost the same, Japanese may perceive syllable stress mainly by relative pitch when the intensity of each syllable is equal." Watanabe (1988:181-186) undertook an experiment to examine whether Japanese subjects perceive stress on the highest pitch syllable in an English utterance. The results show that Japanese subjects "tend to rely on high pitch rather than duration or intensity or even pitch movement for stress judgement."

In Cruttenden (2001:25), Gimson states that "Our hearing mechanism must be thought of in two ways: the physiological mechanism which reacts to the acoustic stimuli...and the psychological activity – which, at the level of the brain, selects from the gross acoustic information that which is relevant in terms of the linguistic system involved." Gimson (2001) states as follows:

> Listeners, without any phonetic training, can, therefore, frequently give valuable guidance by their judgements of synthetic qualities. But it is important to be aware of the limitations of such listeners, so as to be able to make a proper evaluation of their judgements. A listener's reactions are normally conditioned by his experience of handling his own language. (Cruttenden, 2001:25)

It was considered that it seemed to be natural for Js to perceive stress on the higher syllable in pitch because word accent in Japanese was produced by pitch change.

Table 4.20 Comparison of the incorrect answer rates between AEs and Js (Total of Sentence 1 and Sentence 2)

	Correct answer	Incorrect answer	Total	Incorrect answer rate	Correct answer rate
AEs group	1545	255	1800	14.2%	85.8%
Js group	4523	697	5220	13.4%	86.6%
Total	6068	952	7020	13.6%	86.4%

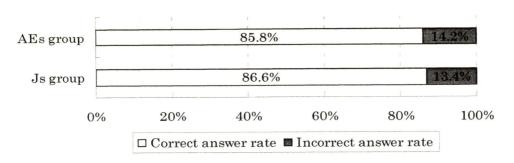

Figure 4.24 Comparison of the incorrect answer rates between AEs and Js (Total of Sentence 1 and Sentence 2)

4.7 Summary

In this chapter, 116 Japanese learners of English (Js) were asked to listen to the nine stimulus types of synthesized utterances, which were synthesized in Chapter 3, five times recorded at random and the result was compared with that of 40 native speakers of American English (AEs).

The result of the analysis of this experiment shows that an average of 86.6% of Js and an average of 85.8% of AEs perceived a stressed word on the higher syllable in F_0. Concerning the simple short sentence used in this research, there was no significant difference in perceiving F_0 changes in English between AEs and Js at the 0.05 significance level. Word accent in Japanese is produced by the F_0 change. It was considered that it is natural for Js to perceive prominence on the higher syllable in F_0 even in English. The purpose of this book was to examine the pitch movements on the stressed syllables, so that only F_0 was changed. It would be interesting to examine how Js perceive prominence for synthesized utterances where the elements of length and intensity were added.

5 Perception of pitch change with a comparison of native speakers of American English, British English and Japanese

5.1 Introduction

In Chapter 2, the movements in pitch on the sentence stress uttered by native speakers of American English (AEs) were explained. In Chapter 3, a stress perception test was undertaken by 40 AEs to examine whether they perceive a stressed word on the higher syllable in the pitch. The result showed that 85.8% of AEs perceived a stressed word on the higher syllable in the pitch. This result confirmed that pitch movement was a parameter in perceiving sentence stress. In Chapter 4, the same test as Chapter 3 was undertaken by 116 Japanese learners of English (Js). The result showed that 86.6% of Js perceived a stressed word on the higher syllable in the pitch. In this chapter, the same test as Chapters 3 and 4 was undertaken by 36 native speakers of British English (BEs). This result was compared with AEs and Js and statistically analyzed.

5.2 Experiment

5.2.1 Purpose
The purpose of the experiment reported in this chapter is twofold. Firstly, it aims to examine whether a higher syllable in pitch is perceived as a stressed word by BEs. Secondly, it aims to compare the results of this experiment with that of AEs and Js.

5.2.2 Method
The same stress perception test as undertaken in Chapters 3 and 4 (see section 3.2) was undertaken by BEs. The subjects were 36 BEs who were university students or university graduates (7 professors, 9 university or graduate students, 15 postgraduates and 5 university graduates) with no hearing and speaking disorder, their ages were between 19 and 69. The perception test was carried out by 41 BEs but only the data of 36 subjects,

150 Perception of pitch change with a comparison of AEs, BEs and Js

who were university students and graduated university were used. Five subjects who never attended university were omitted because the purpose of this experiment in this chapter was to compare the results with AEs (well-educated, their ages between 19 and 69) and Js (university students, their ages between 19 and 29). Thirty-six subjects were asked to listen to nine stimulus types of synthesized utterances five times at random (five stimulus types of "A**VOID** every kind of evil" and four stimulus types of "Ig**NORE** the gloom and doom") where only pitch (F_0) was changed (see p.75). They were asked to listen to forty-five synthesized utterances which were recorded on a micro disk and to choose either one stressed word or if there was no stressed word to choose 'monotone (no stressed words)'.

5.3 Stress perception by native speakers of British English (Group C)

5.3.1 Background theory
(A) Assuming that an event happens k times in a series of n tests, the sample ratio p is:

$$p = k / n \qquad (5.1) \qquad \text{(Inagaki, et al 1996: 138.)}$$

(B) Generally, the probability p in which an event happens x times in n tests is calculated by the binominal distribution.
(C) When the mean np is large in a binominal distribution, the probability is calculated from the fact that the binominal distribution approximates to a normal distribution (np>5 approximately).

$$Z = \{(x/n)-p\} / \{p(1-p)/n\}^{1/2} \quad (5.2) \qquad \text{(Inagaki, et al 1996: 138.)}$$

This approximates to a standard normal distribution. Using this, a test was carried out after setting a critical region of Z.

N (people) random samples were drawn from BEs. These are labeled as Group C. A ratio test was carried out to determine whether the incorrect answer rate p_0 is considered as the incorrect answer rate of Group C. The hypothesis was set as follows:

Null hypothesis $\qquad H_0 : p=p_0$ (the incorrect answer rate of Group C is considered as p_0.)
Alternative hypothesis $\quad H_1 : p \neq p_0$ (the incorrect answer rate of Group C differs from p_0.)
(Inagaki, et al., 1996: 138.)

From the normal distribution table, the critical region $Z_{0.01}=2.58$, $Z_{0.05}=1.96$, and $Z_{0.1}=1.64$ were used (Inagaki, et al., 1996: 65).

5.3.2 Test of incorrect answer rates

As stated in Chapters 3 and 4, the incorrect answers are for expediency defined as:
(1) when subjects listen to the synthesized utterances with a higher pitch (F_0) syllable, they do not answer that there is a stressed syllable on a higher F_0 syllable, and
(2) when subjects listen to the synthesized utterance in which F_0 was decreased uniformly from the beginning to the end, they did not answer that there are no stressed words.

Tables 5.1 and 5.2 show the results in which 36 BEs listened to the nine stimulus types of synthesized utterances five times at random. These are shown graphically in Figures 5.1 and 5.2. Underlined and italic letters show the syllables which were set to higher in F_0.

Table 5.1 The incorrect answer rate of each word by BEs (Group C) <Sentence 1> (The total of each stimulus is 180 (36 (listeners) × 5 (repetitions))).

Higher F0 word	Correct answer	Incorrect answer	Total	Incorrect answer rate (p)	Correct answer rate (1-p)
_e_vil	137	43	180	23.9%	76.1%
'steady'	161	19	180	10.6%	89.4%
kind	162	18	180	10.0%	90.0%
A_void_	166	14	180	7.8%	92.2%
_e_very	168	12	180	6.7%	93.3%
Total	794	106	900	11.8%	88.2%

Table 5.2 The incorrect answer rate of each word by BEs (Group C) <Sentence 2> (The total of each stimulus is 180 (36 (listeners) × 5 (repetitions))).

Higher F0 word	Correct answer	Incorrect answer	Total	Incorrect answer rate (p)	Correct answer rate (1-p)
gloom	132	48	180	26.7%	73.3%
doom	136	44	180	24.4%	75.6%
'steady'	140	40	180	22.2%	77.8%
Ig_nore_	148	32	180	17.8%	82.2%
Total	556	164	720	22.8%	77.2%

Note: Underlined and italic letters show the syllables set to higher. Also 'steady' shows the synthesized utterances that F_0 was decreased uniformly.

A test was carried out to determine whether the incorrect answer rate is considered as 0.2 at a significance level of 0.05 when Group C listened to the synthesized utterance where the word "$\underline{e}$vil" was set to higher in F_0.

  Null hypothesis $H_0 : p=0.2$ (The incorrect answer rate of Group C is considered as 0.2.)

  Alternative hypothesis $H_1 : p \neq 0.2$ (The incorrect answer rate of Group C differs from 0.2.)

Where $Z_{0.05}=1.96$.

Here $n=180$, $x/n=0.239$, $p=0.2$. Entering these values in formula (5.2), the following result was obtained:

$|Z|=1.304$.

Then

$|Z|<1.96 (=Z_{0.05})$.

Therefore, H_0 was accepted because Z was not included in the critical region. This means that the incorrect answer rate is considered as 20% at a level of significance = 0.05.

Tests of other incorrect answer rates were also carried out at a level of significance = 0.05. Tables 5.3 and 5.4 show the results of the test of the incorrect answer rates in Tables 5.1 and 5.2. They were represented in the graph in Figures 5.3 and 5.4.

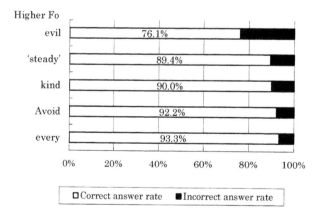

Figure 5.1 The incorrect answer rate of each word by BEs (Group C) <Sentence 1>

5.3 Stress perception by BEs

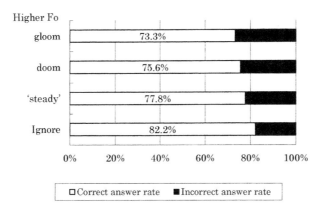

Figure 5.2 The incorrect answer rate of each word by BEs (Group C) <Sentence 2>

Table 5.3 Estimated value of the incorrect answer rate for each word by BEs (Group C) <Sentence 1>

Higher Fo word	Incorrect answer rate (%)
_e_vil	20
'steady'	10
kind	10
A_void_	10
_ev_ery	10

(The level of significance is 0.05)

Table 5.4 Estimated value of the incorrect answer rate for each word by BEs (Group C) <Sentence 2>

Higher Fo word	Incorrect answer rate (%)
gloom	30
doom	20
'steady'	20
Ig_nore_	20

(The level of significance is 0.05)

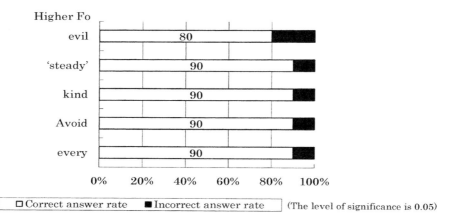

Figure 5.3 Estimated value of the incorrect answer rate for each word by BEs (Group C) <Sentence 1>

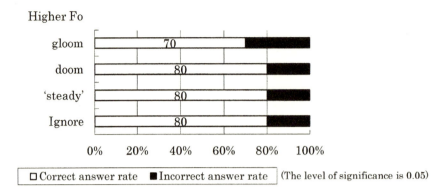

Figure 5.4 Estimated value of the incorrect answer rate for each word by BEs (Group C) <Sentence 2>

5.3.3 Test of difference in incorrect answer rates between words

N_1 and n_2 random samples were chosen from two Groups of BEs (C_1 and C_2). Data were analyzed statistically whether the incorrect answer rate of words, p_1 was equal to p_2.

Null hypothesis $H_0 : p_1=p_2$ (There is no difference in the incorrect answer rate between Group C_1 and Group C_2.)

Alternative hypothesis $H_1 : p_1 \neq p_2$ (There is a difference in the incorrect answer rate between Group C_1 and Group C_2.)

The difference in the incorrect answer rate between Group C_1 and Group C_2 was unknown, so that it was estimated from two sample rates.

$p_1 = x_1 / n_1$ (n_1: a sample number in Group C_1
        x_1: a data number)   (5.3)
$p_2 = x_2 / n_2$ (n_2: a sample number in Group C_2
        x_2: a data number)   (5.4)   (Inagaki, *et al.*, 1996: 139.)

A test of Parameter Variance was carried out. Using the fact that the binominal distribution approximates to a normal distribution:

$$Z = (p_1 - p_2) / [\{p_1(1-p_1)/n_1\} + \{p_2(1-p_2)/n_2\}]^{1/2}$$
$$= \{(x_1/n_1) - (x_2/n_2)\} / [\{(x_1/n_1)(1-x_1/n_1)\}/n_1 + \{(x_2/n_2)(1-x_2/n_2)\}/n_2]^{1/2} \quad (5.5)$$

(Inagaki, *et al.*, 1996: 140.)

This approximates to a standard normal distribution. Using this, a test was carried out after setting a critical region of Z. From the normal distribution table, the critical regions $Z_{0.01}=2.58$, $Z_{0.05}=1.96$, and $Z_{0.1}=1.64$ were used.

(1) A test was carried out to determine whether there was a difference in the incorrect answer rate between "_e_vil" and 'steady' in Sentence 1 at a significance level of 0.05.

    Null hypothesis $H_0 : p_1=p_2$ (There is no difference in the incorrect answer rate between "_e_vil" and 'steady'.)

    Alternative hypothesis $H_1 : p_1 \neq p_2$ (There is a difference in the incorrect answer rate between "_e_vil" and 'steady'.)

Where $Z_{0.05}=1.96$.
Here $n_1=180$, $x_1/n_1=0.239$, $n_2=180$, $x_2/n_2=0.106$. Entering these values in formula (5.5), the following result was obtained:
$|Z|=3.4036$.
Then
$|Z|>1.96 (=Z_{0.05})$.

Therefore, H_0 was rejected and H_1 was accepted. This means that there was a significant difference in the incorrect answer rate between "_e_vil" and 'steady' at a level of significance = 0.05.

(2) A test was carried out to determine whether there was a difference in the incorrect answer rate between 'steady' and "_kind_" in Sentence 1 at a level of significance = 0.05.

    Null hypothesis $H_0 : p_1=p_2$ (There is no difference in the incorrect answer rate between 'steady' and "_kind_".)

    Alternative hypothesis $H_1 : p_1 \neq p_2$ (There is a difference in the incorrect answer rate between 'steady' and "_kind_".)

Where $Z_{0.05}=1.96$.
Here $n_1=180$, $x_1/n_1=0.106$, $n_2=180$, $x_2/n_2=0.100$. Entering these values in formula (5.5), the following result was obtained:
$|Z|=0.1736$.
Then
$|Z|<1.96 (=Z_{0.05})$.

Therefore, H_0 was accepted because Z was not included in the critical region. This means that there was no significant difference in the incorrect answer rate between 'steady' and "*kind*" at a level of significance = 0.05.

(3) A test was carried out to determine whether there was a difference in the incorrect answer rate between "*kind*" and "A*void*" in Sentence 1 at a level of significance = 0.05.

    Null hypothesis $H_0 : p_1=p_2$ (There is no difference in the incorrect answer rate between "*kind*" and "A*void*".)

    Alternative hypothesis $H_1 : p_1 \neq p_2$ (There is a difference in the incorrect answer rate between "*kind*" and "A*void*".)

Where $Z_{0.05}=1.96$.
Here $n_1=180$, $x_1/n_1=0.100$, $n_2=180$, $x_2/n_2=0.078$. Entering these values in formula (5.5), the following result was obtained:
$|Z|=0.7414$.
Then
$|Z|<1.96 (=Z_{0.05})$.

 Therefore, H_0 was accepted because Z was not included in the critical region. This means that there was no significant difference in the incorrect answer rate between "*kind*" and "A*void*" at a level of significance = 0.05.

(4) A test was carried out to determine whether there was a difference in the incorrect answer rate between "A*void*" and "*ev*ery" in Sentence 1 at a level of significance = 0.05.

    Null hypothesis $H_0 : p_1=p_2$ (There is no difference in the incorrect answer rate between "A*void*" and "*ev*ery".)

    Alternative hypothesis $H_1 : p_1 \neq p_2$ (There is a difference in the incorrect answer rate between "A*void*" and "*ev*ery".)

Where $Z_{0.05}=1.96$.
Here $n_1=180$, $x_1/n_1=0.078$, $n_2=180$, $x_2/n_2=0.067$. Entering these values in formula (5.5), the following result was obtained:
$|Z|=0.4073$.
Then
$|Z|<1.96 (=Z_{0.05})$.

 Therefore, H_0 was accepted because Z was not included in the critical region. This means that there was no significant difference in the incorrect answer rate between "A*void*" and "*ev*ery" at a level of significance = 0.05.

5.3 Stress perception by BEs

(5) A test was carried out to determine whether there was a difference in the incorrect answer rate between 'steady' and "*ev*ery" in Sentence 1 at a level of significance = 0.05.

    Null hypothesis $H_0 : p_1 = p_2$ (There is no difference in the incorrect answer rate between 'steady' and "*ev*ery".)

    Alternative hypothesis $H_1 : p_1 \neq p_2$ b(There is a difference in the incorrect answer rate between 'steady' and "*ev*ery".)

Where $Z_{0.05} = 1.96$.
Here $n_1 = 180$, $x_1/n_1 = 0.106$, $n_2 = 180$, $x_2/n_2 = 0.067$. Entering these values in formula (5.5), the following result was obtained:
$|Z| = 0.0389$.
Then
$|Z| < 1.96 \, (= Z_{0.05})$.

   Therefore, H_0 was accepted because Z was not included in the critical region. This means that there was no significant difference in the incorrect answer rate between 'steady' and "*ev*ery" at a level of significance = 0.05.

(6) A test was carried out to determine whether there was a difference in the incorrect answer rate between "*gloom*" and "*doom*" in Sentence 2 at a level of significance = 0.05.

    Null hypothesis $H_0 : p_1 = p_2$ (There is no difference in the incorrect answer rate between "*gloom*" and "*doom*".)

    Alternative hypothesis $H_1 : p_1 \neq p_2$ (There is a difference in the incorrect answer rate between "*gloom*" and "*doom*".)

Where $Z_{0.05} = 1.96$.
Here $n_1 = 580$, $x_1/n_1 = 0.429$, $n_2 = 580$, $x_2/n_2 = 0.293$. Entering these values in formula (5.5), the following result was obtained:
$|Z| = 0.4835$.
Then
$|Z| < 1.96 \, (= Z_{0.05})$.

   Therefore, H_0 was accepted because Z was not included in the critical region. This means that there was no significant difference in the incorrect answer rate between "*gloom*" and "*doom*" at a level of significance = 0.05.

(7) A test was carried out to determine whether there was a difference in the incorrect answer rate between "*doom*" and 'steady' in Sentence 2 at a level of significance = 0.05.

Null hypothesis $H_0 : p_1=p_2$ (There is no difference in the incorrect answer rate between "*doom*" and 'steady'.)

Alternative hypothesis $H_1 : p_1 \neq p_2$ (There is a difference in the incorrect answer rate between "*doom*" and 'steady'.)

Where $Z_{0.05}=1.96$.
Here $n_1=180$, $x_1/n_1=0.244$, $n_2=180$, $x_2/n_2=0.222$. Entering these values in formula (5.5), the following result was obtained:
$|Z|=0.4986$.
Then
$|Z|<1.96 \ (=Z_{0.05})$.

Therefore, H_0 was accepted because Z was not included in the critical region. This means that there was no significant difference in the incorrect answer rate between "*doom*" and 'steady' at a level of significance = 0.05.

(8) A test was carried out to determine whether there was a difference in the incorrect answer rate between 'steady' and "Ig*nore*" in Sentence 2 at a level of significance = 0.05.

Null hypothesis $H_0 : p_1=p_2$ (There is no difference in the incorrect answer rate between 'steady' and "Ig*nore*".)

Alternative hypothesis $H_1 : p_1 \neq p_2$ (There is a difference in the incorrect answer rate between 'steady' and "Ig*nore*".)

Where $Z_{0.05}=1.96$.
Here $n_1=180$, $x_1/n_1=0.222$, $n_2=180$, $x_2/n_2=0.178$. Entering these values in formula (5.5), the following result was obtained:
$|Z|=1.0557$.
Then
$|Z|<1.96 \ (=Z_{0.05})$.

Therefore, H_0 was accepted because Z was not included in the critical region. This means that there was no significant difference in the incorrect answer rate between 'steady' and "Ig*nore*" at a level of significance = 0.05.

(9) A test was carried out to determine whether there was a difference in the incorrect answer rate between "*gloom*" and 'steady' in Sentence 2 at a level of significance = 0.05.

Null hypothesis $H_0 : p_1=p_2$ (There is no difference in the incorrect answer rate between "*gloom*" and 'steady'.)

Alternative hypothesis $H_1 : p_1 \neq p_2$ (There is a difference in the incorrect answer rate between "*gloom*" and 'steady'.)

Where $Z_{0.05}=1.96$.
Here $n_1=180$, $x_1/n_1=0.267$, $n_2=180$, $x_2/n_2=0.222$. Entering these values in formula (5.5), the following result was obtained:
$|Z|=0.9824$.
Then
$|Z|<1.96 \; (=Z_{0.05})$.

Therefore, H_0 was accepted because Z was not included in the critical region. This means that there was no significant difference in the incorrect answer rate between "*gloom*" and 'steady' at a level of significance = 0.05.

(10) A test was carried out to determine whether there was a difference in the incorrect answer rate between "*gloom*" and "Ig*nore*" in Sentence 2 at a level of significance = 0.05.

Null hypothesis $H_0 : p_1=p_2$ (There is no difference in the incorrect answer rate between "*gloom*" and "Ig*nore*".)

Alternative hypothesis $H_1 : p_1 \neq p_2$ (There is a difference in the incorrect answer rate between "*gloom*" and "Ig*nore*".)

Where $Z_{0.05}=1.96$.
Here $n_1=180$, $x_1/n_1=0.267$, $n_2=180$, $x_2/n_2=0.178$. Entering these values in formula (5.5), the following result was obtained:
$|Z|=2.0401$.
Then
$|Z|>1.96 \; (=Z_{0.05})$.

Therefore, H_0 was rejected and H_1 was accepted. This means that there was a significant difference in the incorrect answer rate between "*gloom*" and "Ig*nore*" at a level of significance = 0.05.

(11) A test was carried out to determine whether there was a difference in the incorrect answer rate between "Ig*nore*" and "*doom*" in Sentence 2 at a level of significance = 0.05.

Null hypothesis $H_0 : p_1=p_2$ (There is no difference in the incorrect answer rate between "Ig*nore*" and "*doom*".)

Alternative hypothesis $H_1 : p_1 \neq p_2$ (There is a difference in the incorrect answer rate between "Ig*nore*" and "*doom*".)

Where $Z_{0.05}=1.96$.
Here $n_1=180$, $x_1/n_1=0.267$, $n_2=180$, $x_2/n_2=0.178$. Entering these values in formula (5.5), the following result was obtained:
$|Z|=1.555$.
Then
$|Z|<1.96 (=Z_{0.05})$.

Therefore, H_0 was accepted. This means that there was no significant difference in the incorrect answer rate between "Ig*nore*" and "*doom*" at a level of significance = 0.05.

(12) Summary of Section 5.3.3
Figure 5.5 shows the result of testing to determine whether there was a significant difference in the incorrect answer rate between words in Sentence 1 by BEs and Figure 5.6 shows the result of testing to determine whether there was a significant difference in the incorrect answer rate between words in Sentence 2 by BEs. In Sentence 1, there was only a significant difference in the incorrect answer rate of words at the 0.05 significance level when the last word "*e*vil" was set to higher in F_0 and there was no significant difference between 'steady', "*kind*", "A*void*" and "*ev*ery". In Sentence 2, the incorrect answer rate was the highest when "*gloom*" was set to higher in F_0 and the incorrect answer rate was the lowest when "Ig*nore*" was set to higher in F_0. There was no significant difference in the incorrect answer rate between "*doom*", 'steady' and "Ig*nore*". There was also no significant difference in the incorrect answer rate between "*gloom*", "*doom*" and 'steady'. That is, there was a significant difference in the incorrect answer rate between "*gloom*" and "Ig*nore*".

For Sentence 1, as well as the result of AEs (see section 3.3, p.90-91), there was only a significant difference in the incorrect answer rate at the 0.05 significance level when the last word "*e*vil" was set to higher in F_0 and there was no significant difference between 'steady', "*kind*", "A*void*" and "*ev*ery". It is considered that "*e*vil" was too short in the synthesized utterance for AEs and BEs to perceive stress on "*e*vil" (see section 3.4).

For Sentence 2, For AEs, the incorrect answer rate of the last word "*doom*" was the highest and there was a significant difference at the 0.05 significance level (see section 3.3, p.91). However, concerning BEs, the incorrect answer rate was not the highest when "*doom*" was set to higher in F_0.

The incorrect answer rates between words of AEs with BEs will be compared in the next section.

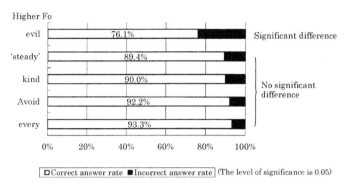

Figure 5.5 Comparison of the incorrect answer rates of words in Sentence 1 by BEs

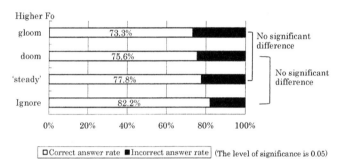

Figure 5.6 Comparison of the incorrect answer rates of words in Sentence 2 by BEs

5.4 Test of difference in incorrect answer rates of words between American subjects and British subjects

A test was carried out to determine whether there was a difference in the incorrect answer rate of words between AEs (Group A) and BEs (Group C). N_1 and n_2 random samples were chosen from the two groups of A and C. Data were analyzed statistically whether the incorrect answer rate of words, p_1 was equal to p_2.

    Null hypothesis $H_0 : p_1=p_2$ (There is no difference in the incorrect answer rate between Group A and Group C.)

    Alternative hypothesis $H_1 : p_1 \neq p_2$ (There is a difference in the incorrect answer rate between Group A and Group C.)

The difference in the incorrect answer rate between Group A and Group C was unknown, so that it was estimated from two sample rates.

$$p_A = x_1/n_1 \quad (n_1\text{: a sample number in Group A,}$$
$$x_1\text{: the number of incorrect answers}) \quad (5.6)$$
$$p_C = x_2/n_2 \quad (n_2\text{: a sample number in Group C,}$$
$$x_2\text{: the number of incorrect answers}) \quad (5.7)$$

A test of Parameter Variance was carried out. Using the fact that the binominal distribution approximates to a normal distribution:

$$Z = (p_1 - p_2) / [\{p_1(1-p_1)/n_1\} + \{p_2(1-p_2)/n_2\}]^{1/2}$$
$$= \{(x_1/n_1) - (x_2/n_2)\} / [\{(x_1/n_1)(1-x_1/n_1)\}/n_1$$
$$+ \{(x_2/n_2)(1-x_2/n_2)\}/n_2]^{1/2} \quad (5.8)$$

This approximates to a standard normal distribution. Using this, a test was carried out after setting a critical region of Z. From the normal distribution table, the critical regions $Z_{0.01}=2.58$, $Z_{0.05}=1.96$, and $Z_{0.1}=1.64$ were used.

(1) Higher "evil" in Sentence 1

Table 5.5 shows the result of the numbers of correct and incorrect answers by AEs (Group A) and BEs (Group C) when subjects listened to the synthesized utterance where the word "evil" was set to higher in F_0.

Table 5.5 Correct and incorrect answer rates by AEs (Group A) and BEs (Group C) when "evil" was set to higher in F_0

evil	Correct answer	Incorrect answer	Total	Incorrect answer rate(%)	Correct answer rate(%)
A	150	50	200	25.0%	75.0%
C	137	43	180	23.9%	76.1%

Entering the result of Table 5.5 in formulae (5.6) and (5.7), the following result was obtained:
$p_A = 0.25$.
$p_C = 0.239$.

Null hypothesis $H_0 : p_1 = p_2$ (There is no difference in the incorrect answer rate between Group A and Group C.)

Alternative hypothesis $H_1 : p_1 \neq p_2$ (There is a difference in the incorrect answer rate between

5.4 Difference between AEs and BEs (words)

Group A and Group C.)
Where $Z_{0.05}=1.96$.
Here $n_1=200$, $x_1/n_1=0.250$, $n_2=180$, $x_2/n_2=0.239$. Entering these values in formula (5.8), the following result was obtained:
$|Z|=0.252$.
Then
$|Z|<1.96 \; (=Z_{0.05})$.

Therefore, H_0 was accepted. This means that there was no significant difference in the incorrect answer rate between Group A and Group C at a level of significance = 0.05.

(2) No stressed words ('steady') in Sentence 1
Table 5.6 shows the result of the numbers of correct and incorrect answers by AEs (Group A) and BEs (Group C) when
s listened to the synthesized utterance where F_0 was decreased uniformly ('steady') in Sentence 1.

Table 5.6 Correct and incorrect answer rates by AEs (Group A) and BEs (Group C) when F_0 was decreased uniformly ('steady') in Sentence 1

'steady'	Correct answer	Incorrect answer	Total	Incorrect answer rate(%)	Correct answer rate(%)
A	182	18	200	9.0%	91.0%
C	161	19	180	10.6%	89.4%

Entering the result of Table 5.6 in formulae (5.6) and (5.7), the following result was obtained:
$p_A=0.09$.
$p_C=0.106$.

    Null hypothesis $H_0 : p_1=p_2$ (There is no difference in the incorrect answer rate between Group A and Group C.)
    Alternative hypothesis $H_1 : p_1 \neq p_2$ (There is a difference in the incorrect answer rate between Group A and Group C.)

Where $Z_{0.05}=1.96$.
Here $n_1=200$, $x_1/n_1=0.090$, $n_2=180$, $x_2/n_2=0.106$. Entering these values in formula (5.8), the following result was obtained:
$|Z|=0.509$.
Then
$|Z|<1.96 \; (=Z_{0.05})$.

Therefore, H_0 was accepted. This means that there was no significant difference in the incorrect answer rate between Group A and Group C at a level of significance = 0.05.

(3) Higher "A*void*" in Sentence 1

Table 5.7 shows the result of the numbers of correct and incorrect answers by AEs (Group A) and BEs (Group C) when "A*void*" was set to higher in F_0.

Table 5.7 Correct and incorrect answer rates by AEs (Group A) and BEs (Group C) when "A*void*" was set to higher in F_0

avoid	Correct answer	Incorrect answer	Total	Incorrect answer rate(%)	Correct answer rate(%)
A	182	18	200	9.0%	91.0%
C	166	14	180	7.8%	92.2%

Entering the result of Table 5.5 in formulae (5.6) and (5.7), the following result was obtained:

p_A=0.09.
p_C=0.078.

    Null hypothesis $H_0 : p_1=p_2$ (There is no difference in the incorrect answer rate between Group A and Group C.)

    Alternative hypothesis $H_1 : p_1 \neq p_2$ (There is a difference in the incorrect answer rate between Group A and Group C.)

Where $Z_{0.05}$=1.96.

Here n_1=200, x_1/n_1=0.250, n_2=580, x_2/n_2=0.093. Entering these values in formula (5.8), the following result was obtained:

Z=0.430.

Then

|Z|<1.96 (=$Z_{0.05}$).

  Therefore, H_0 was accepted. This means that there was no significant difference in the incorrect answer rate between Group A and Group C at a level of significance = 0.05.

(4) Higher "*ev*ery" in Sentence 1

Table 5.8 shows the result of the numbers of correct and incorrect answers by AEs (Group A) and BEs (Group C) when "*ev*ery" was set to higher in F_0.

5.4 Difference between AEs and BEs (words)

Table 5.8 Correct and incorrect answer rates by AEs (Group A) and BEs (Group C) when "e*v*ery" was set to higher in F_0

every	Correct answer	Incorrect answer	Total	Incorrect answer rate(%)	Correct answer rate(%)
A	188	12	200	6.0%	94.0%
C	168	12	180	6.7%	93.3%

Entering the result of Table 5.5 in formulae (5.6) and (5.7), the following result was obtained:
$p_A=0.06$.
$p_C=0.067$.

Null hypothesis $H_0 : p_1=p_2$ (There is no difference in the incorrect answer rate between Group A and Group C.)

Alternative hypothesis $H_1 : p_1 \neq p_2$ (There is a difference in the incorrect answer rate between Group A and Group C.)

Where $Z_{0.05}=1.96$.
Here $n_1=200$, $x_1/n_1=0.060$, $n_2=180$, $x_2/n_2=0.067$. Entering these values in formula (5.8), the following result was obtained:
$Z=0.266$.
Then
$|Z|<1.96 (=Z_{0.05})$.

Therefore, H_0 was accepted. This means that there was no significant difference in the incorrect answer rate between Group A and Group C at a level of significance = 0.05.

(5) Higher "*kind*" in Sentence 1
Table 5.9 shows the result of the numbers of correct and incorrect answers by AEs (Group A) and BEs (Group C) when "*kind*" was set to higher in F_0.

Table 5.9 Correct and incorrect answer rates by AEs (Group A) and BEs (Group C) when "*kind*" was set to higher in F_0.

kind	Correct answer	Incorrect answer	Total	Incorrect answer rate(%)	Correct answer rate(%)
A	190	10	200	5.0%	95.0%
C	162	18	180	10.0%	90.0%

Entering the result of Table 5.5 in formulae (5.6) and (5.7), the following result was obtained:

$p_A=0.05$.
$p_C=0.10$.

    Null hypothesis $H_0 : p_1=p_2$ (There is no difference in the incorrect answer rate between Group A and Group C.)

    Alternative hypothesis $H_1 : p_1 \neq p_2$ (There is a difference in the incorrect answer rate between Group A and Group C.)

Where $Z_{0.05}=1.96$.
Here $n_1=200$, $x_1/n_1=0.050$, $n_2=180$, $x_2/n_2=0.100$. Entering these values in formula (5.8), the following result was obtained:
$Z=1.841$.
Then
$|Z|<1.96 (=Z_{0.05})$.

  Therefore, H_0 was accepted. This means that there was no significant difference in the incorrect answer rate between Group A and Group C at a level of significance = 0.05.

(6) Higher "*doom*" in Sentence 2
Table 5.10 shows the result of the numbers of correct and incorrect answers by AEs (Group A) and BEs (Group C) when "*doom*" was set to higher in F_0.

Table 5.10 Correct and incorrect answer rates by AEs (Group A) and BEs (Group C) when "*doom*" was set to higher in F_0.

doom	Correct answer	Incorrect answer	Total	Incorrect answer rate(%)	Correct answer rate(%)
A	146	54	200	27.0%	73.0%
C	136	44	180	24.4%	75.6%

Entering the result of Table 5.5 in formulae (5.6) and (5.7), the following result was obtained:
$p_A=0.27$.
$p_C=0.244$.

    Null hypothesis $H_0 : p_1=p_2$ (There is no difference in the incorrect answer rate between Group A and Group C.)

    Alternative hypothesis $H_1 : p_1 \neq p_2$ (There is a difference in the incorrect answer rate between Group A and Group C.)

Where $Z_{0.05}=1.96$.
Here $n_1=200$, $x_1/n_1=0.270$, $n_2=180$, $x_2/n_2=0.244$. Entering these values in

5.4 Difference between AEs and BEs (words)

formula (5.8), the following result was obtained:
$Z=0.570$.
Then
$|Z|<1.96\ (=Z_{0.05})$.

Therefore, H_0 was accepted. This means that there was no significant difference in the incorrect answer rate between Group A and Group C at a level of significance = 0.05.

(7) No stressed words ('steady') in Sentence 2

Table 5.11 shows the result of the numbers of correct and incorrect answers by AEs (Group A) and BEs (Group C) when they listened to the synthesized utterance where F_0 was decreased uniformly ('steady') in Sentence 2.

Table 5.11 Correct and incorrect answer rates by AEs (Group A) and BEs (Group C) when F_0 was decreased uniformly ('steady') in Sentence 2

'steady'	Correct answer	Incorrect answer	Total	Incorrect answer rate(%)	Correct answer rate(%)
A	164	36	200	18.0%	82.0%
C	140	40	180	22.2%	77.8%

Entering the result of Table 5.5 in formulae (5.6) and (5.7), the following result was obtained:
$p_A=0.18$.
$p_C=0.222$.

       Null hypothesis $H_0 : p_1=p_2$ (There is no difference in the incorrect answer rate between Group A and Group C.)

       Alternative hypothesis $H_1 : p_1 \neq p_2$ (There is a difference in the incorrect answer rate between Group A and Group C.)

Where $Z_{0.05}=1.96$.
Here $n_1=200$, $x_1/n_1=0.180$, $n_2=180$, $x_2/n_2=0.222$. Entering these values in formula (5.8), the following result was obtained:
$Z=1.025$.
Then
$|Z|<1.96\ (=Z_{0.05})$.

Therefore, H_0 was accepted. This means that there was no significant difference in the incorrect answer rate between Group A and Group C at a level of significance = 0.05.

(8) Higher "*gloom*" in Sentence 2

Table 5.12 shows the result of the numbers of correct and incorrect answers by AEs (Group A) and BEs (Group C) when "*gloom*" was set to higher in F_0.

Table 5.12 Correct and incorrect answer rates by AEs (Group A) and BEs (Group C) when "*gloom*" was set to higher in F_0

gloom	Correct answer	Incorrect answer	Total	Incorrect answer rate	Correct answer rate
A	168	32	200	16.0%	84.0%
C	132	48	180	26.7%	73.3%

Entering the result of Table 5.5 in formulae (5.6) and (5.7), the following result was obtained:
p_A=0.16.
p_C=0.267.

    Null hypothesis $H_0 : p_1=p_2$ (There is no difference in the incorrect answer rate between Group A and Group C.)

    Alternative hypothesis $H_1 : p_1 \neq p_2$ (There is a difference in the incorrect answer rate between Group A and Group C.)

Where $Z_{0.05}$=1.96.
Here n_1=200, x_1/n_1=0.160, n_2=180, x_2/n_2=0.267. Entering these values in formula (5.8), the following result was obtained:
Z=2.544.
Then
$|Z|>1.96 (=Z_{0.05})$.

Therefore, H_0 was rejected and H_1 was accepted because Z was included in the critical region. This means that there was a significant difference in the incorrect answer rate between group A and group C when the level of significance was set at 0.05. The incorrect answer rate of AEs (Group A) was lower than BEs (Group C).

(9) Higher "Ig*nore*" in Sentence 2

Table 5.13 shows the result of the numbers of correct and incorrect answers by AEs (Group A) and BEs (Group C) when "Ig*nore*" was set to higher in F_0.

Table 5.13 Correct and incorrect answer rates by AEs (Group A) and BEs (Group C) when "Ig*nore*" was set to higher in F_0

ignore	Correct answer	Incorrect answer	Total	Incorrect answer rate(%)	Correct answer rate(%)
A	175	25	200	12.5%	87.5%
C	148	32	180	17.8%	82.2%

Entering the result of Table 5.5 in formulae (5.6) and (5.7), the following result was obtained:
$p_A=0.125$.
$p_C=0.178$.

    Null hypothesis $H_0 : p_1=p_2$ (There is no difference in the incorrect answer rate between Group A and Group C.)

    Alternative hypothesis $H_1 : p_1 \neq p_2$ (There is a difference in the incorrect answer rate between Group A and Group C.)

Where $Z_{0.05}=1.96$.
Here $n_1=200$, $x_1/n_1=0.125$, $n_2=180$, $x_2/n_2=0.178$. Entering these values in formula (5.8), the following result was obtained:
$Z=1.432$.
Then
$|Z|<1.96 (=Z_{0.05})$.

Therefore, H_0 was accepted. This means that there was no significant difference in the incorrect answer rate between Group A and Group C at a level of significance = 0.05.

(10) Summary of Section 5.4
Figure 5.7 shows the result of testing to determine whether there was a significant difference in the incorrect answer rate of words in Sentence 1 between AEs (Group A) and BEs (Group C). Each top bar indicates AEs and each bottom bar indicates BEs. There was no significant difference in the incorrect answer rate of any word between AEs and BEs at the 0.05 significance level.

Figure 5.8 shows the result of Sentence 2. Only when "*gloom*" was set to higher in F_0, there was a significant difference in the incorrect answer rate of words between AEs and BEs at the 0.05 significance level. The incorrect answer rate of BEs was higher than AEs. There were no significant differences in the incorrect answer rates when other words were set to higher in F_0 and 'steady'. This raises the question: Why was the number of incorrect answers of BEs largest when "*gloom*" was set to higher in F_0?

F₀ variations of informant B1 (a native speaker of British English: a BE) and informant A1 (a native speaker of American English: an AE), which were uttered with stress placed on each word in Sentence 1 and Sentence 2, will be shown and be compared in the next section.

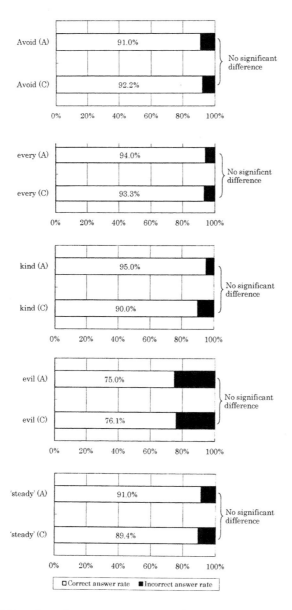

Figure 5.7 Results of testing to determine whether there are significant differences in the incorrect answer rates of words in Sentence 1 between AEs (A) and BEs (C) (The level of significance is 0.05)

5.4 Difference between AEs and BEs (words)   171

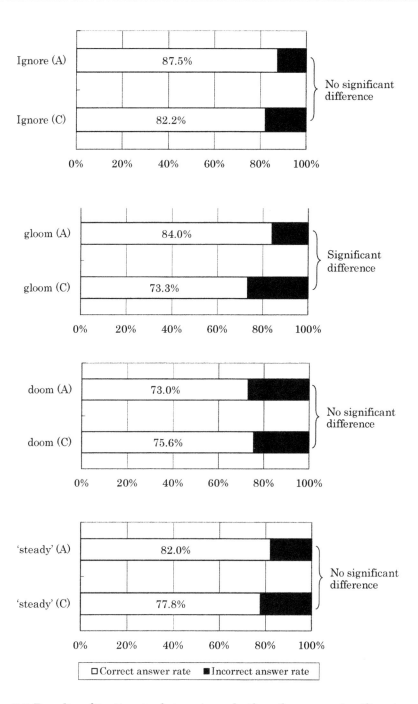

Figure 5.8 Results of testing to determine whether there are significant differences in the incorrect answer rates of words in Sentence 2 between AEs (A) and BEs (C) (The level of significance is 0.05)

5.5 Comparison of pitch movements between American subjects and British subjects

Figures 5.9, 5.11, 5.13 and 5.15 show the F_0 contours stressed on "**AVOID**", "**EV**ery", "**KIND**" and "**E**vil", respectively, in Sentence 1 uttered by a British informant B1. Figures 5.10, 5.12, 5.14 and 5.16 show the F_0 contours stressed on "**AVOID**", "**EV**ery", "**KIND**" and "**E**vil", respectively, in Sentence 1 uttered by an American informant A1. When the F_0 contours of each utterance by a British informant and an American informant are compared, the similar tendency is seen in F_0 contours.

Figures 5.17, 5.19, and 5.21 show the F_0 contours stressed on "Ig**NORE**", "**GLOOM**", and "**DOOM**", respectively, in Sentence 2 uttered by a British informant B1. Figures 5.18, 5.20, and 5.22 show the F_0 contours stressed on "Ig**NORE**", "**GLOOM**", and "**DOOM**" in Sentence 2 uttered by an American informant A1. When the F_0 contours of each utterance by a British informant and an American informant are compared, the difference in the size of F_0 variations on "**GLOOM**" is clear (Figures 5.19 and 5.20). The variation in F_0 on "**GLOOM**" uttered by a British informant is greater than an American informant. A British informant uttered "**GLOOM**" 57 Hz higher in F_0 than the preceding syllable. On the other hand, an American informant uttered "**GLOOM**" only 22 Hz higher in F_0 than the preceding syllable. Because the synthesized utterance is 35 Hz higher in F_0 than the preceding syllables, the variation in F_0 seems to be too small for BEs to perceive stress.

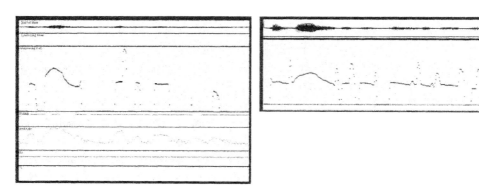

Figure 5.9 F_0 contour of "AVOID every kind of evil" by informant B1 (British informant)

Figure 5.10 F_0 contour of "AVOID every kind of evil" by informant A1 (American informant)

5.5 Comparison between AEs and BEs 173

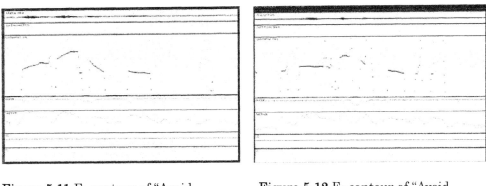

Figure 5.11 F₀ contour of "Avoid EVery kind of evil" by informant B1

Figure 5.12 F₀ contour of "Avoid EVery kind of evil" by informant A1

Figure 5.13 F₀ contour of "Avoid every KIND of evil" by informant B1

Figure 5.14 F₀ contour of "Avoid every KIND of evil" by informant A1

Figure 5.15 F₀ contour of "Avoid every kind of Evil" by informant B1

Figure 5.16 F₀ contour of "Avoid every kind of Evil" by informant A1

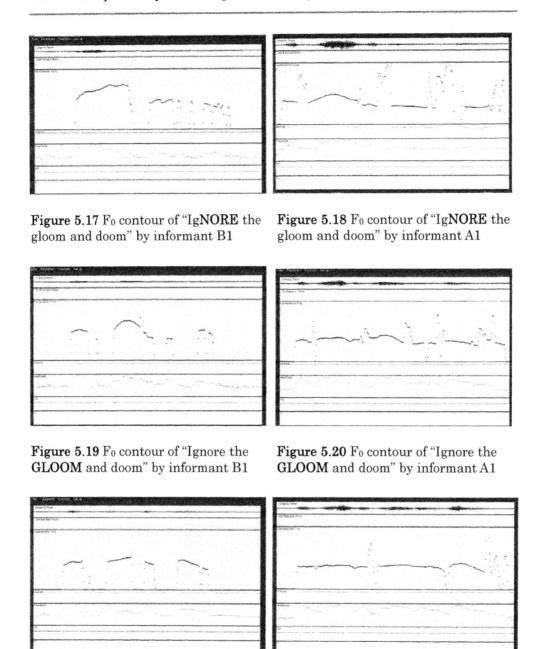

Figure 5.17 F₀ contour of "IgNORE the gloom and doom" by informant B1

Figure 5.18 F₀ contour of "IgNORE the gloom and doom" by informant A1

Figure 5.19 F₀ contour of "Ignore the GLOOM and doom" by informant B1

Figure 5.20 F₀ contour of "Ignore the GLOOM and doom" by informant A1

Figure 5.21 F₀ contour of "Ignore the gloom and DOOM" by informant B1

Figure 5.22 F₀ contour of "Ignore the gloom and DOOM" by informant A1

5.6 Details of answers from American subjects, Japanese subjects and British subjects

In this section, the answers given by subjects in the perception test are shown.

In Figures 5.23 to 5.27, (A) shows the answers of Sentence 1 by 40 AEs, (B) shows the answers of Sentence 1 by 116 Js, and (C) shows the answers of Sentence 1 by 36 BEs.

In Figure 5.26, (C) shows the answers of BEs who listened to the synthesized utterance where "evil" was set to higher in F_0 five times. Seventy-six point one percent answered "there was a stress on evil", 15.6% answered "there were no stressed words", 3.9% answered "there was a stress on Avoid", 2.8% answered "there was a stress on every", and 1.7% answered "there was a stress on kind". In Figure 5.26, (A) shows the answers of AEs who listened to the same synthesized utterance five times. Seventy-five percent answered "there was a stress on evil", 17.0% answered "there were no stressed words", 2.0% answered "there was a stress on Avoid", 2.0% answered "there was a stress on every", 3.5% answered "there was a stress on kind", and 0.5% were invalid because two words were selected or no words were selected. In Figure 5.26, (B) shows the answers of Js who listened to the same synthesized utterance five times. Ninety point seven percent answered "there was a stress on evil", 6.7% answered "there were no stressed words", 1.4% answered "there was a stress on Avoid", 0.5% answered "there was a stress on every", and 0.7% answered "there was a stress on kind".

In natural utterance, when stress is placed on "Evil", the length of "Evil" becomes much longer. Figure 3.28 in Chapter 3 showed that when informant A1 placed stress on "Evil", the length of "Avoid" was 27% and "Evil" was 26% if the length of a whole sentence was 100%. However, the length of "evil" for the synthesized utterance was very short. The length of AVOID" was 43% and "evil" was 11% if the length of a whole sentence was 100%. It was considered that the utterance time of "evil" was too short in the synthesized utterance for AEs and BEs to perceive stress on "evil" even though "evil" was set to higher in F_0.

On the other hand, for Js, there was no significant difference in the incorrect answer rate between when "evil" was set to higher in F_0 and when "every" was set to higher in F_0 (Figure 5.24 (B)), of which the incorrect answer rate was the second highest in Sentence 1. Interestingly, the shortness of the utterance time of "evil" did not seem to influence the perception rate of Js.

Before the experiment, the writer expected that the largest incorrect answer to be made by subjects would be "Avoid", because the utterance time of "Avoid" in synthesized utterance was the longest in Sentence 1. However, Figure 5.26 shows that only 3.9% of BEs, 2.0% of AEs and 1.4% of Js answered "there was a stress on Avoid". The most common incorrect answer made by subjects was that "there were no stressed words" (BEs: 15.6%, AEs: 17.0%, Js: 6.7%).

Figure 5.27 shows the answers of subjects who listened to the synthesized utterance 'steady' five times. For BEs, the incorrect answer "stressed word was Avoid" (5.0%) was slightly greater than other incorrect answers. For Js, the incorrect answer "stressed word was Avoid" (3.1%) was also slightly greater than other incorrect answers.

When "A*void*" was set to higher in F_0 (Figure 5.23), "there were no stressed words" was the highest among the incorrect answers (BEs: 6.1%, AEs: 5.5%, Js: 1.6%). When "*kind*" was set to higher in F_0 (Figure 5.25), the incorrect answer "there were no stressed words" was also the highest among the incorrect answers (BEs: 3.9%, AEs: 2.5%, Js: 1.2%).

In Figures 5.28 to 5.31, (A) shows the answers of Sentence 2 by 40 AEs, (B) shows the answers of Sentence 2 by 116 Js, and (C) shows the answers of Sentence 2 by 36 BEs.

In Figure 5.28, (C) shows the answers of BEs who listened to the synthesized utterance where "Ig*nore*" was set to higher in F_0 five times. Eighty-two point two percent answered "there was a stress on Ig*nore*", 14.4% answered "there were no stressed words", 2.2% answered "there was a stress on gloom", and 1.1% answered "there was a stress on doom". Figure 5.28 (A) shows the answers of AEs and Figure 5.28 (B) shows the answers of Js. "There were no stressed words" was the highest among the incorrect answers (AEs: 9.0%, Js: 7.4%).

When "*gloom*" was set to higher in F_0 (Figure 5.29), "there were no stressed words" was higher than any other incorrect answers (BEs: 11.7%, AEs: 7.5%, Js: 20.9%). When "*doom*" was set to higher in F_0 (Figure 5. 30), "there were no stressed words" was also higher than any other incorrect answers (BEs: 17.8%, AEs: 21.0%, Js: 36.4%).

Before the experiment, the writer expected that the largest incorrect answer to be made by subjects would be "Ignore", because the utterance time of "Ignore" in synthesized utterance was the longest in Sentence 2. However, only 5.6% of BEs, 4.0% of AEs and 4.5% of Js answered "there was a stress on Ignore".

In natural utterance, when stress is placed on any one syllable, the stressed portion tends to have a higher intensity, or the F_0 is changed or the duration tends to be longer than the unstressed syllables. Sometimes two or all three may occur. However, with synthesized utterance, the

5.6 Details of answers   177

longest syllable and a higher F_0 syllable were separated. Therefore it is possible that two stressed words were perceived; or no one syllable was prominent.

Figure 5.31 shows the answers of subjects who listened to the synthesized utterance 'steady' five times. "Stressed word was Ignore" was the highest among the incorrect answers (BEs: 16.7%, AEs: 12.0%, Js: 7.6%).

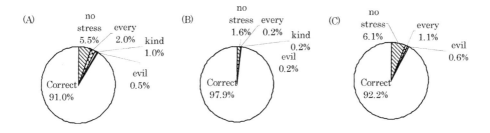

Figure 5.23 Answers by AEs (A), Js (B) and BEs (C) when "A*void*" was set to higher in F_0

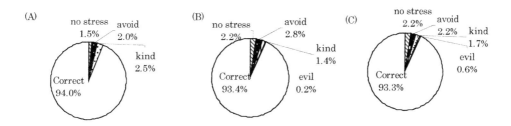

Figure 5.24 Answers by AEs (A), Js (B) and BEs (C) when "*every*" was set to higher in F_0

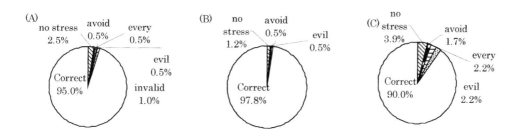

Figure 5.25 Answers by AEs (A), Js (B) and BEs (C) when "*kind*" was set to higher in F_0

178 Perception of pitch change with a comparison of AEs, BEs and Js

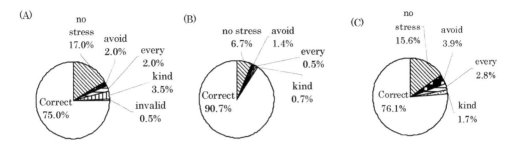

Figure 5.26 Answers by AEs (A), Js (B) and BEs (C) when "_e_vil" was set to higher in F_0

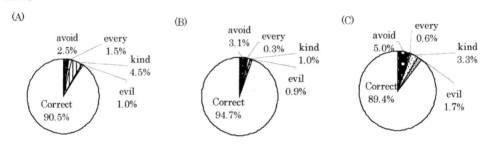

Figure 5.27 Answers by AEs (A), Js (B) and BEs (C) in the case of 'steady' in Sentence 1

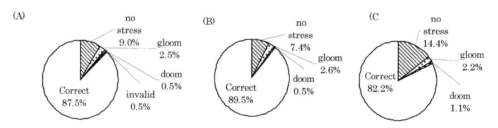

Figure 5.28 Answers by AEs (A), Js (B) and BEs (C) when "Ig_nore_" was set to higher in F_0

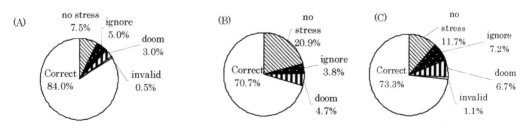

Figure 5.29 Answers by AEs (A), Js (B) and BEs (C) when "_gloom_" was set to higher in F_0

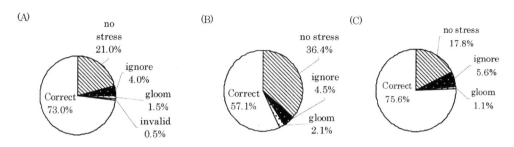

Figure 5.30 Answers by AEs (A), Js (B) and BEs (C) when "*doom*" was set to higher in F₀

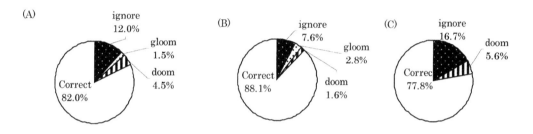

Figure 5.31 Answers by AEs (A), Js (B) and BEs (C) in the case of 'steady' in Sentence 2

In the next section, the writer will examine whether there is a difference in the incorrect answer rates between Sentence 1 and Sentence 2.

5.7 Total perception rates of Sentence 1 and Sentence 2 by British subjects

Table 5.14 and Figure 5.32 show the results of the total perception rates of Sentence 1 and Sentence 2. When 36 BEs listened to the synthesized utterance five times at random where F_0 parameter was changed (5 types of Sentence 1 and 4 types of Sentence 2), an average of 83.3% of subjects perceived stress on the word which was set to higher in F_0.

Table 5.14 The perception rate of Sentence 1 and Sentence 2

	Correct answer	Incorrect answer	Total	Incorrect answer rate (p)	Correct answer rate (1-p)
Sentence 1 + Sentence 2	1350	270	1620	0.167	0.833

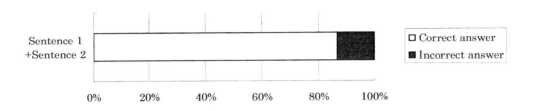

Figure 5.32 The perception rate of Sentence 1 and Sentence 2

5.8 Test of difference in incorrect answer rates of sentences between American subjects and British subjects

A test was carried out to determine whether there was a difference in the incorrect answer rates of Sentence 1 between AEs and BEs. A test was also carried out to determine whether there was a difference in the incorrect answer rates of Sentence 2 between AEs and BEs. Table 5.15 and Figure 5.33 show the results of Sentence 1, and Table 5.16 and Figure 5.34 show the results of Sentence 2.

Entering the result of Table 5.15 in the formulae (5.6) and (5.7) in section 5.4, the following result was obtained:
$p_A=0.108$.
$p_C=0.118$.

> Null hypothesis $H_0 : p_1=p_2$ (There is no difference in the incorrect answer rate between Group A and Group C.)
> Alternative hypothesis $H_1 : p_1 \neq p_2$ (There is a difference in the incorrect answer rate between Group A and Group C.)

Where $Z_{0.05}=1.96$.
Here, $n_1=1000$, $x_1/n_1=0.108$, $n_2=900$, $x_2/n_2=0.118$. Entering these values in the formula (5.8), the following result was obtained:
$|Z|=0.6719$.
Then
$|Z|<1.96 \ (=Z_{0.05})$.

Therefore, H_0 was accepted. This means that there was no significant difference in the incorrect answer rates of Sentence 1 between AEs and BEs when the level of significance was set at 0.05.

Entering the result of Table 5.16 in the formulae (5.6) and (5.7), the following result was obtained:

5.8 Difference between AEs and BEs (sentences)

$p_A=0.184$.
$p_C=0.228$.

Null hypothesis $H_0 : p_1=p_2$ (There is no difference in the incorrect answer rate between Group A and Group C.)

Alternative hypothesis $H_1 : p_1 \neq p_2$ (There is a difference in the incorrect answer rate between Group A and Group C.)

Where $Z_{0.05}=1.96$.

Here, $n_1=800$, $x_1/n_1=0.184$, $n_2=720$, $x_2/n_2=0.228$. Entering these values in the formula (5.8), the following result was obtained:

$|Z|=2.1188$.

Then

$|Z|>1.96 (=Z_{0.05})$.

Therefore, H_0 was rejected and H_1 was accepted. This means that there was a significant difference in the incorrect answer rates of Sentence 2 between AEs and BEs when the level of significance was set at 0.05. It was considered that the number of incorrect answers of AEs was fewer than BEs.

Table 5.15 The incorrect answer rates of Sentence 1 by AEs and BEs

Sentence 1	Correct answer	Incorrect answer	Total	Incorrect answer rate (p)	Correct answer rate (1-p)
AEs (Group A)	892	108	1000	10.8%	89.2%
BEs (Group C)	794	106	900	11.8%	88.2%

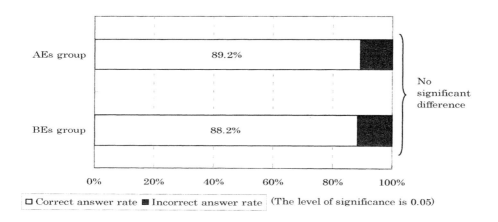

Figure 5.33 Results of testing to determine whether there is a significant difference in the incorrect answer rates in Sentence 1 between AEs and BEs

Table 5.16 The incorrect answer rates of Sentence 2 by AEs and BEs

Sentence 2	Correct answer	Incorrect answer	Total	Incorrect answer rate (p)	Correct answer rate (1-p)
AEs (Group A)	653	147	800	18.4%	81.6%
BEs (Group C)	556	164	720	22.8%	77.2%

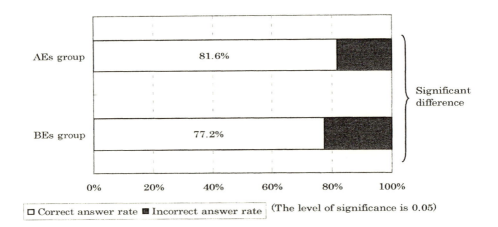

Figure 5.34 Results of testing to determine whether there is a significant difference in the incorrect answer rates in Sentence 2 between AEs and BEs

5.9 Test of difference in incorrect answer rates of words between British subjects and Japanese subjects

A test was carried out to determine whether there was a difference in the incorrect answer rates of words between Js (Group B) and BEs Group C). N_1 and n_2 random samples were chosen from the two groups of B and C. Data were analyzed statistically whether the incorrect answer rates of words, p_B was equal to p_C.

  Null hypothesis H_0 : $p_1 = p_2$ (There is no difference in the incorrect answer rate between Group B and Group C.)

  Alternative hypothesis H_1 : $p_1 \neq p_2$ (There is a difference in the incorrect answer rate between Group B and Group C.)

The difference in the incorrect answer rates between Group B and Group C was unknown, so that it was estimated from two sample rates.

5.9 Difference between BEs and Js (words)

$p_B = x_1 / n_1$ (n_1: a sample number in Group B,
x_1: the number of incorrect answers) (5.9)

$p_C = x_2 / n_2$ (n_2: a sample number in Group C,
x_2: the number of incorrect answers) (5.10)

A test of Parameter Variance was carried out. Using the fact that the binominal distribution approximates to a normal distribution:

$$Z = (p_1 - p_2) / [\{p_1(1-p_1)/n_1\} + \{p_2(1-p_2)/n_2\}]^{1/2}$$
$$= \{(x_1/n_1) - (x_2/n_2)\} / [\{(x_1/n_1)(1-x_1/n_1)\}/n_1 + \{(x_2/n_2)(1-x_2/n_2)\}/n_2]^{1/2} \quad (5.11)$$

This approximates to a standard normal distribution. Using this, a test was carried out after setting a critical region of Z. From the normal distribution table, the critical regions $Z_{0.01}=2.58$, $Z_{0.05}=1.96$, and $Z_{0.1}=1.64$ were used.

(1) Higher "ẹvil" in Sentence 1
Table 5.17 shows the result of the numbers of correct and incorrect answers by Js (Group B) and BEs (Group C) when "ẹvil" was set to higher in F_0.

Table 5.17 Correct and incorrect answer rates by Js (Group B) and BEs (Group C) when "ẹvil" was set to higher in F_0

evil	Correct answer	Incorrect answer	Total	Incorrect answer rate(%)	Correct answer rate(%)
B	526	54	580	9.3%	90.7%
C	137	43	180	23.9%	76.1%

Entering the result of Table 5.17 in the formulae (5.9) and (5.10), the following result was obtained:
$p_B = 0.093$.
$p_C = 0.239$.

Null hypothesis $H_0 : p_1 = p_2$ (There is no difference in the incorrect answer rates between Group B and Group C.)
Alternative hypothesis $H_1 : p_1 \neq p_2$ (There is a difference in the incorrect answer rates between Group B and Group C.)
Where $Z_{0.05} = 1.96$.
Here, $n_1 = 580$, $x_1/n_1 = 0.093$, $n_2 = 180$, $x_2/n_2 = 0.239$. Entering these values in the formula (5.11), the following result was obtained:
$Z = 4.288$.

Then
|Z|>1.96 (=$Z_{0.05}$).

Therefore, H_0 was rejected and H_1 was accepted. This means that there was a significant difference in the incorrect answer rates between Group B and Group C when the level of significance was set at 0.05. The incorrect answer rate of Js (Group B) was lower than BEs (Group C).

(2) No stressed words ('steady') in Sentence 1

Table 5.18 shows the result of the numbers of correct and incorrect answers by Js (Group B) and BEs (Group C) when they listened to the synthesized utterance where F_0 was decreased uniformly ('steady') in Sentence 1.

Table 5.18 Correct and incorrect answer rates by Js (Group B) and BEs (Group C) when F_0 was decreased uniformly ('steady') in Sentence 1

'steady'	Correct answer	Incorrect answer	Total	Incorrect answer rate(%)	Correct answer rate(%)
B	549	31	580	5.3%	94.7%
C	161	19	180	10.6%	89.4%

Entering the result of Table 5.5 in formulae (5.9) and (5.10), the following result was obtained:
p_B=0.053.
p_C=0.106.

Null hypothesis H_0 : $p_1=p_2$ (There is no difference in the incorrect answer rates between Group B and Group C.)
Alternative hypothesis H_1 : $p_1 \neq p_2$ (There is a difference in the incorrect answer rates between Group B and Group C.)

Where $Z_{0.05}$=1.96.
Here, n_1=580, x_1/n_1=0.053, n_2=180, x_2/n_2=0.106. Entering these values in the formula (5.11), the following result was obtained:
Z=2.107
Then
|Z|>1.96 (=$Z_{0.05}$).

Therefore, H_0 was rejected and H_1 was accepted because Z was included in the critical region. This means that there was a significant difference in the incorrect answer rates between Group B and Group C when the level of significance was set at 0.05. The incorrect answer rate of Js (Group B) was lower than BEs (Group C).

5.9 Difference between BEs and Js (words)

(3) Higher "A*void*" in Sentence 1

Table 5.19 shows the result of the numbers of correct and incorrect answers by Js (Group B) and BEs (Group C) when "A*void*" was set to higher in F_0.

Table 5.19 Correct and incorrect answer rates by Js (Group B) and BEs (Group C) when "A*void*" was set to higher in F_0

avoid	Correct answer	Incorrect answer	Total	Incorrect answer rate(%)	Correct answer rate(%)
B	568	12	580	2.1%	97.9%
C	166	14	180	7.8%	92.2%

Entering the result of Table 5.5 in formulae (5.9) and (5.10), the following result was obtained:
$p_B = 0.021$.
$p_C = 0.078$.

      Null hypothesis $H_0 : p_1 = p_2$ (There is no difference in the incorrect answer rates between Group B and Group C.)
      Alternative hypothesis $H_1 : p_1 \neq p_2$ (There is a difference in the incorrect answer rates between Group B and Group C.)
Where $Z_{0.05} = 1.96$.
Here, $n_1 = 580$, $x_1/n_1 = 0.021$, $n_2 = 180$, $x_2/n_2 = 0.078$. Entering these values in the formula (5.11), the following result was obtained:
$Z = 2.742$.
Then
$|Z| > 1.96 (= Z_{0.05})$.

Therefore, H_0 was rejected and H_1 was accepted because Z was included in the critical region. This means that there was a significant difference in the incorrect answer rates between Group B and Group C when the level of significance was set at 0.05. The incorrect answer rate of Js (Group B) was lower than BEs (Group C).

(4) Higher "*ev*ery" in Sentence 1

Table 5.22 shows the result of the numbers of correct and incorrect answers by Js (Group B) and BEs (Group C) when "*ev*ery" was set to higher in F_0.

Table 5.20 Correct and incorrect answer rates by Js (Group B) and BEs (Group C) when "*every*" was set to higher in F_0

every	Correct answer	Incorrect answer	Total	Incorrect answer rate(%)	Correct answer rate(%)
B	542	38	580	6.6%	93.4%
C	168	12	180	6.7%	93.3%

Entering the result of Table 5.5 in formulae (5.9) and (5.10), the following result was obtained:
$p_B=0.066$.
$p_C=0.067$.

        Null hypothesis $H_0 : p_1=p_2$ (There is no difference in the incorrect answer rates between Group B and Group C.)
        Alternative hypothesis $H_1 : p_1 \neq p_2$ (There is a difference in the incorrect answer rates between Group B and Group C.)
Where $Z_{0.05}=1.96$.
Here, $n_1=580$, $x_1/n_1=0.066$, $n_2=180$, $x_2/n_2=0.067$. Entering these values in the formula (5.11), the following result was obtained:
$Z=0.054$.
Then
$|Z| <1.96 (=Z_{0.05})$.

Therefore, H_0 was accepted. There was no significant difference in the incorrect answer rates between Group B and Group C when the level of significance was set at 0.05.

(5) Higher "*kind*" in Sentence 1
Table 5.23 shows the result of the numbers of correct and incorrect answers by Js (Group B) and BEs (Group C) when "*kind*" was set to higher in F_0.

Table 5.21 Correct and incorrect answer rates by Js (Group B) and BEs (Group C) when "*kind*" was set to higher in F_0

kind	Correct answer	Incorrect answer	Total	Incorrect answer rate(%)	Correct answer rate(%)
B	567	13	580	2.2%	97.8%
C	162	18	180	10.0%	90.0%

Entering the result of Table 5.5 in formulae (5.9) and (5.10), the following result was obtained:
$p_B=0.022$.
$p_C=0.100$.

Null hypothesis $H_0 : p_1=p_2$ (There is no difference in the incorrect answer rates between Group B and Group C.)
Alternative hypothesis $H_1 : p_1 \neq p_2$ (There is a difference in the incorrect answer rates between Group B and Group C.)

Where $Z_{0.05}=1.96$.
Here, $n_1=580$, $x_1/n_1=0.022$, $n_2=180$, $x_2/n_2=0.100$. Entering these values in the formula (5.11), the following result was obtained:
$Z=3.346$.
Then
$|Z|>1.96 (=Z_{0.05})$.

Therefore, H_0 was rejected and H_1 was accepted because Z was included in the critical region. This means that there was a significant difference in the incorrect answer rates between Group B and Group C when the level of significance was set at 0.05. The incorrect answer rate of Js (Group B) was lower than BEs (Group C).

(6) Higher "*doom*" in Sentence 2
Table 5.24 shows the result of the numbers of correct and incorrect answers by Js (Group B) and BEs (Group C) when "*doom*" was set to higher in F_0.

Table 5.22 Correct and incorrect answer rates by Js (Group B) and BEs (Group C) when "*doom*" was set to higher in F_0

doom	Correct answer	Incorrect answer	Total	Incorrect answer rate(%)	Correct answer rate(%)
B	331	249	580	42.9%	57.1%
C	136	44	180	24.4%	75.6%

Entering the result of Table 5.24 in formulae (5.9) and (5.10), the following result was obtained:
$p_B=0.429$.
$p_C=0.244$.

Null hypothesis $H_0 : p_1=p_2$ (There is no difference in the incorrect answer rates between Group B and Group C.)
Alternative hypothesis $H_1 : p_1 \neq p_2$ (There is a difference in the incorrect answer rates between Group B and Group C.)

Where $Z_{0.05}=1.96$.
Here, $n_1=580$, $x_1/n_1=0.429$, $n_2=180$, $x_2/n_2=0.244$. Entering these values in the formula (5.11), the following result was obtained:
$Z=4.857$.
Then

$|Z|>1.96$ ($=Z_{0.05}$).

Therefore, H_0 was rejected and H_1 was accepted because Z was included in the critical region. This means that there was a significant difference in the incorrect answer rates between Group B and Group C when the level of significance was set at 0.05. The incorrect answer rate of BEs (Group C) was lower than Js (Group B).

(7) No stressed words ('steady') in Sentence 2
Table 5.25 shows the result of the numbers of correct and incorrect answers by Js (Group B) and BEs (Group C) when they listened to the synthesized utterance where F_0 was decreased uniformly ('steady') in Sentence 2.

Table 5.23 Correct and incorrect answer rates by Js (Group B) and BEs (Group C) when F_0 was decreased uniformly ('steady') in Sentence 2

'steady'	Correct answer	Incorrect answer	Total	Incorrect answer rate(%)	Correct answer rate(%)
B	511	69	580	11.9%	88.1%
C	140	40	180	22.2%	77.8%

Entering the result of Table 5.5 in formulae (5.9) and (5.10), the following result was obtained:
$p_B=0.119$.
$p_C=0.222$.

   Null hypothesis H_0 : $p_1=p_2$ (There is no difference in the incorrect answer rates between Group B and Group C.)
   Alternative hypothesis H_1 : $p_1 \neq p_2$ (There is a difference in the incorrect answer rates between Group B and Group C.)

Where $Z_{0.05}=1.96$.
Here, $n_1=580$, $x_1/n_1=0.119$, $n_2=180$, $x_2/n_2=0.222$. Entering these values in the formula (5.11), the following result was obtained:
$Z=3.057$.
Then
$|Z|>1.96$ ($=Z_{0.05}$).

Therefore, H_0 was rejected and H_1 was accepted because Z was included in the critical region. This means that there was a significant difference in the incorrect answer rates between Group B and Group C when the level of significance was set at 0.05. The incorrect answer rate of Js (Group B) was lower than BEs (Group C).

5.9 Difference between BEs and Js (words)

(8) Higher "*gloom*" in Sentence 2

Table 5.26 shows the result of the numbers of correct and incorrect answers by Js (Group B) and BEs (Group C) when "*gloom*" was set to higher in F_0.

Table 5.24 Correct and incorrect answer rates by Js (Group B) and BEs (Group C) when "*gloom*" was set to higher in F_0

gloom	Correct answer	Incorrect answer	Total	Incorrect answer rate(%)	Correct answer rate(%)
B	410	170	580	29.3%	70.7%
C	132	48	180	26.7%	73.3%

Entering the result of Table 5.5 in formulae (5.9) and (5.10), the following result was obtained:
$p_B=0.293$.
$p_C=0.267$.

     Null hypothesis $H_0 : p_1=p_2$ (There is no difference in the incorrect answer rates between Group B and Group C.)
     Alternative hypothesis $H_1 : p_1 \neq p_2$ (There is a difference in the incorrect answer rates between Group B and Group C.)

Where $Z_{0.05}=1.96$.
Here, $n_1=580$, $x_1/n_1=0.293$, $n_2=180$, $x_2/n_2=0.267$. Entering these values in the formula (5.11), the following result was obtained:
$Z=0.696$.
Then
$|Z|<1.96 (=Z_{0.05})$.

Therefore, H_0 was accepted. There was no significant difference in the incorrect answer rates between Group B and Group C when the level of significance was set at 0.05.

(9) Higher "Ig*nore*" in Sentence 2

Table 5.27 shows the result of the numbers of correct and incorrect answers by Js (Group B) and BEs (Group C) when "Ig*nore*" was set to higher in F_0.

Table 5.25 Correct and incorrect answer rates by Js (Group B) and BEs (Group C) when "Ig*nore*" was set to higher in F_0

ignore	Correct answer	Incorrect answer	Total	Incorrect answer rate(%)	Correct answer rate(%)
B	519	61	580	10.5%	89.5%
C	148	32	180	17.8%	82.2%

Entering the result of Table 5.5 in formulae (5.9) and (5.10), the following result was obtained:
$p_B=0.105$.
$p_C=0.178$.

    Null hypothesis $H_0 : p_1=p_2$ (There is no difference in the incorrect answer rates between Group B and Group C.)
    Alternative hypothesis $H_1 : p_1 \neq p_2$ (There is a difference in the incorrect answer rates between Group B and Group C.)

Where $Z_{0.05}=1.96$.
Here, $n_1=580$, $x_1/n_1=0.105$, $n_2=180$, $x_2/n_2=0.178$. Entering these values in the formula (5.11), the following result was obtained:
$Z=2.326$.
Then
$|Z|>1.96 (=Z_{0.05})$.

   Therefore, H_0 was rejected and H_1 was accepted because Z was included in the critical region. This means that there was a significant difference in the incorrect answer rates between Group B and Group C when the level of significance was set at 0.05. The incorrect answer rate of Js (Group B) was lower than BEs (Group C).

(10) Summary of Section 5.9
Figures 5.35 and 5.36 show the results of testing whether there was a significant difference in the incorrect answer rates of words between BEs and Js. There was no significant difference in the incorrect answer rates at a level of significance = 0.05 when "*ev*ery" was set to higher in F_0 in Sentence 1. There was a significant difference in the incorrect answer rates between words when other words were set to higher in F_0 and 'steady'. The perception rate of Js was higher than BEs when "A*void*", "*kind*" and "*ev*il" was set to higher in F_0 and 'steady'.

   In Sentence 2, there was no significant difference in the incorrect answer rates when "*gloom*" was set to higher in F_0. There was a significant difference in the incorrect answer rates between words when other words were set to higher in F_0 and 'steady'. The perception rate of Js was higher than BEs when "Ig*nore*" was set to higher in F_0 and 'steady'. When "*doom*" was set to higher in F_0, the perception rate of BEs was higher than Js.

5.9 Difference between BEs and Js (words)

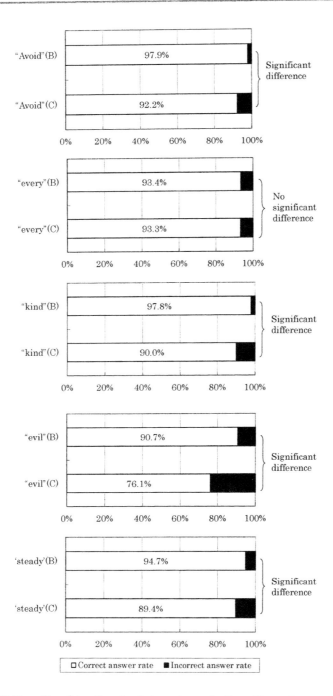

Figure 5.35 Results of testing to determine whether there is a significant difference in the incorrect answer rates of words in Sentence 1 between Js (B) and BEs (C) (The level of significance is 0.05)

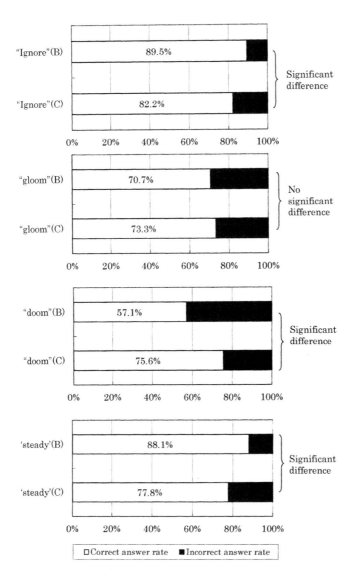

Figure 5.36 Results of testing to determine whether there is a significant difference in the incorrect answer rates of words in Sentence 2 between Js (B) and BEs (C) (The level of significance is 0.05)

5.10 Test of difference in incorrect answer rates of sentences between British subjects and Japanese subjects

A test was carried out to determine whether there was a significant difference in the incorrect answer rates in Sentence 1 between BEs and Js. A

5.10 Difference between BEs and Js (sentences)

test was also carried out to determine whether there was a significant difference in the incorrect answer rates in Sentence 2 between BEs and Js. Table 5.26 and Figure 5.37 show the results of Sentence 1 by BEs and Js. Table 5.27 and Figure 5.38 show the results of Sentence 2 by BEs and Js.

Entering the result of Table 5.26 in the formulae (5.9) and (5.10) described in section 5.9, the following result was obtained:
$p_B=0.051$.
$p_C=0.118$.

  Null hypothesis $H_0 : p_1=p_2$ (There is no difference in the incorrect answer rates between Group B and Group C.)
  Alternative hypothesis $H_1 : p_1 \neq p_2$ (There is a difference in the incorrect answer rates between Group B and Group C.)

Where $Z_{0.05}=1.96$.
Here, $n_1=2900$, $x_1/n_1=0.051$, $n_2=900$, $x_2/n_2=0.118$. Entering these values in the formula (5.11), the following result was obtained:
$|Z|=5.8059$.
Then
$|Z|>1.96 (=Z_{0.05})$.

Therefore, H_0 was rejected and H_1 was accepted. This means that there was a significant difference in the incorrect answer rates in Sentence 1 between BEs and Js when the level of significance was set at 0.05. The number of incorrect answers of Js was fewer than BEs.

Entering the result of Table 5.27 in the formulae (5.9) and (5.10), the following result was obtained:
$p_B=0.237$.
$p_C=0.228$.

  Null hypothesis $H_0 : p1 = p2$ (There is no difference in the incorrect answer rates between Group B and Group C.)
  Alternative hypothesis $H_1 : p1 \neq p2$ (There is a difference in the incorrect answer rates between Group B and Group C.)

Where $Z_{0.05}=1.96$.
Here, $n_1=2320$, $x_1/n_1=0.237$, $n_2=720$, $x_2/n_2=0.228$. Entering these values in the formula (5.11), the following result was obtained:
$|Z|=0.4936$.
Then
$|Z|<1.96 (=Z_{0.05})$.

Therefore, H_0 was accepted. This means that there was no significant difference in the incorrect answer rates in Sentence 2 between BEs and Js when the level of significance was set at 0.05.

Table 5.26 The incorrect answer rates of Sentence 1 by Js and BEs

Sentence 1	Correct answer	Incorrect answer	Total	Incorrect answer rate (p)	Correct answer rate (1-p)
Js (Group B)	2752	148	2900	5.1%	94.9%
BEs (Group C)	794	106	900	11.8%	88.2%

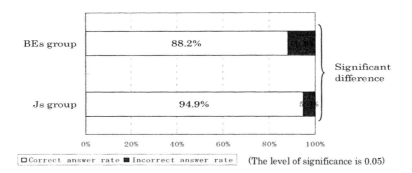

Figure 5.37 Results of testing to determine whether there is a significant difference in the incorrect answer rates in Sentence 1 between Js and BEs

Table 5.27 The incorrect answer rates of Sentence 2 by Js and BEs

Sentence 2	Correct answer	Incorrect answer	Total	Incorrect answer rate (p)	Correct answer rate (1-p)
Js (Group B)	1771	549	2320	23.7%	76.3%
BEs (Group C)	556	164	720	22.8%	77.2%

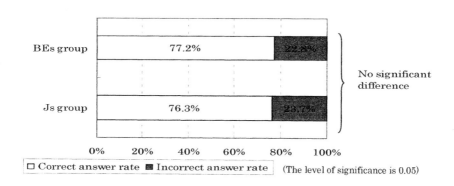

Figure 5.38 Results of testing to determine whether there is a significant difference in the incorrect answer rates in Sentence 2 between Js and BEs

5.11 Test of difference in incorrect answer rates between American subjects, Japanese subjects and British subjects (total of Sentence 1 and Sentence 2)

A test was carried out to determine whether there was a significant difference in the incorrect answer rates between AEs, Js and BEs. Table 5.28 shows the result of tallying up their incorrect answer rates and perception rates.

Entering the results of AEs and BEs from Table 5.28 into the formulae (5.9) and (5.10) described in section 5.9, the following result was obtained:
$p_A=0.142$.
$p_C=0.167$.

Null hypothesis $H_0 : p_1=p_2$ (There is no difference in the incorrect answer rate between Group A and Group C.)

Alternative hypothesis $H_1 : p_1 \neq p_2$ (There is a difference in the incorrect answer rate between Group A and Group C.)

Where $Z_{0.05}=1.96$.
Here, $n_1=5220$, $x_1/n_1=0.134$, $n_2=1620$, $x_2/n_2=0.167$. Entering these values in the formula (5.11), the following result was obtained:
$|Z|=2.019$.
Then
$|Z|>1.96 (=Z_{0.05})$.

Therefore, H_0 was rejected and H_1 was accepted. This means that there was a significant difference in the incorrect answer rates between AEs and BEs when the level of significance was set at 0.05. The number of incorrect answers of AEs was smaller than BEs.

Table 5.28 Comparison of the incorrect answer rates between AEs, Js and BEs (Total of Sentence 1 and Sentence 2)

Subjects	Correct answer	Incorrect answer	Total	Incorrect answer rate (p)	Correct answer rate (1-p)
AEs (Group A)	1,545	255	1,800	14.2%	85.8%
Js (Group B)	4,523	697	5,220	13.4%	86.6%
BEs (Group C)	1,350	270	1,620	16.7%	83.3%
Total	7,418	1,222	8,640	14.1%	85.9%

Next, entering the results of Js and BEs from Table 5.28 into the formulae (5.9) and (5.10), the following result was obtained:

$p_B = 0.134$.
$p_C = 0.167$.

    Null hypothesis $H_0 : p_1 = p_2$ (There is no difference in the incorrect answer rate between Group B and Group C.)
    Alternative hypothesis $H_1 : p_1 \neq p_2$ (There is a difference in the incorrect answer rate between Group B and Group C.)

Where $Z_{0.05} = 1.96$.
Here, $n_1 = 5220$, $x_1/n_1 = 0.134$, $n_2 = 1620$, $x_2/n_2 = 0.167$. Entering these values in the formula (5.11), the following result was obtained:
$|Z| = 3.191$.
Then
$|Z| > 1.96 \, (= Z_{0.05})$.

Therefore, H_0 was rejected and H_1 was accepted. This means that there was a significant difference in the incorrect answer rates between Js and BEs when the level of significance was set at 0.05. The number of incorrect answers of Js was smaller than BEs.

Section 4.6 considered whether there was a significant difference in the perception rates between AEs (Group A) and Js (Group B) from Table 4.20 titled as "Comparison of the incorrect answer rates between AEs and Js (Total of Sentence 1 and Sentence 2)". The result showed that there was no significant difference between them at the 0.05 significance level.

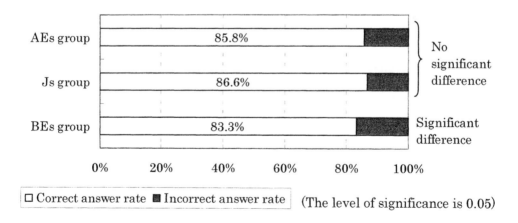

Figure 5.39 The significant difference in perception rates between AEs, Js and BEs

Figure 5.39 shows that in this experiment where the utterance by an AE was synthesized, there was no significant difference in the perception rates between AEs and Js. However, there were significant differences in the perception rates between both AEs (Group A) and BEs (Group C) and between Js (Group B) and BEs (Group C). The perception rates of both AEs and Js were higher than BEs.

The reason that the perception rate of BEs was slightly less than AEs may be that the variation in F_0 of synthesized utterance was less than ordinary variation in F_0 used by BEs, so that it was hard for them to perceive sentence stress in the synthesized utterance.

5.12 Summary

Forty native speakers of American English (AEs), 116 Japanese learners of English (Js) and 36 native speakers of British English (BEs) listened to synthesized utterances where the F_0 parameter was changed. The result of this experiment showed that an average of 85.8% of AEs, 86.6% of Js and 83.3% of BEs perceived sentence stress on the higher syllables in F_0. On average, 85.9% of all subjects perceived stress on the higher syllables in F_0. This indicates that the variation in F_0 is a key factor in perceiving sentence stress for AEs, Js and BEs.

There was no significant difference between AEs and Js at a level of significance = 0.05. However, there was a significant difference in the perception rates between AEs and BEs and between BEs and Js at the 0.05 significance level. The reason that the perception rate of BEs was less than AEs is considered that the variation in F_0 of synthesized utterances was less than ordinary variation in F_0 used by BEs, so that it seemed to be hard for them to perceive sentence stress in the synthesized utterances. Deutsch (1994:130) states that 'it is reasonable to assume from the existing data that the overall pitch range for British English speech is higher than that for Californian speech.'

This result suggests that when talking to BEs, it is probably better to make the F_0 range wider than when talking to AEs.

6 Relationship between perception of pitch change in speech and ability to distinguish pitch levels in music

6.1 Introduction

In the experiment undertaken in Chapter 3, the utterances were synthesized in nine different ways depending on where the higher pitch (F_0) syllable was placed. Forty native speakers of American English (AEs) were asked to listen to nine types of synthesized utterances five times at random and an average of 85.8% subjects perceived stress on the higher syllable in F_0. This indicated that the F_0 parameter was one of the key factors in perceiving sentence stress in English.

In the experiment undertaken in Chapters 4 and 5, 116 Japanese learners of English (Js) and 36 native speakers of British English (BEs) listened to the same synthesized utterance five times at random and an average of 86.6% of Js and 83.3% of BEs perceived stress on the higher syllable in F_0. This means that an average of 13.4% of Js and 16.7% of BEs did not perceive stress on the higher syllable in F_0.

The possible reasons that subjects did not perceive stress were considered as follows:

(1) The utterance time of higher word in F_0 in the synthesized utterance was shorter than with the natural stress. As the longest word and the higher F_0 word were separate in the synthesized utterance, it seems to be perceived either to have two words that were stressed, or to have "no stress" because no one word was perceived to stand out (Chapter 3).
(2) The variation of F_0 was too small to perceive stress (Chapter 5).
(3) The synthesized utterances in which F_0 was changed were hard to hear because it was different from natural human utterances.
(4) Subjects could not perceive the changes in F_0.

In this chapter, the writer focuses on the fourth cause. Do some people find it difficult to perceive F_0 changes? The writer hypothesizes that subjects who were unable to perceive fundamental frequency (pitch, F_0) changes in synthesized utterances would also have difficulty in distinguishing between high and low pitches in music.

In this chapter, we examine whether there is a relationship between the ability to distinguish between high and low pitch in music and the ability to perceive F_0 variations in synthesized utterances. Two statements and two questions of a native speaker of American English were synthesized using speech processing software Praat. The F_0 parameter was controlled in each sentence. Eighty-one Japanese learners of English listened to 88 synthesized utterances and 72 piano tones at controlled pitch levels. The correlation between the ability to distinguish between pitch levels in music and the ability to perceive the prominent pitch change in speech is examined.

6.2. Purpose

The purpose of this experiment is to examine the relationship between the ability to perceive the pitch (F_0) change in synthesized utterances and the ability to distinguish between pitch levels in music.

6.3 Experiment 1

A specialist in music was asked to develop a test to measure the ability to distinguish between high and low pitch in music. Eighteen kinds of 5 high and low tone rows (abbreviated as 5 tones) and eighteen kinds of 6 high and low tone rows (abbreviated as 6 tones) were played on the piano. Only one tone was the highest in each row. They were recorded on a mini disk (MD). All of the sounds were digitized (16 bits; speed: 11.025 KHz) and stored. The output for the sounds maintained the same precision using a D/A converter (16bits; speed: 11.025 KHz). Eighteen kinds of 5 tones were recorded twice each in random order (Table 6.3 (1), p.205) and eighteen kinds of 6 tones were recorded twice each in random order (Table 6.3 (2)) on a micro disk. From 1 to 6 in Table 6.3 show the highest sound in each tone row. For example, "1" means the first tone is the highest, "2" means the second tone is the highest and "6" means the sixth tone is the highest in each row.

The scale used in this experiment is from the Center C to an octave higher C. The tone rows from 1) to 3) in Table 6.3 (1) are illustrated from 1) to 3) in Figure 6.1 (1) and the tone rows from 1) to 3) in Table 6.3 (2) are illustrated from 1) to 3) in Figure 6.1 (2).

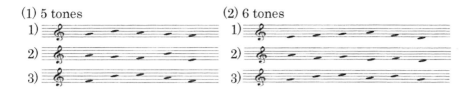

Figure 6.1 Examples of piano tones

6.4 Experiment 2

One male native speaker of American English (informant A1) and one male native speaker of British English (informant B1) were asked to utter two statements, a yes-no question, and a wh question. "You may go in now.", "I always knew you were alive.", "Are you all well?", and "Now where are we going?", with emphasis placed each time on a different word. These four sentences were used to synthesize because they contained only the voiced phonemes. Voiceless phonemes interrupt the smooth contours on the time axis.

These sentences were cited from conversations in movies. The contexts were as follows.

(1) ALL: Oh, how do you solve a problem like Maria?
ALL: How do you hold a moonbeam in your hand?
Margaretta: <u>You may go in now</u>, Maria.
Mother Abbess: Come here, my child. (Lehman 1996: 16)

(2) KELLY: Chuck! Chuck!
KELLY: <u>I always knew you were alive.</u> I knew it.
But everybody said I had to stop saying that… (Broyles 2001: 126)

(3) BROR: … <u>Are you all well?</u>
KAREN: They say I'm cured. I won't have children. (Luedtke 1991: 38)

(4) NICOLE: <u>Now where are we going?</u>
SIMON: My apartment. (Harashima 2002: 50)

"You may go in now." is abbreviated as Statement 1, "I always knew you were alive." is abbreviated as Statement 2, "Are you all well?" is abbreviated as Question 1 and "Now where are we going?" is abbreviated as Question 2.

Though twenty kinds of utterances by two native speakers were recorded on a mini disk (see Table 7.1 below, p.217), only the following four

utterances by informant A1 were synthesized.
- "You may go in **NOW**." (Statement 1)
- "I **AL**ways knew you were alive." (Statement 2)
- "Are you all **WELL**?" (Question 1)
- "Now **WHERE** are we going?" (Question 2)

These utterances were used because F_0 movements were relatively bigger than other utterances. Capitalized and bold letters show the stressed syllables.

When emphatic stress was placed on "**NOW**" in Statement 1, "**NOW**" was uttered at a frequency 26.9 Hz higher than the preceding syllable, "in" by informant A1 and 55.5 Hz higher by informant B1.

Forty-four stimulus types of synthesized utterances were produced from four recorded utterances by informant A1 with speech processing software Praat. The F_0 parameter was changed so that one high-F_0 syllable was produced in each sentence. The utterance time and intensity were not changed.

The output for the 44 synthesized digitized speech signals maintained the same precision using a D/A converter (16 bits; speed: 11.025 KHz). They were divided between statements (Table 6.1, p.204) and questions (Table 6.2, p.205), which are separately recorded twice in random order on an audio magnetic disk.

The following is an example of how to synthesize Statement 1, "You may go in **NOW**."

Figure 6.2 shows the contour of the utterance stressed on "**NOW**" by informant A1. At first, F_0 was decreased uniformly from the beginning to the end (Figure 6.4). Figure 6.5 shows an illustration of F_0 contour in Figure 6.4 with the value of F_0. The utterance by informant A1 begins at 121.2 Hz and ends at 80.8 Hz (Figure 6.2), so that the beginnings of eleven contours in Statement 1 were set to 121.2 Hz and the ends of them were set to 80.8 Hz (Figure 6.5, p.202 and Figures 6.16 to 6.25, p.206).

Stressed syllable, "**NOW**" was uttered at a frequency 26.9 Hz higher than the preceding syllable, "in" by informant A1, so that the high-syllables, "*You*" in Figure 6.6, "*may*" in Figure 6.8, "*go*" in Figure 6.10, "*in*" in Figure 6.12, and "*now*" in Figure 6.14 were set to 26.9 Hz higher than the preceding syllables, respectively, on the basis of Figure 6.4. Figure 6.16, Figure 6.18, Figure 6.20, Figure 6.22, and Figure 6.24 show illustrations of F_0 contours. Underlined and italic letters show the syllables which were set to higher in F_0.

In order to examine whether the perception rate was higher where the F_0 variation was greater, larger F_0 variation of speech was also synthesized, respectively.

Stressed syllable, "**NOW**" was uttered at a frequency 55.5 Hz higher than the preceding syllable by informant B1 (Figure 6.3), so that the high-syllables, "*You*" in Figure 6.7, "*may*" in Figure 6.9, "*go*" in Figure 6.11, "*in*" in Figure 6.13, and "*now*" in Figure 6.15 were set to 55.5 Hz higher than the preceding syllables one by one. Figure 6.17, Figure 6.19, Figure 6.21, Figure 6.23, and Figure 6.25 show illustrations of F_0 contours. The F_0 variations uttered by informant A1 were defined as "small variation" and the F_0 variations uttered by informant B1 were defined as "large variation".

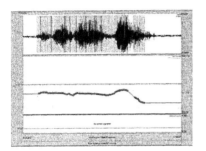

Figure 6.2 F_0 contour and waveform of A1 stressed on "**NOW**"

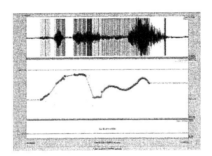

Figure 6.3 F_0 contour and waveform of B1 stressed on "**NOW**"

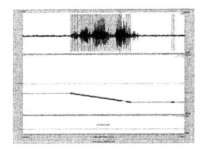

Figure 6.4 No prominent synthesized contour

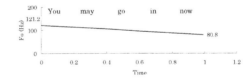

Figure 6.5 Illustration of contour in Figure 6.4

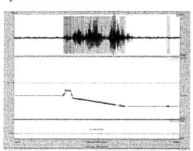

Figure 6.6 "*You*" is set to 26.9 Hz higher

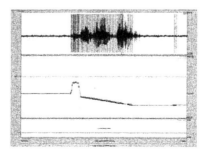

Figure 6.7 "*You*" is set to 55.5 Hz higher

204 Perception of pitch change in speech and pitch levels in music

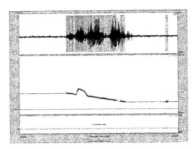

Figure 6.8 "_may_" is set to 26.9 Hz higher than "you"

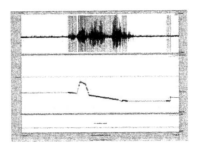

Figure 6.9 "_may_" is set to 55.5 Hz higher than "you"

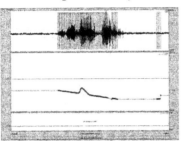

Figure 6.10 "_go_" is set to 26.9 Hz higher than "may"

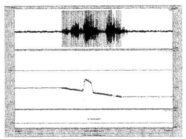

Figure 6.11 "_go_" is set to 55.5 Hz higher than "may"

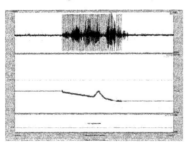

Figure 6.12 "_in_" is set to 26.9 Hz higher than "go"

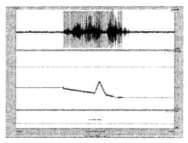

Figure 6.13 "_in_" is set to 55.5 Hz higher than "go"

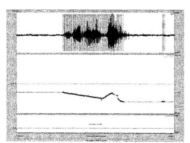

Figure 6.14 "_now_" is set to 26.9 Hz higher than "in"

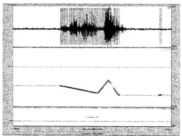

Figure 6.15 "_now_" is set to 55.5 Hz higher than "in"

Table 6.1 List of recorded synthesized utterances: Statement 1 and Statement 2

Examples	Prominent
i You may go *in* now.	small
ii I always knew you *were* alive.	small
iii I always knew you were alive.	no

#	Utterance	Prominent	#	Utterance	Prominent
1	You may *go* in now.	small	25	You may go *in* now.	large
2	I always knew you were a*live*.	large	26	I *al*ways knew you were alive.	small
3	You may go in *now*.	large	27	*You* may go in now.	small
4	*I* always knew you were alive.	large	28	I always knew you were a*live*.	small
5	*You* may go in now.	large	29	*I* always knew you were alive.	small
6	I always *knew* you were alive.	large	30	You *may* go in now.	large
7	I *al*ways knew you were alive.	large	31	I always *knew* you were alive.	small
8	You may go in now.	no	32	I always knew you were alive.	no
9	I always knew you were a*live*.	small	33	You may *go* in now.	small
10	You *may* go in now.	large	34	You may go *in* now.	large
11	*I* always knew you were alive.	large	35	I always knew you *were* alive.	large
12	I always knew you *were* alive.	large	36	You *may* go in now.	small
13	I *al*ways knew you were alive.	small	37	I always knew you were a*live*.	large
14	I always *knew* you were alive.	large	38	I always knew you were alive.	no
15	You may *go* in now.	large	39	You may go *in* now.	small
16	I always knew *you* were alive.	small	40	I always knew *you* were alive.	large
17	You *may* go in now.	small	41	*You* may go in now.	small
18	I always knew you *were* alive.	small	42	You may go in *now*.	small
19	*You* may go in now.	large	43	You may *go* in now.	large
20	I *al*ways knew you were alive.	large	44	You may go in now.	no
21	You may go in *now*.	large	45	I always knew *you* were alive.	large
22	I always *knew* you were alive.	small	46	You may go *in* now.	small
23	I always knew you *were* alive.	small	47	You may go in *now*.	small
24	I always knew *you* were alive.	small	48	*I* always knew you were alive.	small

Note: Underlined and italic letters show the syllables which were set to higher in Fo.

Table 6.2 List of recorded synthesized utterances: Question 1 and Question 2

	Examples	Prominent
i	Are *you* all well?	small
ii	Now where *are* we going?	small
iii	Now where are we going?	no

1	Now where are *we* going?	small	21	*Now* where are we going?	large
2	Are you all *well*?	large	22	Are you *all* well?	small
3	Now where are we *go*ing?	small	23	Now where are *we* going?	large
4	*Are* you all well?	large	24	Are you all *well*?	small
5	Now where *are* we going?	small	25	Are you all well?	no
6	*Now* where are we going?	large	26	Now where are *we* going?	large
7	Are you all *well*?	small	27	Now where *are* we going?	large
8	Now *where* are we going?	large	28	*Now* where are we going?	small
9	Are *you* all well?	small	29	Now where *are* we going?	large
10	*Are* you all well?	small	30	Now *where* are we going?	small
11	Now where are we *go*ing?	large	31	Are you all *well*?	large
12	Now where are *we* going?	small	32	Now where are we going?	no
13	Are you *all* well?	large	33	Are *you* all well?	large
14	Now where *are* we going?	small	34	Now where are we *go*ing?	small
15	Are *you* all well?	small	35	*Are* you all well?	large
16	Now *where* are we going?	large	36	Now where are we going?	no
17	*Are* you all well?	small	37	Now *where* are we going?	small
18	Are you *all* well?	small	38	Are *you* all well?	large
19	Now where are we *go*ing?	large	39	Are you *all* well?	large
20	Are you all well?	no	40	*Now* where are we going?	small

Note: Underlined and italic letters show the syllables which were set to higher in Fo.

Table 6.3 List of piano tones
(1) 5   (2) 6

1)	2	1)	4
2)	4	2)	1
3)	3	3)	3
4)	1	4)	1
5)	5	5)	2
6)	5	6)	6
7)	1	7)	3
8)	3	8)	5
9)	2	9)	2
10)	5	10)	6
11)	4	11)	1
12)	4	12)	5
13)	5	13)	1
14)	4	14)	2
15)	2	15)	5
16)	3	16)	2
17)	3	17)	4
18)	1	18)	4
19)	4	19)	1
20)	1	20)	1
21)	5	21)	6
22)	3	22)	5
23)	5	23)	6
24)	4	24)	5
25)	4	25)	2
26)	3	26)	2
27)	1	27)	4
28)	2	28)	4
29)	3	29)	3
30)	5	30)	2
31)	1	31)	3
32)	2	32)	2
33)	4	33)	1
34)	5	34)	1
35)	2	35)	5
36)	3	36)	4

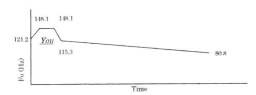

Figure 6.16 Illustration of contour in Figure 6.6

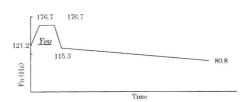

Figure 6.17 Illustration of contour in Figure 6.7

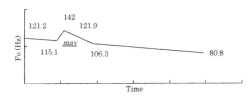

Figure 6.18 Illustration of contour in Figure 6.8

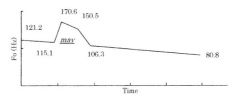

Figure 6.19 Illustration of contour in Figure 6.9

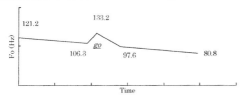

Figure 6.20 Illustration of contour in Figure 6.10

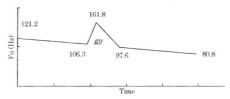

Figure 6.21 Illustration of contour in Figure 6.11

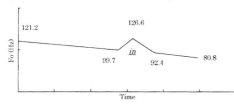

Figure 6.22 Illustration of contour in Figure 6.12

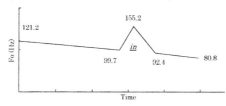

Figure 6.23 Illustration of contour in Figure 6.13

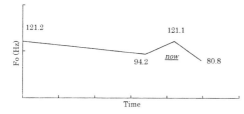

Figure 6.24 Illustration of contour in Figure 6.14

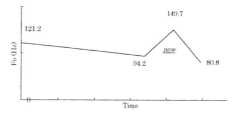

Figure 6.25 Illustration of contour in Figure 6.15

Statement 2, Question 1 and Question 2 uttered by informant A1 are synthesized in the same way as Statement 1.

The high-syllables in Statement 2 were set to 41.6 Hz (small variation) and 94.3 Hz (large variation) higher than the preceding syllables, respectively, because when emphatic stress was placed on "**AL-**", "**AL-**" was uttered at a frequency 41.6 Hz higher than the preceding syllable by informant A1 and 94.3 Hz higher by informant B1.

The high-syllables in Question 1 were set to 23.2 Hz (small variation) and 59.4 Hz (large variation) higher than the preceding syllables, respectively, because when emphatic stress was placed on "**WELL**", "**WELL**" was uttered at a frequency 23.2 Hz higher than the preceding syllable by informant A1 and 59.4 Hz higher by informant B1.

The high-syllables in Question 2 were set to 53.9 Hz (small variation) and 103 Hz (large variation) higher than the preceding syllables, respectively, because when emphatic stress was placed on "**WHERE**", "**WHERE**" was uttered at a frequency 53.9 Hz higher than the preceding syllable by informant A1 and 103 Hz higher by informant B1. These synthesized F_0 variations in Hz are shown in Table 6.4.

Table 6.4 List of synthesized F_0 variations in Hz

	small variation (Hz)	large variation (Hz)
Statement 1: "You may go in **NOW**."	26.9	55.5
Statement 2: "I **AL**ways knew you were alive."	41.6	94.3
Question 1: "Are you all **WELL**?"	23.2	59.4
Question 2: "Now **WHERE** are we going?"	53.9	103.0

6.5 Method

Eighty-one Japanese learners of English, 28 males and 53 females (18 to 29 years), were given the questionnaire illustrated in Figure 6.26 and asked to listen to 72 piano tones (Table 6.3) and 88 synthesized utterances shown in Table 6.1 and Table 6.2. The piano tones were generated by a specialist in music in order to measure the music ability to distinguish between high and low pitch in music. The synthesized utterances (48 statements and 40 questions) were produced with one or no prominent high-F_0 syllable in each utterance using speech processing software Praat.

All subjects indicated which piano tone was the highest in each tone row (Figure 6.26, II) and chose either one prominent / emphasized word or, if there was no prominent / emphasized word, chose 'no prominent word' in synthesized utterances (Figure 6.26, I).

6.5 Method

Name	
Age	10's 20's 30's 40's 50's 60's 70's
Sex	Male Female
Educational Background	High school Vocational School College Graduate School
Major	
Have you ever learned to play an instrument?	Yes No
Have you ever learned *solfeggio*?	Yes No

A tape will be played once. After listening to the tape, please select one word (I) or one number (II) for each question.

Example
  I 1) You / will / never / be / (one) / of / them. // "no prominent word"
    2) These / animals l / are / driving / me / crazy. // ("no prominent word")
  II 1) 1 — 2 — 3 — 4 — (5)
    2) 1 — (2) — 3 — 4 — 5

I(1) Please listen to the following sentences and circle one prominent or emphasized word in each sentence. If there is no prominent or emphasized word in a sentence, please circle "no prominent word". Please listen to the following 3 examples:
  i. You / may / go / in / now. // "no prominent word"
  ii. I / always / knew / you / were / alive.// "no prominent word"
  iii. I / always / knew / you / were / alive.// "no prominent word"
Let's start.
1) You / may / go / in / now. // "no prominent word"
2) I / always / knew / you / were / alive. // "no prominent word"
⋮
48) I / always / knew / you / were / alive. // "no prominent word"

I(2) Please listen to the following sentences and circle one prominent or emphasized word in each sentence. If there is no prominent or emphasized word in a sentence, circle "no prominent word". Listen to the following 3 examples:
  i. Are / you / all / well? // "no prominent word"
  ii. Now / where / are / we / going? // "no prominent word"
  iii. Now / where / are / we / going? // "no prominent word"
Let's start.
1) Now / where / are / we / going? // "no prominent word"
2) Are / you / all / well? // "no prominent word"
⋮
40) Now / where / are / we / going? // "no prominent word"

II(1) Please circle which of the 5 tones you think is the highest tone. Listen to the following 3 examples:
  i. 1 — 2 — 3 — 4 — 5
  ii. 1 — 2 — 3 — 4 — 5
  iii. 1 — 2 — 3 — 4 — 5
Let's start.
1) 1 — 2 — 3 — 4 — 5
2) 1 — 2 — 3 — 4 — 5
⋮
36) 1 — 2 — 3 — 4 — 5

II(2) Please circle which of the 1 to 6 tones you think is the highest tone. Listen to the following 3 examples:
  i. 1 — 2 — 3 — 4 — 5 — 6
  ii. 1 — 2 — 3 — 4 — 5 — 6
  iii. 1 — 2 — 3 — 4 — 5 — 6
Let's start.
1) 1 — 2 — 3 — 4 — 5 — 6
2) 1 — 2 — 3 — 4 — 5 — 6
⋮
36) 1 — 2 — 3 — 4 — 5 — 6

Thank you very much for participating in this research.

Figure 6.26 Questionnaire

Then the perception rates of piano tones and synthesized utterances were analyzed.

6.6 Analysis

Table 6.5 shows the perception rates of piano tones and perception rates of synthesized utterances by 81 subjects. The perception rate of the synthesized statements was 54.9%, of the questions was 57.3%, and of the average was 56.0%. The perception rate of 5 piano tones was 85.5%, of 6 piano tones was 69.4%, and of the average was 77.5%.

Table 6.5 Perception rates of piano tones and of synthesized utterances

Perception rates of synthesized utterances			Perception rates of piano tones		
Statements	Questions	Average	5 tones	6 tones	Average
54.9%	57.3%	56.0%	85.5%	69.4%	77.5%

6.6.1 Correlation coefficient between the perception rates of piano tones and the perception rates of synthesized utterances

Table 6.6 shows the perception rates of the highest piano tone on the horizontal axis (x) and the perception rates of the prominent / emphasized word in synthesized utterances on the vertical axis (y). This means, for example, among the subjects whose perception rates of the piano tone are 100%, there are 2 subjects whose perception rates of the synthesized utterances are 80%, there are 2 subjects whose perception rates of the synthesized utterances are 70%, and there is 1 subject whose perception rate of the synthesized utterances is 40%. Table 6.7 shows the result of calculating the equations from (1) to (7) to analyze the distribution in Table 6.6 (see Inagaki, et al., 1996: 40-44).

6.6 Analysis

Table 6.6 Distribution of perception rates of piano tones and of synthesized utterances

Perception rates of synthesized utterances y	v \ u	Perception rates of piano tones x	10 / -7	20 / -6	30 / -5	40 / -4	50 / -3	60 / -2	70 / -1	80 / 0	90 / 1	100 / 2
10	-5					2	1					
20	-4							2	1			
30	-3						1	2		2		
40	-2				1	1	2	6	1	3	1	1
50	-1						1	6	3	6	5	
60	0						1	2	4	3	7	
70	1						1	1		1	5	2
80	2										3	2
90	3										1	

$$\begin{cases} f_{.j} = \sum_{i=1}^{k} f_{ij}, & f_{i.} = \sum_{j=1}^{l} f_{ij} \\ \\ n = \sum_{j=1}^{l} \sum_{i=1}^{k} f_{ij} = \sum_{j=1}^{l} f_{.j} = \sum_{i=1}^{k} \sum_{j=1}^{l} f_{ij} = \sum_{i=1}^{k} f_{i.} \\ \\ X_j = \sum_{i=1}^{k} f_{ij} x_i, & Y_i = \sum_{j=1}^{l} f_{ij} y_j \end{cases} \quad (1)$$

For Table 6.6 where $k = 10$, $l = 9$, and $n = 81$, are entered in equation (1). To facilitate the calculation, the following variable transformation is used.

$$\begin{cases} x_i = x_0 + a u_i \\ y_j = y_0 + b v_j \end{cases} \quad (2)$$

For convenience, $x_0 = 80$, $a = 10$, $y_0 = 60$, and $b = 10$ are set in equation (2).

$$\begin{cases} T_u = \sum_{i=1}^{k} f_{i\cdot} u_i \\ \\ T_v = \sum_{j=1}^{l} f_{\cdot j} v_j \\ \\ \bar{u} = T_u/n \\ \\ \bar{v} = T_v/n \end{cases} \quad (3)$$

Table 6.7 The analysis result of Table 6.6

Perception rates of synthesized utterances y	Perception rates of piano tones x	v \ u	10	20	30	40	50	60	70	80	90	100	$f_{\cdot j}$	$f_{\cdot j} v_j$	$f_{\cdot j} v_j^2$	$U_j = \Sigma f_{ij} u_i$	$v_j U_j$
			-7	-6	-5	-4	-3	-2	-1	0	1	2					
10		-5	0	0	0	2	1	0	0	0	0	0	3	-15	75	-11	55
20		-4	0	0	0	0	0	2	1	0	0	0	3	-12	48	-5	20
30		-3	0	0	0	1	2	0	0	2	0	0	5	-15	45	-10	30
40		-2	0	0	1	1	2	6	1	3	1	1	16	-32	64	-25	50
50		-1	0	0	0	0	1	6	3	6	5	0	21	-21	21	-13	13
60		0	0	0	0	0	1	2	4	3	7	0	17	0	0	-4	0
70		1	0	0	0	0	1	1	0	1	5	2	10	10	10	4	4
80		2	0	0	0	0	0	0	0	0	3	2	5	10	20	7	14
90		3	0	0	0	0	0	0	0	0	1	0	1	3	9	1	3
$f_{i\cdot}$			0	0	1	4	8	17	9	15	22	5	81	-72	292	-56	189
$f_{i\cdot} u_i$			0	0	-5	-16	-24	-34	-9	0	22	10	-56				
$f_{i\cdot} u_i^2$			0	0	25	64	72	68	9	0	22	20	280				
$V_i = \Sigma f_{ij} v_j$			0	0	-2	-15	-15	-25	-9	-17	7	4	-72				
$u_i V_i$			0	0	10	60	45	50	9	0	7	8	189				

Here $k=10$, $l=9$, and N=81. Entering these values in equation (3), the following result is obtained:
$T_u = -56$, $T_v = -72$, $\bar{u} = -56/81 = -0.691$, $\bar{v} = -72/81 = -0.889$.
The obtained mean is shown in (4) and the obtained standard deviation is shown in (6.5) and (6.6).

$$\begin{cases} \bar{x} = 80 + 10\bar{u} & (=80+10\times(-0.691)=73.09) \quad \bar{x}=73.09 \\ \\ \bar{y} = 60 + 10\bar{v} & (=60+10\times(-0.889)=51.11) \quad \bar{y}=51.11 \end{cases} \quad (4)$$

$$\begin{cases} s_u^2 = (1/n) \sum_{i=1}^{k} f_{i.} u_i^2 - \bar{u}^2 & (=(1/81) \times 280 - (-0.691)^2 = 2.979) \\ \\ s_x = 10 s_u & (=10 \times (2.979)^{1/2} = 17.3) \qquad s_x = 17.3 \end{cases} \qquad (5)$$

For Table 6.7 where $k=10$, is entered in equation (6.5).

$$\begin{cases} s_v^2 = (1/n) \sum_{j=1}^{l} f_{.j} v_j^2 - \bar{v}^2 & (=(1/81) \times 292 - (-0.889)^2 = 2.815) \\ \\ s_y = 10 s_v & (=10 \times (2.815)^{1/2} = 16.8) \qquad s_y = 16.8 \end{cases} \qquad (6)$$

For Table 6.7 where $l=9$, is entered in equation (6.6).

$$\begin{cases} U_j = \sum_{i=1}^{k} f_{ij} u_i & (=-56) \\ \\ V_i = \sum_{j=1}^{l} f_{ij} v_j & (=-72) \end{cases} \qquad (7)$$

For Table 6.7 where $k=10$ and $l=9$ are entered in equation (7).
Entering the results from equations (1) to (7) in equation (8), the correlation coefficient, r_{xy} in Table 6.6 is obtained as follows. Using both equations in (8), r_{xy} is obtained in order to confirm that the calculation is correct, though either equation can be used in equation (8).

$$r_{xy} = r_{uv} = \{(1/n) \sum_{i=1}^{k} u_i V_i - T_u T_v / n^2\} / s_u s_v \qquad (=\{(1/81) \times 189 - ((-56) \times (-72))/81^2\}/(1.73 \times 1.68)$$
$$= 0.59)$$

$$= \{(1/n) \sum_{j=1}^{l} v_j U_j - T_u T_v / n^2\} / s_u s_v \qquad (=\{(1/81) \times 189 - ((-56) \times (-72))/81^2\}/(1.73 \times 1.68)$$
$$= 0.59)$$

$$r_{xy} = 0.59 \qquad (8)$$

For Table 6.7 where k 10, l =9 and n=81 are entered in equation (8). This result shows that the correlation coefficient between x (the perception rates of piano tones; 10~100) and y (the perception rates of synthesized utterances; 10~90) is r_{xy}* =0.59.

* Correlation coefficient, r_{xy}: Although it is not clearly stated what degree is determined as a high correlation, it is generally accepted that;

      very high correlation : $|r| \geq 0.7$
      high correlation : $0.4 \leq |r| \leq 0.7$
      low correlation : $0.2 \leq |r| \leq 0.4$
      almost no correlation : $|r| \leq 0.2$ (Inagaki, *et al.*, 1996: 40).

6.6.2 Regression line of the perception rates of piano tones and the perception rates of synthesized utterances

A regression line is obtained to show more clearly the correlation coefficient obtained in 6.6.1. The result obtained in 6.6.1 is as follows:
$\bar{x}$=73.09, $\bar{y}$=51.11, r_{xy}=0.59, s_x=17.3, s_y=16.8
For the regression line, y=cx+d   (9)
where
      $c = r_{xy} (s_y / s_x)$
      $d = \bar{y} - c\bar{x}$

Entering the result of 6.6.1 in the above equation, the following result is obtained:

      c=0.59×(16.8/17.3)=0.573.
      d=51.11-0.573×73.09=9.229.

Therefore, the regression line is obtained as follows:

      y=0.573x+9.229.   (10)

The above result (10) is illustrated in Figure 6.27. X indicates the perception rate of piano tones and Y indicates the perception rate of synthesized utterances. This shows that the more ability in music to distinguish between pitch levels subjects have, the higher their perception rate of the F_0 change in synthesized utterances.

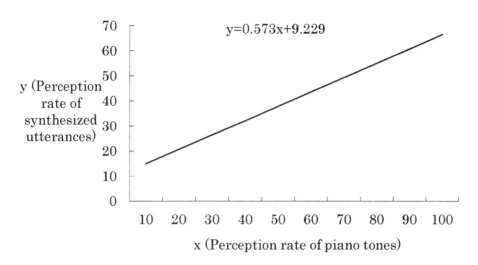

Figure 6.27 Regression line of x and y (Data from Table 6.6)

6.6.3 Test of correlation coefficient between the perception rates of piano tones and the perception rates of synthesized utterances

A test of no correlation (see Inagaki, *et al.*, 1996: 135) was carried out at the level of significance, α= 0.05 to determine whether there was a correlation between x and y in Table 6.6 (see section 6.6.1).
Entering the results of equation (8) (r_{xy}=0.59 and n=81) in the following formula:
$t_{n-2} = r\{(n-2)/(1-r^2)\}^{1/2}$ (t distribution: Degrees of freedom is n−2)

The following result was obtained:
$\quad t_{79} = 0.59[79/\{1-(0.59)^2\}]^{1/2}$
$\quad\quad = 0.59 \times 11.01 = 6.50.$
$\quad t_{0.05,\,79} \fallingdotseq 1.98$ (From the t distribution).
($t_{0.1,\,79} \fallingdotseq 1.658$, $t_{0.01,\,79} \fallingdotseq 2.617$ is obtained from the t distribution.)

Then
$|t_{79}| > t_{0.05,\,79}$.
H_0 was rejected and H_1 was accepted. Therefore, there was a high correlation between x and y at the 5% significance level. (There was also a correlation at the 1% significance level.) This means that subjects who had a better music ability to distinguish between pitch levels more easily perceived the prominent F_0 change in synthesized utterances.

6.7 Summary

The purpose of this chapter is to examine the relationship between the ability to perceive pitch changes in synthesized utterances (changes in fundamental frequency) and music ability (ability to distinguish between pitch levels in music).

The hypothesis is that a subject who is unable to perceive pitch changes in synthesized utterances will also have a lower ability to distinguish between high and low pitches in music. Eighty-one Japanese learners of English listened to synthesized utterances and piano tones at controlled pitch levels.

The perception rates of pitch changes in synthesized utterances and piano tones were analyzed. There was a high correlation between pitch perception in speech and musical pitch sensitivity, with a correlation coefficient of 0.59. This suggests that those who have a good ability to distinguish between high and low pitches in music also tend to have a good ability to perceive pitch changes in synthesized utterances.

7 Relationship between perception of sentence stress and ability to distinguish pitch levels in music

7.1 Introduction

Chapter 6 examined whether there was a relationship between the ability to distinguish between high and low F_0 in music and the ability to perceive F_0 changes in synthesized utterances. The result showed that there was a high correlation between them, with a correlation coefficient of 0.59. Is there also a relationship between music ability and human utterance which is not synthesized utterances?

In the present study in this chapter, 150 Japanese learners of English listened not to synthesized utterances but to 80 utterances by two native speakers of English and 72 piano tones. Then the relationship between the ability to perceive English sentence stress and the ability to distinguish between pitch levels in music was analyzed.

7.2 Purpose

The purpose of this chapter is to examine the relationship of the ability to perceive sentence stress in speech with the ability to distinguish between pitch levels in music.

7.3 Method

In Chapter 6, one male native speaker of American English (informant A1) and one male native speaker of British English (informant B1) were asked to utter two statements, a yes-no question, and a wh question with emphasis placed each time on a different word. Sentences were "You may go in now." (Statement 1), "I always knew you were alive." (Statement 2), "Are you all well?" (Question 1) and "Now where are we going?" (Question 2) (see 6.4, p.200). Twenty kinds of utterances uttered by two native speakers were recorded on a mini disk (see Table 7.1). Capitalized and bold letters show the emphatic syllables. All of the utterances were digitized (16 bits; speed: 11.025 KHz) and stored. The output for the utterances maintained the same precision using a D/A converter. They were divided between statements (Table 7.2 (1)) and questions (Table 7.2 (2)), which are separately recorded twice in random order on an audio magnetic disk. The way the 72 piano tones were developed is described in section 6.3.

Table 7.1 Change of emphasis in test sentences

Statement 1	**YOU** may go in now.
	You **MAY** go in now.
	You may **GO** in now.
	You may go **IN** now.
	You may go in **NOW**.
Statement 2	I always knew you were alive.
	I **AL**ways knew you were alive.
	I always **KNEW** you were alive.
	I always knew **YOU** were alive.
	I always knew you **WERE** alive.
	I always knew you were a**LIVE**.
Question 1	**ARE** you all well?
	Are **YOU** all well?
	Are you **ALL** well?
	Are you all **WELL**?
Question 2	**NOW** where are we going?
	Now **WHERE** are we going?
	Now where **ARE** we going?
	Now where are **WE** going?
	Now where are we **GO**ing?

A group of 150 Japanese learners of English (18 to 29 years old) were examined. All subjects were different from the 81 subjects in Chapter 6 (section 6.5). They were given the questionnaire illustrated in Figure 7.1 and asked to listen to 72 piano tones, which were generated in Chapter 6 (see section 6.3), and 80 utterances with emphasis placed each time on a different word by two native speakers of English (Table 7.2). The perception rate of piano tones and the perception rate of sentence stress uttered by native speakers of English were analyzed.

All subjects indicated which piano tone was the highest in each tone row (Figure 6.26 II) and chose one prominent or emphasized word in each sentence. In this chapter, the questionnaire did not include a 'no prominent word' item (see Figure 7.1).

Table 7.2 List of sentences by native speakers of English
(1) Statement 1 and Statement 2

Examples		Informant
i	You may **GO** in now.	A1
ii	I always **KNEW** you were alive.	B1

1	You may go **IN** now.	A1
2	**YOU** may go in now.	B1
3	**I** always knew you were alive.	A1
4	I always knew **YOU** were alive.	A1
5	You may go **IN** now.	B1
6	I **AL**ways knew you were alive.	A1
7	**YOU** may go in now.	A1
8	**I** always knew you were alive.	B1
9	You may **GO** in now.	A1
10	I always knew **YOU** were alive.	B1
11	You **MAY** go in now.	A1
12	I **AL**ways knew you were alive.	B1
13	I always **KNEW** you were alive.	A1
14	**YOU** may go in now.	B1
15	I always knew you **WERE** alive.	A1
16	You may go in **NOW**.	B1
17	**I** always knew you were alive.	A1
18	You may **GO** in now.	B1
19	You may go in **NOW**.	B1
20	I always knew you were a**LIVE**.	A1
21	You **MAY** go in now.	B1
22	I always **KNEW** you were alive.	A1
23	You may **GO** in now.	A1
24	I always knew you **WERE** alive.	B1
25	You **MAY** go in now.	A1
26	**I** always knew you were alive.	B1
27	You may go in **NOW**.	A1
28	I always knew you were a**LIVE**.	B1
29	You may go **IN** now.	A1
30	I always knew you **WERE** alive.	B1
31	You may **GO** in now.	B1
32	I **AL**ways knew you were alive.	A1
33	You may go in **NOW**.	A1
34	I always knew you were a**LIVE**.	B1
35	You may go **IN** now.	B1
36	I **AL**ways knew you were alive.	B1
37	I always **KNEW** you were alive.	B1
38	I always knew **YOU** were alive.	A1
39	I always knew you were a**LIVE**.	A1
40	I always knew **YOU** were alive.	B1
41	I always knew you **WERE** alive.	A1
42	I always **KNEW** you were alive.	B1
43	You **MAY** go in now.	B1
44	**YOU** may go in now.	A1

(2) Question 1 and Question 2

Examples		Informant
i	Are you **ALL** well?	A1
ii	Now where are we **Going**?	B1

1	Now where are **WE** going?	B1
2	Are you all **WELL**?	B1
3	**NOW** where are we going?	A1
4	Now where are we **GO**ing?	B1
5	**ARE** you all well?	A1
6	Now **WHERE** are we going?	B1
7	Are **YOU** all well?	B1
8	Now where **ARE** we going?	A1
9	Now where are **WE** going?	A1
10	Are **YOU** all well?	B1
11	**NOW** where are we going?	B1
12	Are you **ALL** well?	B1
13	Now where are we **GO**ing?	A1
14	Now where **ARE** we going?	B1
15	Are you **ALL** well?	A1
16	**NOW** where are we going?	A1
17	Are **YOU** all well?	A1
18	Now **WHERE** are we going?	B1
19	**NOW** where are we going?	B1
20	Are you **ALL** well?	B1
21	Now **WHERE** are we going?	A1
22	Now where are we **GO**ing?	B1
23	**ARE** you all well?	A1
24	Are you all **WELL**?	B1
25	Now where are we **GO**ing?	A1
26	Are you **ALL** well?	A1
27	Now where are **WE** going?	A1
28	Now where **ARE** we going?	A1
29	Now **WHERE** are we going?	A1
30	Are **YOU** all well?	A1
31	Are you all **WELL**?	A1
32	Now where **ARE** we going?	B1
33	**ARE** you all well?	B1
34	Now where are **WE** going?	B1
35	Are you all **WELL**?	A1
36	**ARE** you all well?	B1

Note: Capitalized and bold letters show the emphatic syllables in each sentence.

Age	10's 20's 30's 40's over 50
Sex	Male Female
Educational Background	High school Vocational School College Graduate
Have you ever learned to play an instrument?	Yes No
Have you ever learned *solfeggio*?	Yes No

I. Two sentences, "You may go in now." and "I always knew you were alive." will be played repeatedly. Please listen to the 44 sentences and circle one prominent or emphasized word in each sentence. If you select two or more words, your answer will not be counted.   Listen to the following 2 examples:

    i. You / may / go / in / now.
    ii. I / always / knew / you / were / alive.

Let's start.
1. You / may / go / in / now.
2. You / may / go / in / now.
3. I / always / knew / you / were / alive.
⋮
44. You / may / go / in / now.

II. Two sentences, "Are you all well?" and "Now where are we going?" will be played repeatedly. Please listen to the 36 sentences and circle one prominent or emphasized word in each sentence. If you select two or more words, your answer will not be counted.   Listen to the following 2 examples:

    i. Are / you / all / well?
    ii. Now / where / are / we / going?

Let's start.
1. Now / where / are / we / going?
2. Are / you / all / well?
⋮
36. Are / you / all / well?

III. Listen to the 5 tones and circle which of the 5 tones you think is the highest tone. If you select two or more tones, your answer will not be counted.
Please listen to the following 3 examples:
    i. 1—－2—－3—－4—－5
    ii. 1—－2—－3—－4—－5
    iii. 1—－2—－3—－4—－5
Let's start.
1) 1—－2—－3—－4—－5
2) 1—－2—－3—－4—－5
⋮
36) 1—－2—－3—－4—－5

IV. Listen to the 6 tones and circle which of the 6 tones you think is the highest tone. If you select two or more tones, your answer will not be counted.
Please listen to the following 3 examples:
    i. 1—－2—－3—－4—－5—－6
    ii. 1—－2—－3—－4—－5—－6
    iii. 1—－2—－3—－4—－5—－6
Let's start.
1) 1—－2—－3—－4—－5—－6
2) 1—－2—－3—－4—－5—－6
⋮
36) 1—－2—－3—－4—－5—－6

Figure 7.1 Questionnaire

7.4 Analysis

Table 7.3 and Table 7.4 show the results of this experiment by 150 Japanese learners of English. Table 7.3 shows the perception rates of sentence stress uttered by informant A1 and informant B1. The perception rate of the sentence stress in statements uttered by informant A1 was 66.1%, in questions was 66.9%, and on average was 66.4%. The perception rate of the sentence stress in statements uttered by informant B1 was 82.3%, in questions was 83.0%, and on average was 82.7%.

Table 7.4 shows the total perception rates of sentence stress from Table 7.3 and the perception rates of 72 piano tones. The perception rate of statements by the two informants was 74.2% and the perception rate of questions was 74.9%, and their average was 74.5%. The perception rate of 5 piano tones was 84.4%, of 6 piano tones was 72.4%, and of the average was 78.4%.

For reference, the perception rate of 5 piano tones by 81 Japanese learners of English in the previous experiment was 85.5%, the perception rate for 6 piano tones was 69.4%, and their average was 77.5% (see Table 6.5, p.209).

7.4.1 Correlation coefficient between the perception rates of piano tones and the perception rates of sentence stress

Table 7.5 shows the perception rate of the highest piano tone on the horizontal axis (x) and the perception rate of sentence stress on the vertical axis (y). For example, among the subjects whose perception rates of the piano tones are 100%, there are 5 subjects each whose perception rates of sentence stress are 70%, 80%, and 90%. Among the subjects whose perception rates of the piano tone are 90%, 2 subjects' perception rates of sentence stress are 50%, 4 subjects' perception rates are 60%, 7 subjects' perception rates are 70%, 11 subjects' perception rates are 80%, and 6 subjects' perception rates are 90%.

That is, there are 15 subjects whose perception rates for the piano tones are 100%, and all of their perception rates of sentence stress are more than 70%. In addition, among the 30 subjects whose perception rates of the piano tones are 90%, there are 24 subjects whose perception rates of sentence stress are more than 70%.

Table 7.6 shows the result of analyzing the distribution in Table 7.5 (see Inagaki, *et al.*, 1996: 40-44).

222 Perception of sentence stress and pitch levels in music

Table 7.3 Perception rates of sentence stress by 150 Japanese subjects

		Stressed syllables	Correct Answer			Incorrect Answer			Perception rate		
			A1	B1	Total	A1	B1	Total	A1	B1	Total
Statements	1	YOU	219	276	495	81	24	105	73.0%	92.0%	82.5%
		MAY	241	275	516	59	25	84	80.3%	91.7%	86.0%
		GO	240	273	513	60	27	87	80.0%	91.0%	85.5%
		IN	156	228	384	144	72	216	52.0%	76.0%	64.0%
		NOW	204	162	366	96	138	234	68.0%	54.0%	61.0%
		Total	1,060	1,214	2,274	440	286	726	70.7%	80.9%	75.8%
	2	I	87	238	325	213	62	275	29.0%	79.3%	54.2%
		ALways	198	273	471	102	27	129	66.0%	91.0%	78.5%
		KNEW	227	273	500	73	27	100	75.7%	91.0%	83.3%
		YOU	195	227	422	105	73	178	65.0%	75.7%	70.3%
		WERE	165	210	375	135	90	225	55.0%	70.0%	62.5%
		aLIVE	249	282	531	51	18	69	83.0%	94.0%	88.5%
		Total	1,121	1,503	2,624	679	297	976	62.3%	83.5%	72.9%
	Subtotal		2,181	2,717	4,898	1,119	583	1,702	66.1%	82.3%	74.2%
Questions	1	ARE	157	237	394	143	63	206	52.3%	79.0%	65.7%
		YOU	140	268	408	160	32	192	46.7%	89.3%	68.0%
		ALL	254	175	429	46	125	171	84.7%	58.3%	71.5%
		WELL	195	267	462	105	33	138	65.0%	89.0%	77.0%
		Total	746	947	1,693	454	253	707	62.2%	78.9%	70.5%
	2	NOW	264	289	553	36	11	47	88.0%	96.3%	92.2%
		WHERE	216	278	494	84	22	106	72.0%	92.7%	82.3%
		ARE	232	209	441	68	91	159	77.3%	69.7%	73.5%
		WE	228	267	495	72	33	105	76.0%	89.0%	82.5%
		GOing	119	252	371	181	48	229	39.7%	84.0%	61.8%
		Total	1,059	1,295	2,354	441	205	646	70.6%	86.3%	78.5%
	Subtotal		1,805	2,242	4,047	895	458	1,353	66.9%	83.0%	74.9%
Grand total			3,986	4,959	8,945	2,014	1,041	3,055	66.4%	82.7%	74.5%

7.4 Analysis

Table 7.4 Perception rates of sentence stress and of piano tones

				Correct answer	Incorrect answer	Perception rate
Sentences	Statements		1	2,274	726	75.8%
			2	2,624	976	72.9%
			total	4,898	1,702	74.2%
	Questions		1	1,693	707	70.5%
			2	2,354	646	78.5%
			total	4,047	1,353	74.9%
	Total			8,945	3,055	74.5%
Piano tones		5 tones		4,558	842	84.4%
		6 tones		3,909	1,491	72.4%
	Total			8,467	2,333	78.4%

Table 7.5 Distribution of perception rates of piano tones and of sentence stress

Perception rate of sentence stress y	v	Perception rate of piano tones x	u	10 -7	20 -6	30 -5	40 -4	50 -3	60 -2	70 -1	80 0	90 1	100 2
10	-6												
20	-5												
30	-4			1				2					
40	-3					2							
50	-2						3	3	3	2	3	2	
60	-1						5	3	6	5	7	4	
70	0						1	2	6	11	12	7	5
80	1						1	3		11	10	11	5
90	2								1		2	6	5

The correlation coefficient, r_{xy} in Table 7.5 is obtained from the following equation (see Inagaki, et al., 1996: 40-44). Using both equations, r_{xy} is obtained in order to confirm that the calculation is correct, though either equation can be used.

The result shows that the correlation coefficient between x (the perception rate of piano tones; 10~100) and y (the perception rate of sentence stress; 10~90) is $r_{xy}^* = 0.55$.

$$r_{xy} = r_{uv} = \{(1/n) \sum_{i=1}^{k} u_i V_i - T_u T_v / n^2\}/s_u s_v \quad (= \{(1/150) \times 203 - ((-97) \times (-11))/150^2\}/(1.818 \times 1.307) = 0.55)$$

$$= \{(1/n) \sum_{j=1}^{l} v_j U_j - T_u T_v / n^2\}/s_u s_v \quad (= \{(1/150) \times 203 - ((-97) \times (-11))/150^2\}/(1.818 \times 1.307) = 0.55)$$

$r_{xy} = 0.55$

Table 7.6 The analysis result of Table 7.5

Perception rate of sentence stress y	Perception rate of piano tones x	u \ v	10 -7	20 -6	30 -5	40 -4	50 -3	60 -2	70 -1	80 0	90 1	100 2	$f_{.j}$	$f_{.j}v_j$	$f_{.j}v_j^2$	$U_j = \Sigma f_{ij}u_i$	$v_j U_j$
10		-6											0	0	0	0	0
20		-5											0	0	0	0	0
30		-4	1		2						3		-12	48	-13	52
40		-3		2							2		-6	18	-10	30
50		-2			3	3	3	2	3	2			16	-32	64	-27	54
60		-1			5	3	6	5	7	4			30	-30	30	-42	42
70		0			1	2	6	11	12	7	5		44	0	0	-16	0
80		1			1	3		11	10	11	5		41	41	41	-3	-3
90		2					1		2	6	5		14	28	56	14	28
$f_{i.}$			1	0	2	10	13	16	29	34	30	15	150	-11	257	-97	203
$f_{i.}u_i$			-7	0	-10	-40	-39	-32	-29	0	30	30	-97				
$f_{i.}u_i^2$			49	0	50	160	117	64	29	0	30	60	559				
$V_i = \Sigma f_{ij}v_j$			-4	0	-6	-10	-14	-10	2	1	15	15	-11				
$u_i V_i$			28	0	30	40	42	20	-2	0	15	30	203				

* Correlation coefficient, r_{xy}: Although it is not clearly stated what degree is determined as a high correlation, it is generally accepted that;
  very high correlation : $|r| \geq 0.7$
  high correlation : $0.4 \leq |r| \leq 0.7$
  low correlation : $0.2 \leq |r| \leq 0.4$
  almost no correlation : $|r| \leq 0.2$ (Inagaki, et al., 1996: 40).

7.4.2 Regression line of the perception rates of piano tones and the perception rates of sentence stress

A regression line (see Inagaki, et al., 1996: 159-160) is obtained to show more clearly the correlation coefficient obtained in 7.4.1. The result ob-

tained in 7.4.1 is as follows:
$\bar{x}=73.5$, $\bar{y}=69.3$, $r_{xy}=0.55$ $s_x=18.18$, $s_y=13.07$

For the regression line, y=cx+d
where
$c = r_{xy} (s_y / s_x)$
$d = \bar{y} - c\bar{x}$

Entering the result of 7.4.1 in the above equation, the following result is obtained:
 c = 0.55×(13.07 / 18.18) = 0.4.
 d = 69.3-0.4 × 73.5 = 40.
Therefore, the regression line is as follows:
 y = 0.4x + 40.
This is illustrated in Figure 7.2. X indicates the perception rate of piano tones and Y indicates the perception rate of sentence stress. This shows that the more music ability to distinguish between pitch levels subjects have, the higher their perception rate of sentence stress in English.

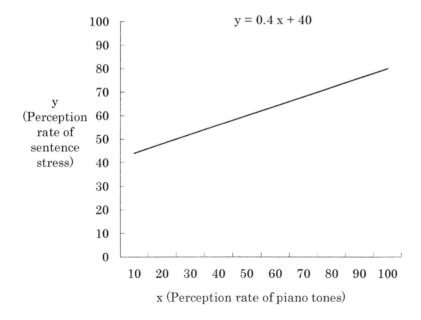

Figure 7.2 Regression line of x and y (Data from Table 7.5)

7.4.3 Test of correlation coefficient between the perception rates of piano tones and the perception rates of sentence stress

A test of no correlation (see Inagaki, *et al.*, 1996: 135) was carried out to determine whether there was a correlation between x and y in Table 7.5 (section 7.4.1). The result showed that there was a high correlation between x and y at the 5% significance level. This means that subjects who had a better ability to distinguish between pitch levels in music more easily perceived the sentence stress in English.

7.5 Summary

The relationship between the perception of sentence stress produced by native speakers of English and the ability to distinguish pitch levels in music is examined. One hundred and fifty Japanese learners of English listened to 80 sentences with emphasis placed each time on a different word by two native speakers of English and were asked to choose one prominent or emphasized word in each sentence. They also listened to 72 piano tones and indicated which piano tone was the highest in each tone row.

The correlation between the perception rates of sentence stress and piano tones at controlled pitch levels was analyzed, which showed that there was a high correlation between them with a correlation coefficient of 0.55. This suggests that for the Japanese learners of English, those who have the ability to distinguish between high and low pitches in music also tend to have the ability to perceive sentence stress in English.

Conclusion

Before the development of acoustic equipment, English word stress was defined as more forceful utterance (Bloomfield, 1933). However, owing to developments in acoustic equipment, word stress of disyllables has been examined acoustically and research shows that word stress syllables are marked by greater intensity, a higher pitch (fundamental frequency), greater duration, or more clearly defined vowel qualities (D.B.Fry, 1955, 1958, 1965; Lieberman, 1960; Nakatani and Aston, 1978; Beckman, 1986). Among these factors, pitch and duration are powerful factors in a listener's perception of word stress (Roach, 2000). Although word stress has been studied, sentence stress has not been the subject of research. This book chose to examine, thus, the effect of pitch (F_0) of stress at the sentence level.

This book, showing that pitch variations play an important role in both producing and perceiving sentence stress (nucleus, nuclear stress, contrastive accent, accent marking, contrastive and emphatic stress, prosodic contrasts) in English, consists of three parts. Firstly, in Chapter 2, English pitch patterns of sentence stress uttered by native speakers of English are studied acoustically from the production point of view. The author devised a new pitch contour (F_0 contour S) in order to compare visually the pitch patterns on the stressed syllables of native speakers of English with those of learners of English. The author also drew the average pitch contours of native speakers group and Japanese learners group. Pitch contours showed that sentence stress produced by native speakers of English tended to be marked by greater intensity, a higher pitch or greater duration. On the other hand, sentence stress produced by Japanese learners of English who were not accustomed to speaking English well was not prominent.

Secondly, Chapters 3−5 examine whether English pitch parameter is also an important factor for perceiving sentence stress (contrastive accent). Utterances of a native speaker of English are separated into sound source information (F_0 and amplitude) and track resonance information by PARCOR analysis; and F_0 only is controlled using the speech processing software. Forty native speakers of American English (AEs), 36 native speakers of British English (BEs) and 116 Japanese learners of English (Js) listened to nine stimulus types of synthesized utterances five times in random order to examine whether they perceive sentence stress (emphatic stress) on the higher pitch syllables. The results show that an average of 85.8% of AEs and 83.3% of BEs perceived sentence stress (prominence) on the syllable with higher pitch. This result indicates that pitch is an important factor in perceiving sentence stress (accent marking) as well as word stress. The following conclusion is obtained:

(a) AEs did not perceive sentence stress (nuclear stress) on the higher pitchEd word where the duration was too short. This seems to show that the duration parameter should also not be disregarded in stress (Chapter 3).
(b) When the pitch variation is too small, lower BEs perceived sentence stress (nuclear stress) than AEs (Chapter 5).

An average of 86.6% of Js perceived sentence stress on the higher pitch. Concerning the simple utterances used in this experiment, there was no significant difference between AEs and Js at the 0.05 significance level. It may be that Js perceive English sentence stress on the higher pitch because Japanese word accent is produced by pitch change.

Thirdly, because the successful perception rate of some subjects was very low in the second research in Chapters 3−5, the author hypothesized that subjects who did not perceive pitch variations easily had poor ability in music and examined the relationship between the perception rate of pitch variations and subjects' musical pitch sensitivity. Chapters 6 and 7 examine the relationship between the perception of English and the subjects' music ability. Though music seems to enhance spatial-temporal reasoning abilities, such as mathematics and science (Rauscher, *et.al.*, 1997), the relationship between music and language (Patel, 2008; Pastuszek- Lipinska, 2007; Magne, *et al.*, 2006) has not been extensively studied.

Chapter 6 examines the relationship between ability in music and pitch perception of synthesized utterances. The two declarative and the two interrogative utterances of a native speaker of English were synthesized by Praat. Eighty-one Js listened to 44 stimulus types of synthesized utterances and 36 piano tones at controlled pitch levels twice at random. The result showed that there was a high correlation between pitch perception of synthesized utterances and musical pitch sensitivity, with a correlation coefficient of 0.59. This suggests that listeners who have a good ability to distinguish between high and low pitches in music also tend to have a good ability to perceive pitch changes in synthesized utterances.

Chapter 7 examines the relationship between musical pitch sensitivity and perception of sentence stress in English. The 150 Js listened to 80 utterances with emphasis placed each time on a different word by two native speakers of English and 72 piano tones at controlled pitch levels. The correlation between perception of English sentence stress and the ability to distinguish between pitch levels is analyzed. The result showed a high correlation between the perception rate of sentence stress and piano tones, with a correlation coefficient of 0.55. This suggests that listeners who have the ability to distinguish between high and low pitches in music also tend to have a greater ability to perceive sentence stress in English.

The following eight points are the main conclusions of this book:

(1) The syllables of sentence stress uttered by AEs are higher in F_0 than in preceding syllables. This is interpreted to mean that F_0 is closely related to production of sentence stress in English. F_0 variations are hardly found on lexical word stresses when the nucleus is placed on another word (Chapter 2).
(2) For some Js who do not speak English well, sentence stress does not stand out because variation in F_0 of the sentence stress tends to be too small to be prominent (Chapter 2).
(3) For some other Js who do not speak English well, the sentence stress is not emphasized because they tend to change F_0 equally on each word so that there is no prominent word in a sentence (Chapter 2).
(4) F_0 cue is an effective parameter in order to perceive sentence stress in English (Chapters 3 and 5).
(5) Sentence stress is not perceived on the word where the duration of higher F_0 is too short (Chapter 3).
(6) Js perceive sentence stress in English on the higher F_0 because Japanese word accent is produced by F_0 change (Chapter 4).
(7) BEs do not perceive nucleus where F_0 variation is too small (Chapter 5).
(8) There is a high correlation between pitch perception of synthesized utterances and piano tones, with a correlation coefficient of 0.59. There is also a high correlation between the perception of sentence stress and piano tones, with a correlation coefficient of 0.55. This suggests that listeners' musical pitch sensitivity affects perception of pitch changes in synthesized utterances and sentence stress in English (Chapters 6 and 7).

The following four suggestions on teaching and learning English sentence stress for Japanese learners of English can be made based on the above conclusions:

(i) It is important for students to be instructed in sentence stress as well as word stress in order for them to speak English naturally.
(ii) Students should be instructed in pitch pattern in a whole sentence because pitch variation is an important cue to perceive the emphasized word in American and British English.
(iii) Students should be instructed not to produce significant pitch changes on non-focused lexical stresses in order to make the focused word stand out.
(iv) It is effective for students to be instructed both aurally and visually about the difference of pitch patterns between native speakers of English and Japanese learners of English.

Although research was not undertaken of duration cue for sentence stress for this book, further research conducted by Sasaki (2013a, 2013b, 2013c) examines how duration and pitch variations are important cues for perceiving sentence stress in English. The results showed that both the pitch variations and the duration parameter were important in perceiving sentence stress. The longer words whose pitch variations are large were perceived as sentence stress at the rate of more than 90%. The shorter words whose pitch variations are large enough were perceived as sentence stress at the rate of 61% to 90%. Even the longer words with no pitch variations were perceived as sentence stress at the rate of 46% to 80%. The lengthened words tended to be perceived as emphasized words at a high rate and there was a correlation between the length and sentence stress perception, with a correlation coefficient of 0.44. The words whose pitch variations are large tended to be perceived as emphasized words at a high rate and there was a high correlation between the pitch variations and sentence stress perception, with a correlation coefficient of 0.74.

In Japan, English intonation has not been adequately taught and Japanese learners of English often speak English using Japanese intonation. In order to avoid being misunderstood by native speakers or making them feel discomfort, students should learn natural English intonation. One hopes that the new pitch contour devised in this book will be useful in learning and teaching about sentence stress and intonation in English.

References

Beckman, Mary E. 1986. *Stress and Non-Stress Accent*, Holland: Foris Publications.
Beckman, Mary E. and Pierrehumbert, Janet B. 1986. "Intonational Structure in Japanese and English", *Phonology Yearbook* 3, 255-309.
Bloomfield Leonard. 1933. *Language*, The University of Chicago Press.
Bolinger, Dwight. 1958. "A Theory of Pitch Accent in English," *Word* 14, 109-149.
Bronstein, Arthur, J. 1960. *The Pronunciation of American English: An Introduction to Phonetics*, Prentice-Hall.
Brown, Gillian, Currie, Karen, L. and Kenworthy, Joanne. 1985. *Questions of Intonation*, London & Sydney: Groom Helm Ltd.
Brown, W. S Jr. and McGlone, Robert E. 1974. "Aerodynamic and acoustic study of stress in sentence productions", *the Journal of the Acoustic Society of America*, vol.56, No.3. , 971-974.
Broyles, William, Jr. 2001. *Cast Away*, Screenplay, FOUR-IN Creative. Products Corp. (Broyles, William, Jr. 2001. *Cast Away*, スクリーンプレイ出版, フォーイン・クリエイティブ プロダクツ)
Catford, J.C. 2001. *A Practical Introduction to Phonetics*, 2nd ed. Oxford University Press.
Clark, John and Yallop, Colin. 1995. *An introduction to phonetics and phonology*, 2nd ed. Oxford: B. Blackwell.
Cruttenden, Alan. 1997. *Intonation,* 2nd ed. Cambridge University Press.
   2001. *Gimson's Pronunciation of English*, 6th ed. revised, London: Arnold.
Crystal, David, 2003. *A Dictionary of Linguistics & Phonetics*, 5th ed. Blackwell Publishing.
Denes, Peter B. and Elliot N. Pinson. 1993. *The Speech Chain: The Physics and Biology of Spoken Language*, W.H. Freeman and Company.
Deutsch, Diana. 1990. "A link between music perception and speech production" *the Journal of the Acoustic Society of America*, vol.88, Suppl.1, 139.

1991. "The Tritone Paradox: An Influence of Language on Music Perception", *Music Perception*, vol. 8, No. 4, 335-347.

1994. "The Tritone Paradox: Some Further Geographical Correlates", *Music Perception*, vol. 12, No. 1, 25-136.

Fry, D.B. 1955. "Duration and Intensity as Physical Correlates of Linguistic Stress", Reprinted from *the Journal of the Acoustic Society of America*, vol.27, No.4, 765-768.

1958. "Experiments in the Perception of Stress", *Language and Speech*, vol.1, 126-152.

1965. "The Dependence of Stress Judgments on Vowel Formant Structure", in E. Zwirner and W. Bethge (eds.), *Proceedings of the 6th International Congress of Phonetic Sciences*, Karger, 306-311.

Fudge, Erik, 1984. *English Word-Stress*, London: George Allen & Unwin Publishers Ltd.

Fujisaki, Hiroya, Sugito, Miyoko, Hirose, Keikichi and Takahashi Noboru. 1982. "Word Accent and Sentence Intonation in Foreign Language Learning", *Reprints of Papers, Working Group on Intonation, 16 International Congress of Linguistics*, Tokyo. I.

Harashima, Kazuo. 2002. *English from Movies*, Japan Times（原島一男 2002『映画の英語 心にのこる名場面・名せりふ』ジャパンタイムズ）

Hirasaka, Fumio. 2000. "Speech Processing Software for Personal Computer", *English Phonetics* No.3, The English Phonetic Society of Japan.（平坂文男 2000「パーソナルコンピュータを用いた分析・編集処理ソフトウェアについて」学術論文集『英語音声学』第3号, 日本英語音声学会, 323-343.）

Imai, Kunihiko. 1989. *English Pronunciation Teaching Using a New Approach*, Tokyo: Taishukan.
（今井邦彦 1989「新しい発想による英語発音指導」大修館書店）

Inagaki, Nobuo, Yamane, Yoshikazu and Yoshida, Mitsuo. 1996. *Introduction to Statistics*, Tokyo: Shokabo.
（稲垣宣生、山根芳和、吉田光雄 1996「統計学入門」東京：裳華房）

Itakura, Fumitada. 1971. "Extraction of Speech Features using Statistical Techniques", *Speech Data Processing* II-5, pp.1-12.（板倉文忠 1971 "統計的手法による音声の特徴抽出"「音声情報処理」II-5, 1-12.）

Kent, Ray D. and Read, Charles. 1992. *The Acoustic Analysis of Speech*, San Diego: Singular Publishing Group.

Kingdom, Roger. 1959. *The Groundwork of English Stress*, London: Longmans.

Kubozono, Haruo and Ohta, Satoshi. 1998. *Phonological Structure and Accent*. Tokyo: Kenkyusha Publishing.（窪薗晴夫、太田聡 1998『日英語比較選書 音韻構造とアクセント』研究社出版）

Ladefoged, Peter. 2001. *Vowels and Consonants: An Introduction to the Sounds of Languages*, Blackwell Publishers Inc.

Laver, John. 1994. *Principles of Phonetics*. New York: Cambridge University Press.

Lehman, Ernest. 1996. *The Sound of Music*, Screenplay, FOUR-IN Creative. (Lehman, Ernest. 1996. *The Sound of Music*, スクリーンプレイ出版, フォーイン・クリエイティブ プロダクツ)

Lieberman, Philip. 1960. "Some Acoustic Correlates of Word Stress in American English", *Journal of the Acoustic Society of America*, vol.32, 451-454.

―― 1967. *Intonation, Perception, and Language*, The M.I.T. Press.

Luedtke, Kurt. 1991. *Out of Africa*, Screenplay, FOUR-IN Creative. (Luedtke, Kurt. 1991. *Out of Africa*, スクリーンプレイ出版, フォーイン・クリエイティブ プロダクツ)

Magne, C., Schön, D., and Besson, M. 2006. "Musician children detect pitch violations in both music and language better than nonmusician children: behavioral and electrophysiological approaches", *Journal of Cognitive Neuroscience* 18: 2, 199-211.

Maidment, John. 2002. "The Structure of Intonation Patterns", UCL Summer Course in English Phonetics.

Medress, Mark, Skinner, T. E. and Anderson, D. E. 1972. "Acoustic correlates of word stress," *Journal of the Acoustic Society of America*, vol.51, 101 (A).

Misono, Kazuo. 1995. *A Study of English Phonetics: Theory and Application*, Tokyo: Wako Publishing. (御園和夫 1995『英語音声学研究』和広出版)

Mitchell, Margaret. 1994. *Gone with the Wind*, vol. 1, Tokyo: Movie Bunko, 92.
(マーガレット・ミッチェル 1994『風と共に去りぬ[上]』英話対訳映画文庫)

Mizutani, Osamu. 1990. "Learning Method of Accent and Intonation", *Japanese Phonetics and Phonology*, vol. 3 of *Course in Japanese and Japanese Teaching* (Part II), Tokyo: Meiji Shoin.
(水谷修 1990「アクセントとイントネーションの習得法」『講座日本語と日本語教育』第3巻日本語の音声・音韻(下)』明治書院)

Mok, P.K. Peggy and Zuo, Donghui. 2012. "The separation between music and speech: Evidence from the perception of Cantonese tones", *The Journal of the Acoustical Society of America* 132 (4), 2711-2720.

Morton, John and Eiktor Jassem. 1965. "Acoustic correlates of stress", *Language and Speech 8*, 159-181.

Nakatani, Lloyd, H. and Aston, Carletta, H. 1978. "Perceiving the stress patterns of words in sentences", *The Journal of the Acoustical Society of America* 63, Suppl. No.1, Spring.

Ohman, S. 1967. "Word and sentence intonation: A quantitative model", *Speech Transmission Laboratory Quarterly Progress and Status Report*, STL-QPSR 2-3, 20-54.

Ohyama, Ghen, Suzuki, Hiroshi, and Kiritani, Shigeru. 1989. "A Study on the Prosody of the English Spoken by Japanese Speakers", *Sound Speech III*. (大山玄、鈴木博、桐谷滋 1989「日本人が発話した英語のプロソディーに関する一検討」『音声言語III』)

Pastuszek-Lipinska, Barbara. 2007. "Musicians outperform nonmusicians in a study with shadowing speech", *ICPhS*, XVI, 821-824.

Patel, A. D. 2008. *Music, Language, and the Brain*, Oxford: Oxford University Press.

Pike, Kenneth, L. 1943. *Phonetics*, University of Michigan Press.

── 1948. *Tone Languages*, University of Michigan Press.

Rauscher, Frances, H; Shaw, Gordon, L; Levine, Linda, J; Wright, Eric, L; Dennis, Wendy R and Newcomb, Robert, L. 1997. "Music training causes long-term enhancement of preschool children's spatial- temporal reasoning", *Neurological Research*, 19, no.1, 2, 2-8.

Roach, Peter. 2000. *English Phonetics and Phonology*, 3rd ed. Cambridge University Press.

Sasaki, Saeko. 2002 a. "Fundamental Frequency Patterns in Producing Sentence Stress in American English", *English Phonetics* No.5, The English Phonetic Society of Japan, 259-278.

── 2002 b. "Analysis of the Perception of Sentence Stress and Pitch Changes in American English", *English Phonetics* No.5, The English Phonetic Society of Japan, 433-451.
(佐々木彩子 2002 b「アメリカ英語における文ストレスの知覚と高さの動きの分析」学術論文集『英語音声学』第5号, 日本英語音声学会, 433-451.)

── 2003 a. "Perception of Fundamental Frequency Patterns", *English Phonetics* No.6, The English Phonetic Society of Japan, 163-180.

── 2003 b. "Perception of Fundamental Frequency Patterns and Music Ability", *English Phonetics* No.6, The English Phonetic Society of Japan, 181-198.

── 2004 a. "The Relationship between Perception of Pitch and Music Ability", *Silphe* No.43, The Silphe Society, 24-43.
(佐々木彩子 2004 a「ピッチの知覚と音感との相関関係」『シルフェ』第43号, シルフェ英語英米文学会, 24-43.)

2004 b. *Fundamental Frequency Pattern and Sentence Stress in English: From Acoustic Point of View*, PhD dissertation, Kanto Gakuin University.

2004 c. "Comparison of the Perception of Pitch by Native Speakers of American English with Native Speakers of Japanese", *OLIVA* No.10, Kanto Gakuin University, 49-68.（佐々木彩子 2004 c「アメリカ英語母語話者と日本語母語話者のピッチの知覚の分析と比較」『OLIVA』第 10 号，関東学院大学文学部英語英米文学会，49-68.）

2005. "Perception of Sentence Stress in English by Japanese Learners of English", *English Phonetics* No.7, The English Phonetic Society of Japan, 125-144.（佐々木彩子 2005「日本人英語学習者による英語の文強勢の知覚」学術論文集『英語音声学』第 7 号，日本英語音声学会，125-144.）

2006. "Prominence and Fundamental Frequency Movement", *English Phonetics*, a double issue for No.9 / No.10, The English Phonetic Society of Japan, 161-179.
（佐々木彩子 2006「プロミネンスと基本周波数の変動」学術論文集『英語音声学』第 9 号・10 号合併号，日本英語音声学会，161-179.）

2007. "Perception of Sentence Stress in English by Native Speakers of American English", *Silphe* No.46, The Silphe Society, 115-134.
（佐々木彩子 2007「英語母語話者による英語の文強勢知覚」『シルフェ』第 46 号，シルフェ英語英米文学会，115-134.）

2008. "Relationship between Perception of Pitch Changes in Speech and Music Ability", *English Phonetics*, a double issue for No.11 / No.12, The English Phonetic Society of Japan, 129-139.
（佐々木彩子 2008「音声の聞き取りと音楽的能力との関係」学術論文集『英語音声学』第 11 号・12 号合併号，日本英語音声学会，129-139.）

2009. "Perception of Sentence Stress in English and Ability to Distinguish between High and Low Pitches", *English Phonetics* No.13, The English Phonetic Society of Japan, 365-378.
（佐々木彩子 2009「英語の文強勢と音高識別能力」『英語音声学』第 13 号，日本英語音声学会，365-378.）

2013 a. "The Influence of Length on English Sentence Stress: A Theoretical Framework", *OLIVA* No. 19, Kanto Gakuin University, 59-71.
（佐々木彩子 2013 a「英語の文強勢における長さの役割：理論的枠組み」『OLIVA』第 19 号，関東学院大学人文学会英語英米文学部会，59-71.）

2013 b. "The Influence of Length and Pitch on English Sentence Stress: from an Acoustic Point of View", *English Phonetics* No.18, The English Phonetic Society of Japan, 201-210.
（佐々木彩子 2013 b「英語の文強勢における長さとピッチの役割―音響的見地から―」学術論文集『英語音声学』第 18 号，日本英語音声学会，201-210.）

2013 c. "The Perception of English Sentence Stress: Importance of Pitch and Length", *English Phonetics* No.18, The English Phonetic Society of Japan, 487-499.
(佐々木彩子 2013 c「英語の文強勢の知覚―ピッチと長さの重要性―」学術論文集『英語音声学』第 18 号，日本英語音声学会，487-499.)
Schön, D., Magne, C., and Besson, M. 2004. "The music of speech: Music training facilitates pitch processing in both music and language" *Psychophysiology* 41, 341-349.
Sugito, Miyoko. 1990. "Accent and Intonation of Japanese and English", *Japanese Phonetics and Phonology*, Part II, vol. 3 of *Course in Japanese and Japanese Teaching*, Tokyo: Meiji Shoin.
(杉藤美代子 1990「日本語と英語のアクセントとイントネーション」『講座日本語と日本語教育 第 3 巻日本語の音声・音韻（下）』明治書院）
Sweet, Henry. 1906. *A Primer of Phonetics*, 3rd ed. revised, London: Oxford University Press.
Thompson, W. F., Schellenberg, E. G., and Husain, G. 2003. "Perceiving prosody in speech: Effects of music lessons" In: Avanzini, G., Faienza, C., Minciacchi, D., Lopez, L., & Majno, M. (eds), *The Neurosciences and Music*. New York: The New York Academy of Sciences, vol. 999, 530-532.
Tiffany, William R., Carrell, James.1977. *Phonetics: Theory and Application*, 2nd ed. McGraw-Hill Book Company.
Watanabe, Kazuyuki. 1988. "Sentence stress perception by Japanese students", *Journal of Phonetics* 16, 181-186.
1994. *English Rhythm and Intonation Teaching*, Tokyo: Taishukan.
(渡辺和幸 1994『英語のリズム・イントネーションの指導』大修館書店）
Wells, J.C. 2000. *Longman Pronunciation Dictionary* (Pearson Education Limited, 2000).
Wong, Patrick. 2007. "Ability to learn a second language in adulthood linked to brain anatomy", http://www.medicalnewstoday.com/articles/77942.php.
Yabuuchi, Satoshi and Satoi, Hisateru. 2000. "Prosodic features of reading aloud by Japanese learners of English: Comparison between good readers and poor readers", Tokyo: Japanese Phonetic Society, 1-10.
(藪内智、里井久輝 2000「日本人英語学習者の音読課題におけるプロソディ特性 good readers と poor readers を比較して」日本音声学会第 302 回例会，1-10.)

The Daily Yomiuri. Friday, May 5, 2000. 10.
The New Testament, New International Version. 1978. "The first letter of Paul to the Thessalonians", Chapter 5, 610.

Index

accent, 1, 3, 5, 6, 10-2, 14-7, 20, 22-7, 40, 147, 148, 227-30
Beckman, 2, 19, **22**-25, 227
Bloomfield, 18, 227
Bolinger, 20, 21
Bronstein, 10, 11
Brown and McGlone, 21
Catford, 15
Clark and Yallop, 17
compounds and phrases, 12
content word, 7, **9**
correlation coefficient, 210, 213-7, 221, 223, **224**, 226, 228-30
Cruttenden, 1, 5, 10, **15**-7, 147
Denes and Pinson, 17
Deutsch, 27, 197
duration, 1, 2, 7, 11, 15, 17-24, 29, 31-3, 41, 67, 68, 95, 101, 106, 147, 176, 227-30
emphatic stress, 6, 7, 227-9
F_0, **2**-4, 21-5, 29-75, 78-86, 91-114, 126-36, 141-52, 160-79, 183-90, 197-203, 208, 214-217, 227, 229
F_0 Contour S, **31**, 32, 33, 41, 227
focused word, 2, 4, 25, 39-41, 111, 230
Fry, 1, 2, **19**-22, 227
Fudge, 6, 26
Fujisaki, Sugito, *et al.*, 1
function word, 7, 9
fundamental frequency, 1-3, 18-21, 29, 39, 67, 200, 216, 227
Gillian Brown, *et al.*, 7
Gimson, 1, 5, 10, 15, 147

head, 8
Imai, 1
Inagaki, *et al.*, 78, 86, 112, 113, 117, 127, 150, 154, 210, 214, 215, 221, 223, 224, 226
intelligibility, 1, 26
intensity, 1, 16-24, 27, 29, 67, 69, 106, 110, 147, 148, 176, 202, 227
intonation, 1, 5, 6, 12, 17, **25**, 230
isochronism, 26
isochronous, 26
isochrony, 6, 26
Kent and Read, 2
Kingdom, 19
Kubozono and Ohta, 24, 26
Ladefoged, 14, 15
Laver, 6
length, 2, 5, 11-14, 17, 93-5, 99, 100, 110, 143-8, 175, 230
lexical stress, 6, 7, 9
Lieberman, 2, **17**, 18, **21**, 227
linguistic, 11, 16, 17, 28, 147
loudness, 7, 11, 13, 14, 16-8, 22
Magne, *et al.*, 2, 27, 228
Misono, 5, 6, 8-10
Mizutani, 25
Mok, *et al.*, 28
monotone, **24**, 39, 74, 78, 94, 112, 150
mora-timed rhythm, 26
Morton and Jassem, 21
music, 2-5, **27**, 28, **199**, 200, 208, 214-7, 225, 226, 228, 229
Nakatani and Aston, 2, **22**, 40, 227

nuclear stress, 2, 6, 227, 228
nucleus, 2, 6-9, 227, 229
Ohyama, Suzuki, *et al.*, 1, 23
Pastuszek-Lipinska, 2, 27, 28, 228
Patel, 2, 27, 228
perceive, 3, 4, 16-20, 24, 67, 94, 96, 100-6, 109-12, 126, 143, 145-9, 160, 172, 175, 177, 179, 197-200, 215-7, 226-30
perception, 2, 3, 11, 13, 19, 22-7, 67, 70, 74, 77, 78, 99, 108-12, 126, 143-6, 149, 150, 175, 179, 190, 195-9, 202, 210, 211, 214-8, 221-30
phonetician, 1, 17-21
phonetics, 11
phonology, 6
Pike, 19, 25
pitch, 1-5, 7-17, 20, 22-29, 31, 32, 40, 41, 67, 68, 92, 111, 147-51, 172, 197-200, 208, 214-7, 225-30
pitch accent, 16, 20, 23, **24**
pitch pattern, 2-4, 23, 25, 28, 41, 227, 230
pitch variation, 1-3, 24, 111, 147, 227, 228, 230
Praat, 4, 200, 202, 208, 228
prehead, 8
primary stress, 6-8, 12
production, 3, 11, 13, 21-3, 27, 40, 110, 227, 229
prominence, 6, 8, 11, 13-20, 25, 39-40, 148, 228, 230
prominent, 2, 5-7, 11-6, 39-41, 106, 111, 177, 200, 203, 208-10, 215, 218, 219, 226-9
prosodic features, 1, 3, 5, 15, **24**
prosody, 24, 27
Rauscher, *et.al.*, 2, 228
rhythm, 1, 5, 6, 9, 10, 17, **26**
Roach, 2, 10, 11, **13**, 14, 227
Sasaki, 3, 230
Schön, *et al.*, 27

segmental phonemes, 5
sentence stress, 6, 19, 25, 26, 28, 29, 40, 41, 67, 110, 111, 149, 197, 199, 217, 218, 221-30
sound spectrograph, 19
steady, **70**, 71-5, 78-80, 83, 87-91, 95, 96, 101, 102, 105, 113-25, 128, 129, 133, 134, 136-9, 142, 144, 146, 151-63, 167, 169, 176-9, 184, 188, 190-2
stress, 1-31, 34-41, 67-70, 74, 75, 78, 80, 83, 92-113, 126, 128, 133, 141-51, 160, 163, 167, 170, 172, 175-9, 184, 188, 197, 199, 202, 203, 208, 227-30
stress accent, 22-4
stress shift, 8, 12, 26
stressed syllable, 1-21, 26, 28, 29, 34-41, 67-70, 78, 92, 99, 110, 112, 113, 148, 151, 176, 202, 203, 227
stress-timed rhythm, 6, 26
Sugito, 25-7
suprasegmental phonemes, 1, 5
Sweet, 18
syllable-timed rhythm, 26
tail, 8
Thompson, *et al.*, 27
tone, 1, 4-9, 12, 25, 200, 201, 206-11, 216-8, 221-6, 228
tonic, 2, 7
vowel quality, 1, 11, 20, 23, 67, 227
Watanabe, 24, 147
weak form, 6, 10, 41
Wells, 8, 9, 11-2
Wong, *et al.*, 28
word stress, 1, 2, 5, 6, 16, 19-26, 39-41, 111, 227-30
Yabuuchi and Satoi, 24

著者略歴
佐々木 彩子（ささき さえこ）
文学博士。専門は英語音声学。現在、神奈川大学、早稲田大学、日本大学生物資源科学部などで非常勤講師。

Acquiring English Sentence Stress:
Pitch and Musical Sensitivity

2016年12月25日　初版発行

著作者　　佐々木 彩 子　　　　　　　　ⓒ 2016
　　　　　Saeko Sasaki

発行所　　丸善プラネット株式会社
　　　　　〒101-0051　東京都千代田区神田神保町2-17
　　　　　電話（03）3512-8516
　　　　　http://planet.maruzen.co.jp/

発売所　　丸善出版株式会社
　　　　　〒101-0051　東京都千代田区神田神保町2-17
　　　　　電話（03）3512-3256
　　　　　http://pub.maruzen.co.jp/

印刷・製本／大日本印刷株式会社

ISBN 978-4-86345-310-4 C3382